# Natural Resources and the New Frontier

# Natural Resources and the New Frontier

## Constructing Modern China's Borderlands

JUDD C. KINZLEY

The University of Chicago Press
Chicago and London

The University of Chicago Press, Chicago 60637
The University of Chicago Press, Ltd., London
© 2018 by The University of Chicago
Published 2018
Printed in the United States of America

27  26  25  24  23  22  21  20  19  18      1  2  3  4  5

ISBN-13: 978-0-226-49215-5 (cloth)
ISBN-13: 978-0-226-49229-2 (paper)
ISBN-13: 978-0-226-49232-2 (e-book)
DOI: https://doi.org/10.7208/chicago/9780226492322.001.0001

Library of Congress Cataloging-in-Publication Data

Names: Kinzley, Judd C., author.
Title: Natural resources and the new frontier : constructing modern China's
    borderlands / Judd C. Kinzley.
Description: Chicago ; London : The University of Chicago Press, 2018. |
    Includes bibliographical references and index.
Identifiers: LCCN 2017044567 | ISBN 9780226492155 (cloth : alk. paper) |
    ISBN 9780226492292 (pbk. : alk. paper) | ISBN 9780226492322 (e-book)
Subjects: LCSH: Natural resources—China—Xinjiang Uygur Zizhiqu. | China—
    Foreign economic relations—Soviet Union. | Soviet Union—Foreign economic
    relations—China. | Industrialization—China.
Classification: LCC HC428.X56 K57 2018 | DDC 333.70951/6—dc23
LC record available at https://lccn.loc.gov/2017044567

# Contents

# Acknowledgments

While conducting the research for this book, I received support from the University of California, San Diego's Institute for International, Comparative and Area Studies and from the Fulbright Hays Program. The writing process was generously supported by the All University of California Group in Economic History program, the Association for Asian Studies, and particularly from the American Council of Learned Societies China Studies/Henry Luce Foundation. Additional support was provided by the University of Wisconsin–Madison Office of the Vice Chancellor for Research and Graduate Education with funding from the Wisconsin Alumni Research Foundation. I have presented portions of this work at the Chinese Academy of Social Sciences, Duke University, Harvard University, University of Heidelberg, the Hoover Institution at Stanford University, Hong Kong University of Science and Technology, Humboldt University of Berlin, Ludwig Maximilian University of Munich, the University of Michigan, the University of South Carolina, the University of Wisconsin-Madison, and Xinjiang Normal University. I benefited greatly from the comments and questions I received at each.

I have been working on this project in some shape or form for more than a decade. Over that time, I have accumulated a lot of debts to individuals in China, Taiwan, the United States, the United Kingdom, Moscow, and elsewhere. Acknowledging their generosity with their time, insights, knowledge, and support is the least that I can do. In particular, I am indebted to various teachers for inspiring and supporting me. I would like to thank all of my Chinese language instructors at various institutions in China, Taiwan, and the United States over the past twenty years. I am also very thankful for all of those teachers who have helped shepherd me through my study of Chinese history over the course of my academic career, including Gardner Boving-don, Suzanne Cahill, Sherry Gray, Robert Hegel, Lu Weijing, Barry Naughton, Jeremy Prestholdt, Sarah Schneewind, Yue Him Tam, and others I am surely forgetting. I am particularly thankful for having had the opportunity to work so closely with Joseph Esherick and Paul Pickowicz. Their comments and critiques served to motivate and inspire, and I continue to learn from their advice and ongoing mentorship. They are model teachers and research-ers, and this book would not have been possible without the two of them.

During my time in China I had the good fortune to be affiliated with the Chinese Academy of Social Sciences, Research Center for Chinese Border-land History and Geography. While there, I benefited from the advice and introductions provided by Li Sheng, Adili Aini, Xu Jianying, and particularly my friend Jia Jianfei. In addition, Shen Zhihua gave me access to a handful of critical sources for this project and was very generous in introducing me to an assortment of helpful people. In Xinjiang, Meng Nan at Xinjiang University offered me a piece of critical advice at a critical time and I have continued to benefit from the support and friendship of Cao Meng and others whom I will not name. In Taiwan, Mike (Shi-yung) Liu at the Academia Sinica has helped a great deal at various stages of the research and writing process. Ethan (Yit-ing) Zheng has been a wonderful friend, and he and his family have been a source of support whenever I find myself in Taipei. And in Moscow, I received generous support from the National Research University Higher School for Economics and particularly from Liudmila Novikova. My time in Moscow would have much less productive and pleasant without the help and friend-ship provided by Irina Pichugina.

Various friends and colleagues gave me their time and attention while I worked away at this book over the last ten years. I benefited a great deal from my colleagues in the modern Chinese history program at UCSD, including Emily Baum, Jeremy Brown, David Cheng Chang, Maggie Greene, Miriam Gross, Dahpon Ho, Ellen Huang, Matt Johnson, Jeremy Murray, and Xiao-wei Zheng, and a particular thanks goes to Justin Jacobs, who pointed me to a number of key sources and has read most everything I have written on Xinjiang at one point or another. Additional thanks to Angie Chau, Benny Cohen, Liz Mikos, and Ryan Reft. I would also like to thank Maura Dyks-tra, Agnieszka Joniak-Luthi, Charles Kraus, Ben Levy, Ken Pomeranz, Jon Schlesinger, Wu Yulian, and many others who have supported me along the way. In Wisconsin, friends and colleagues have been generous with their time and I am grateful for their ongoing support and friendship. I would like to thank Emily Callaci, Shelly Chan, Kathryn Ciancia, Joe Dennis, Victor Gold-gel, Pablo Gomez, Liz Hennessey, Toshi Higuchi, Charles Kim, Viren Murthy,

John Nimis, Max Sauban, Sarah Thal, Louise Young, and Stephen Young, all of whom helped in their own ways. I would also like to thank Priya Nelson at the University of Chicago Press for helping shepherd this book through, as well as Shellen Xiao Wu and Peter Perdue, both of whom provided critical advice on the manuscript in its later stages.

This book would not have been possible without the love and support from my family. I am particularly indebted to my late grandmother Velma Lee Creighton, brother Patrick Kinzley, and parents William Dean Kinzley and Alma Creighton, all of whom have helped me however they were able. My father has always been willing to read and offer comments on whatever I write. In addition to having read every chapter of this book multiple times and in multiple forms, he has also been a source of wisdom and insight on topics related to academia and beyond—I am profoundly grateful. My wife Coco has been a companion and confidant since well before I began working on this book. I am deeply indebted to her for her love and support and also for the world that we, along with our son Xavier and daughter Axelle, have created for ourselves. The fact that this world is insulated from Xinjiang, Chinese history, and long days in my office has made the process of moving this book forward all the more pleasant. The research and the writing of this book took me away from them for long stretches and often occupied my mind even when I was around. So for them, I am happy to announce that the book is finally finished. It does little to repay my debts for their patience, but I dedicate the book to them.

# Resources, Competition, and the Layers of the State

Passing through the Jade Gate and setting foot in the Qing empire's western-most province of Xinjiang in 1911, the imperial official Yuan Dahua carefully noted the rocky desert (*gebi*), harsh unrelenting climate, and lack of vegetation. Summing up the landscape of this region located a long and dusty 1,500 miles from Beijing in a memorial to the imperial court, he wrote, "The scattered, bleached bones of men and horses lie strewn in this place." In that same document, however, Yuan, who served as the last Qing governor of Xinjiang, also noted that those capable of braving the brutal landscape and willing to sweep aside the bones, move the rocks, and sift the arid soil, could catch a glimpse of a different vision of this region—one that glittered.[1]

Qing armies conquered Xinjiang, which means "New Frontier" in Chinese, in 1759, and for more than a century afterward, travelers, prisoners, soldiers, and officials from the "inner lands" (*neidi*, or what I will also refer to in this book as China-proper) tended to depict the region as a vast unredeemable "wasteland" (*huang*).[2] The distance, the terrain, and the difficult climate were significant obstacles to the integration of this border region into the empire. In spite of this, a whole host of highly sought-after lucrative local products, including Kazakh horses, black otter pelts, white jade, and bolts of gold-threaded satin, attracted the interest and attention of Qing officials throughout the late eighteenth and early nineteenth centuries. By the twentieth, the allure of gold, petroleum, wool, various animal parts, and rare minerals caught the attention of officials from the Qing dynasty, as well as the Republic of China and the People's Republic, all of whom were eager to try to stake their own claims to these products.

The dynamic pull of its local products and the push of its natural environment have shaped Xinjiang's relationship to the modern Chinese nation-state.

Today, Xinjiang, now known as the Xinjiang Uyghur Autonomous Region, is a major producer of petroleum and various lucrative industrial minerals critical for fueling China's economic rise. This position, however, is merely the end point of more than a century of struggle, as China-based officials struggled to bridge Xinjiang's distance from infrastructural networks, institutions, and markets in China-proper, and grappled with the severe difficulties of operating in the often harsh and unforgiving landscape. The natural obstacles forced successive generations of Qing and later Chinese officials from the late nineteenth century well into the second half of the twentieth, to undertake complex and often surprising alliances with the agents of foreign powers and largely autonomous local and regional leaders in order to stake some semblance of a claim to the region's rich local products.

In this book, these local products and natural resources sit at the center of a broader narrative that seeks to understand the development of the institutions of Chinese state power in this border region. By focusing on the resources themselves, along with the surveying, extraction and processing facilities, transportation infrastructure, and institutions of state control that were established to oversee their production, I reveal a new narrative of Chinese state building in Xinjiang. Far from a process of inexorable state-centered integration over the course of the twentieth century, which is the narrative that has been aggressively endorsed by the Chinese Communist Party today, this work finds that in fact the process was nonlinear, transnational, and highly contingent. Well into the 1950s, faced with high price tags and competing priorities, Chinese officials left much of the work of infrastructural development and institution building in Xinjiang to a shifting alliance of imperial agents, local officials, and Chinese technocrats. The result is not a unified, centralized program of state building, but rather the accumulation of a disjointed mishmash of infrastructure and institutions that ran counter to Chinese state interests as often as they supported them.

This work makes three major contributions. First, it reveals the deep seated but often overlooked connection that exists between resources, resource extraction regimes, and long-term patterns of economic development and state institutionalization. Secondly, over the ensuing seven chapters, I offer a new "layered" model of state formation that binds the efforts not only of state planners, but also largely autonomous local officials and the representatives of foreign powers into one singular, transnational narrative. What this model reveals is that in peripheral regions like Xinjiang, surveys, capital investments, and institutions begun by one regime to facilitate the extraction of natural resources often served as a blueprint for future regimes to follow. Eager to facilitate production quickly and cheaply, subsequent regimes layered their own surveys, investments, and infrastructure atop these earlier layers, thereby shaping long-term patterns of state investment, infrastructural development, and ultimately political institutionalization in ways that continue to resonate. Finally, this work also offers a unique perspective on the origins of a simmering discontent among indigenous groups in Xinjiang. Connected to patterns of state investment and institutionalization that were shaped by resource extraction campaigns developed over the course of the twentieth century, this discontent has increasingly manifested itself in a growing ethno-nationalism, religious fundamentalism, and antistate violence.

## China and Xinjiang

Xinjiang was first conquered by the armies of the Qing dynasty in order to exert greater control over their western frontier. Well into the nineteenth century, however, rather than undertaking an aggressive integrationist policy in this region, the court retained it as a frontier "dependency" (*fanshu*) overseen by Qing military officials working with a network of indigenous local headmen.[3] As the proponents of what has come to be called "New Qing History" have forcefully argued, this border policy was a product of the court's pluralistic vision of empire.[4] But in addition, practical concerns about the cost and difficulty of undertaking a large-scale program of settlement and administrative expansion paired with a fear of destabilizing the delicate ethnocultural balance in this region made up primarily of various groups of Turkic Muslims ensured that Qing officials into the 1860s were content to retain their policy of keeping Xinjiang as a dependency, rather than transforming it into a fully integrated province of the empire.

Maintaining even a light grip on Xinjiang, however, cost the court substantial amounts of treasure. The need to station large numbers of troops in this arid region with a small population and meager and widely dispersed plots of arable land meant that Qing officials in the region had to rely on annual shipments of silver bullion from the imperial treasury to keep their fiscal heads above water. Desperate to lighten the heavy financial burden of empire, these shipments, referred to as "interprovincial assistance" (*xiexiang*), were a major source of frustration for Qing officials in the years following the conquest.[5] Compounding this situation, a series of uprisings among Turkic Muslim ethnocultural groups in southern Xinjiang in the first half of the nineteenth century increased the burden of empire in the region and inspired a new generation of thinkers to experiment with new approaches to the administration of empire.

In the early to mid-nineteenth century, a new group of Han thinkers, influenced by "statecraft" (*jingshi*) approaches, called on the court to abandon pluralism in the empire's border regions and adopt an assimilationist approach.[6] In an 1820 essay, the influential statecraft thinker Gong Zizhen, urged the imperial court to adopt a new border policy that centered around aggressively investing in agricultural reclamation, importing large numbers of immigrant settlers from China-proper, and eliminating the administrative differences between Xinjiang and the lands "inside the pass" by establishing the region as an official province and also implementing the prefecture-county (*jun-xian*) system of local administration.[7] By creating a stable population of taxpaying immigrants who would be overseen by a proven system of governance, Gong and other statecraft advocates argued that the court could resolve the fiscal and ethnic problems simultaneously. The Qing military commander Zuo Zongtang, himself a committed adherent to statecraft approaches, was particularly influenced by Gong's essay on Xinjiang. Zuo was tapped to head the Qing military campaign to reconquer the region after a decade-long rebellion in the 1860s. After the successful reconquest of Xinjiang in 1878, he was in a position to advocate for much of Gong's program. Pushed by Zuo's advocacy, the Qing court established Xinjiang as an official province in 1884.

By the late nineteenth century, the integrationist impulse was not confined simply to statecraft thinkers. New ideas about the state and empire, many of which were imported from the West, prompted many reformist Qing officials to begin calling for even greater integration of border regions like Xinjiang. All across the empire they sought to transform imperial frontiers into national borderlands through political reforms and the development of transportation infrastructure, as well as education and cultural campaigns.[8] This impulse continued in the years following the overthrow of the Qing in 1911, and the establishment of the Republic of China the next year, as early Republican modernizers like Sun Yatsen sought to fundamentally transform these former imperial frontiers into integrated corners of the newly established Chinese Republic. There was no shortage of integrationist plans for Xinjiang from leaders in the late Qing and early Republican periods, including the development of large-scale rail networks, the construction of agricultural settler communities, and aggressive surveys of Xinjiang's resource wealth. But despite these plans, and the vocal commitment to carrying them out, both late Qing officials and their Republican counterparts lacked the political and economic capital to implement them. From the late Qing period well into the Republic, central government officials tended to prioritize efforts in the Han Chinese heartland of eastern and central China, and the bulk of the plans drawn up for Xinjiang never existed outside of the paper they were written on.

The inability and often unwillingness of officials in the new Republic to tangibly support this effort in the far west meant that Chinese officials retained a light grip on Xinjiang. Indeed, the priorities of the Republican government on developing areas of China-proper over investing in border regions, the cutting off of interprovincial assistance in 1912, and the long distances that stood between Xinjiang and the rest of China helped ensure that a succession of Han Chinese provincial leaders, who governed the region from the time of the revolution into the mid-1940s, operated with almost complete autonomy. In addition, this hands-off border policy by officials in the Chinese Republic also allowed for the emergence of new competitors for power in Xinjiang. In the early twentieth century, British, Russian and later Soviet, and even American agents jousted over access to the region's resource wealth. By the late 1920s, armed with an advantageous topography and a willingness to invest in transportation infrastructure in neighboring Central Asia, Soviet planners had large eclipsed their imperial rivals. Well into the 1950s, Soviet officials were actively involved in the task of accessing Xinjiang's lucrative resource wealth. Eager to control its natural resources without shouldering the costly burden of annexing it, Soviet officials effectively transformed Xinjiang into a nearly textbook example of "informal empire."[9] For their part, the largely autonomous provincial officials who were desperate for aid, support, and infusions of cash and commodities to prop up their isolated economy were more than willing to work closely with their Soviet counterparts even as they continued to proclaim their allegiance to the Chinese Republic. This dynamic continued well into the post-1949 People's Republic period, as Chinese officials enthusiastically offered up access to Xinjiang's resources in exchange for material support and aid in the region.

Despite the autonomy of local officials and the growing boldness of foreign powers, officials in the central government of the Republic of China repeatedly asserted their sovereign claims to Xinjiang. These claims were backed up with little more than aggressive rhetoric, however. In his work on Republican-era Tibet, Lin Hsiao-ting argues that Chinese officials simply asserted an "imagined sovereignty" that was "based on a sort of political imagination that was engineered to maintain its Nationalist façade and political legitimacy."[10] A similar imagination was at play in Xinjiang, as rhetorical claims by Republican officials and to a lesser extent their counterparts in the Chinese Communist Party (CCP) rarely matched realities on the ground. This inability or often unwillingness of the state to exert a totalizing control over state integration is not uncommon in distant border regions. As Richard White notes in his work on empire in North America, power weakens at the periphery: "At the center are hands on the levers of power, but the cables have, in a sense, been badly frayed or even cut." As in North America, in Xinjiang this opened the door to a wide assortment of state and nonstate actors all competing for resources and influence. As White writes, along these peripheries, "minor agents, allies, and even subjects at the periphery often guide the course of empire."[11]

Moving from the world of rhetoric and discourse to the political and economic realities on the ground in Xinjiang, my work reveals the weakness of Chinese border policy in the twentieth century. When it comes to the embattled Republic of China, weakness is a common trope of historical scholarship. Whether or not one points to Chiang Kaishek's administrative inadequacies, the corruption at the heart of Chinese political elites, the impact of Japanese aggression throughout the 1930s, or some other factor, weakness is frequently seen to sit at the center of the Republican project.[12] As far as its policy in border regions was concerned, this assessment is undeniably true. The period from 1911 to 1949 was witness to the secession of Outer Mongolia, the seizure of Manchuria by Japan, and the autonomy if not de facto independence of both Tibet and Xinjiang. While Qing officials exerted control over border regions and the early People's Republic was able to stake clearer sovereign claims to various borderlands in ways that their Republican counterparts could not, my work reveals that in a practical sense, weakness remained a central element of border policy from the late nineteenth century well into the 1960s.

Unlike much of the previous scholarship on Republican weakness, which is driven by a desire to ascertain the roots of the CCP's 1949 victory over Chiang Kaishek's Guomindang Party (GMD), this work does not focus on the factors that led to Qing and later Chinese weakness in Xinjiang. Instead, I am more interested in the consequences of this weakness. What impact does the inability or unwillingness of Qing and Republican leaders to invest in the integration of Xinjiang have in shaping this border region's relationship to China-based regimes in the twentieth century? This simple question lies at the heart of this book. In pursuing it, I reveal the complex concessions, alliances, and negotiations between provincial officials, local elites, the agents of imperial powers, Chinese officials, and representatives of international markets in the late nineteenth century and much of the twentieth. This perspective places Xinjiang into a broader transnational context and highlights a contingency that lay at the heart of China's twentieth-century state building project in the far west that has lasting implications for this border region.

## Resources and the State

This moment of Chinese weakness coincided with the development of a global, integrated resource market. As a consequence, beginning in the late nineteenth century but continuing throughout the twentieth, Xinjiang's rich natural resources were a siren song attracting the attentions of foreign powers, Chinese planners, and provincial officials. Whether it was gold and petroleum in the late nineteenth and early twentieth centuries; wool, hides, and furs with high value on international markets in the 1910s and 1920s; industrial minerals with military application including beryllium and tungsten in the 1930s and 1940s; or the pursuit of petroleum and rare nonferrous metals in more recent years, the potential profit that these local products were capable of generating drew in large numbers of interested parties. The efforts to gain access to Xinjiang's local products served as a critical but largely overlooked factor in shaping the region's connections to China, regional neighbors, and indeed the world.

Qing officials had long been interested in quantifying tributary goods and identifying taxable products throughout the realm. But the growing dominance of the imperial powers in the nineteenth century, and a new belief that the key to the West's so-called "wealth and power" (*fuqiang*) lay in their efforts to acquire resources and minerals in particular, prompted Qing reformist officials in the latter part of the nineteenth century to begin aggressively promoting new state-sponsored scientific surveys to accurately assess the resource wealth of the empire.[13] The late nineteenth-century campaigns to make Xinjiang's complex landscape more "legible," to borrow from James C. Scott, were part of a larger effort to rationalize China's territory and facilitate the extraction of lucrative natural resources that could be used to fill state coffers.[14] Intended to rationalize and bureaucratize Xinjiang's landscape with the goal of promoting the generation of revenue, these efforts can be placed squarely within one definition of modern state making and what I refer to in this work as state formation or alternatively state building.[15] In contrast to much of the work on twentieth-century Xinjiang, which has tended to focus on political campaigns, ethnic policy, and agriculture-based settler colonialism, I find that the engine shaping the political, economic, and social contours of the Chinese state in Xinjiang was the desire to gain access to the region's resources by a wide assortment of state and nonstate actors in the twentieth century.

The efforts to exploit, process, and transport a variety of natural resources resonated well beyond the minerals extracted, the wool sheered, petroleum drilled, or skins cured. The campaigns to gain access to natural resources left a firm imprint, the outline of which remains visible on Xinjiang's landscape, its political and transport infrastructure, and demography. In order to understand the power of Xinjiang's resources in shaping state power in the region we must understand the materiality of these resources. In his work on fossil fuels, Timothy Mitchell argues that previous scholarship focused almost exclusively on petroleum as a unit of value. This perspective has obscured, "the ways in which oil is extracted, processed, shipped and consumed, the power of oil as a concentrated source of energy, or the apparatus that turns this fuel into forms of affluence and power," Mitchell writes.[16] By considering the material qualities of oil rather than viewing it simply as a unit of value, we are reminded of its weight and its liquidity, both of which make long-distance transport difficult and expensive, as well as the need to add heat to make raw petroleum usable in combustion engines. In the modern world, these qualities mean that among the preconditions for profiting off of the production of petroleum are the construction of paved roads, the purchase of tanker trucks, the construction of rail lines, the development of pipeline networks, and the establishment of large-scale refining operations. In some ways, petroleum is unique; its material qualities require an unusually complex and expensive apparatus in order to generate revenue. But that does not mean that other resources, whether industrial ores, animal pelts, wool, or cotton do not require similar infrastructure to facilitate the ability of the state to produce, process, and transport these products.

Historians of technology in particular have convincingly pointed to the socioeconomic and political power of infrastructure. As Christopher Jones notes in his work on the role of infrastructure in shaping energy regimes, "canals, pipelines, and wires must be seen as more than simply material assemblages of earth, water, concrete, steel, and copper."[17] In this work I argue that the material foundation constructed to produce, process, and transport Xinjiang's resource wealth are the all-too-often overlooked bones of state power and authority in the region. In twentieth-century Xinjiang, the road networks, lithium ore sorting stations, and petroleum refineries all serve as the brick and mortar framework upon which political institutions, capital investment, and new immigrant populations rest.[18] Focusing on oil production in the Niger Delta, Michael Watts argues that the oil complex "provides the setting, at once institutionally dense and politically cogent, within which new governable spaces are manufactured."[19] In Xinjiang, this insight can be extrapolated beyond petroleum, as the institutions used to centralize Chinese government control and produce governable space, including party organs, police and military forces, and immigrant communities were grafted atop the

infrastructures established to facilitate the production of a shifting assortment of resources and local products.[20] The abilities of various state agents,
local officials, and imperial representatives to profit off of these products demanded the establishment of interlocking institutions and infrastructure that
also served as the foundation of state power in this border region.

My work reveals that in distant and rugged but resource-rich regions like
Xinjiang, the desire for resources shaped the development of institutions of
the state. Geological and planning surveys often served as some of earliest
comprehensive surveys of Xinjiang, the desire to protect claims to local products facilitated the establishment of early political and coercive institutions in
resource-rich areas, the need to transport bulky local products led state planners to fund the construction of long-distance transport networks that could
be used for political as well as economic purposes, and the effort to control
production prompted the promotion of immigration and the establishment
of settler communities in resource-rich areas. Here, the economic efforts to
identify, extract, process, and transport local products were carefully inter-
twined with the more nakedly political efforts to control populations as well
as centralize and enforce state authority.

In an influential 2003 article, Karen Barad argues that "language has been
granted too much power." She continues, "Language matters. Discourse matters. Culture matters. There is an important sense in which the only thing
that does not matter anymore is matter."[21] At its core, this work is an attempt
to resubstantiate the material side of what geographers have referred to as the
production of "territory," a process that I argue is about more than symbolic
representations of space through maps, the crafting of historical narratives,
or the performance of identities.[22] Indeed, these symbolic representations,
which have dominated much of the recent work on the integration of border
regions, merely represent often idealized conceptions of national power and
state authority. They reflect little on the complex logics that support the development of institutions and infrastructure. By tracking the connections between state investment, institutions, and the production of local products and
raw materials, this work reveals the process by which territory is inscribed
and ascribed, and points to the historical contingency and human agency that
lies at the core of this process.

### Transnational "Layers"

In trying to assess twentieth-century Chinese state formation in Xinjiang
from the perspective of resource extraction, one runs into a prominent obstacle. Namely, most of the earlier efforts surrounding the exploitation of

local products and natural resources were undertaken by provincial officials, foreign powers, and imperial agents who had little inclination to aid in Chinese efforts to centralize their control over this border region. Indeed, largely autonomous provincial officials, as well as Russian, Soviet, and British representatives spearheaded the earliest surveys, extraction operations, and infrastructural development in Xinjiang in the late nineteenth and early twentieth centuries. The question then is how do the efforts of various imperial powers to exploit Xinjiang's raw materials fit into a broader framework of Chinese state formation? Or, to put the question in a slightly different way, how can we construct a unified narrative of local production, resource exploitation, and state formation in this contested border region?

In this book I will argue that in distant, largely unintegrated border regions like Xinjiang, which have multiple competitors eager to gain access to lucrative resources, we should adopt a "layered" model of state formation. In this model, the efforts of powerful states or empires to facilitate the outflow of local products and raw materials served as an enduring production blueprint for subsequent planners. In places like Xinjiang, the high cost of fielding surveying teams, establishing resource extraction enterprises, and developing transport networks meant that rather than distributing capital widely in an effort to uncover all of the region's resource wealth, in order to quickly and cheaply ramp up production, states often simply tracked the earlier efforts of their predecessors. The desire to maximize investments meant that these layers channeled state interest and capital away from other resource-rich sites in other areas. Repeated over a long time frame, the result is a layering of surveys, capital investments, political institutions, and transportation infrastructure into a handful of discrete production sites.

In Xinjiang, the initial layers were shaped by the emergence of global resource markets in the late nineteenth century. These markets prompted an outflow of Western explorers and surveyors into the region. In their travels, these explorers discovered a multitude of resources scattered throughout this vast province, from the Kunlun Mountain range in the south, to the Turfan Depression in the east, to the foothills of the Tianshan Mountains in central Xinjiang, to the Altay range in the far north. But the desire to facilitate the outflow of lucrative resources ensured that by the early twentieth century, imperial planners, most notably from the Russian Empire and later the Soviet Union, prioritized capital investments into a small handful of sites located along their border and near extant transport networks. Repurposing Frederick Cooper's evocative metaphor about power in colonized spaces, I find that in resource-rich, imperialized spaces like Xinjiang, capital flows too should

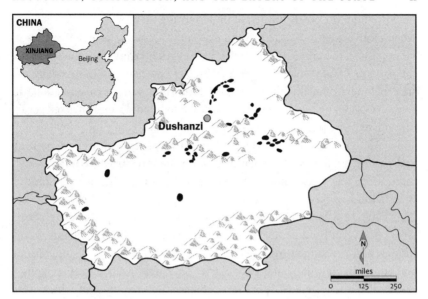

MAP 1.1 The major oil fields in Xinjiang. Source: Xinjiang Weiwu'er zizhiqu difangzhi bianzuan wei-yuanhui, ed., *Xinjiang tongzhi: shiyou gongye* (vol. 40) (Urumqi: Xinjiang Renmin Chubanshe, 1999). Reproduction by Debbie Newell.

not be seen as "capillary"; they were in fact "arterial."[23] Meaning, rather than distributing capital widely throughout the territory in an effort to uncover resources from even the most far-flung but resource-rich locality, eager to gain access to raw materials quickly and inexpensively, imperial powers mainlined capital directly to Xinjiang's most easily accessible and proven, resource sites. For Russian and Soviet explorers, who dominated the region's raw materials markets in the early twentieth century, this capital was concentrated at a handful of sites in the northern stretches of the province. Map 1.1 illustrates the various known oilfields in Xinjiang. Russian/Soviet, British, and Chinese planners were all well aware of the existence of many of these fields scattered throughout the region's vast territory. Yet surveys undertaken by Russian geologists in the late Qing period and subsequent efforts to exploit the oil wealth they discovered at a place called Dushanzi, prompted the layering of future surveys, capital investment, and infrastructure in a tight circumference around this single area throughout the twentieth century.

The high cost of labor, material, and equipment in Xinjiang, as well as a desire for quick profit off of the region's rich local products, prompted successive waves of foreign actors, local and provincial officials, and Chinese state agents in the twentieth century to build upon their predecessors' work rather than shoulder the costly burden of underwriting their own new efforts. Even when clear evidence pointed to the existence of equally productive sites in other parts of the province, the power of the earlier layers continued to shape the patterns of later state investments. To cite one example, in 1953, Chinese state planners officially closed several promising petroleum operations in southern Xinjiang, explaining that "production should be restricted to areas with existing [refining] equipment."[24] This decision to concentrate capital and attention on sites that had already been well surveyed, well capitalized, and well integrated into regional transportation infrastructure repeats itself throughout this work. Indeed, throughout the twentieth century, Chinese, British, Russian, Soviet, and local provincial officials all sought to concentrate their capital investments in order to minimize costs and maximize short-term returns on production. The accretion of layers of infrastructure, institutions, and investment into specific resource sites served to channel funds and efforts into a small handful of discrete, geographically narrow regions.[25] Focused at a few isolated spots in northern Xinjiang, most of which were located near the border with Russian and later Soviet Central Asia, these sites siphoned off nearly all of the state investment earmarked for resource extraction operations in the region for much of the twentieth century.

By focusing on the creation of a transnational blueprint for local production, my work reveals the critical role of collaboration and negotiation in the formation of modern Xinjiang. This collaboration and negotiation, indeed the very layers upon which Chinese administration in the region has been constructed, stands in stark contrast to a long-held narrative of Xinjiang's history, which sees the region simply as a pawn in a wider geopolitical struggle. Xinjiang has long been placed within a broader "great game" framework characterized by a zero-sum imperial struggle for control between the British, Russian, and Qing empires. Since Owen Lattimore's pathbreaking 1950 work on Xinjiang, *Pivot of Asia*, scholars have expanded the great game framework beyond the late nineteenth and early twentieth centuries into the Cold War era.[26] While competition was unquestionably an element that has shaped the region, these studies leave little room for an economic collaboration and negotiation that had an equally significant, if not greater, impact on Xinjiang. In this work, I reveal that the efforts of British, Soviet, American, GMD, and Chinese Communist actors to profit off of Xinjiang's rich natural resources and local products are part of a single, unified narrative. This perspective helps uncover the underlying logics that have shaped enduring state priorities and long-term spatial patterns of investment and institutionalization in this corner of the Chinese nation-state.

By excavating the layers of modern Xinjiang, I seek to reveal the long-term legacies of formal and informal empires all along China's long borders, an issue I will return to in greater detail in the conclusion. Much of the previous work on the role of foreign powers operating in Chinese border regions has tended to be studies of empire. As such, these works are often too temporally delimited to fully reveal the long-term resonance of the surveys, capital, investments, and infrastructural development undertaken by these imperial powers. They therefore fail to reveal the ways in which Chinese and local officials worked with and built upon the efforts of foreign powers.[27] Imperial competition raged across resource-rich Chinese borderlands in the nineteenth and twentieth centuries, from Manchuria and Inner Mongolia in the north, to Taiwan in the southeast, to Yunnan and Guangxi in the south, to Tibet in the southwest. This competition had a lasting resonance, as the desire to gain access to certain lucrative raw materials and the layers that were laid to extract them helped shape long-term patterns of industrial production, infrastructural development, and institutionalization. Pulling back the layers of twentieth-century Xinjiang offers new perspectives on the integration of China's border regions, by prying them out of a China-centered narrative and integrating them more clearly into a truly transnational one.

Beyond China, the case of Xinjiang also speaks directly to the broader experiences of states in Asia, Africa, Latin America, and other places in the global south that continue to grapple with the complex legacies of formal and informal empire. The influx of imperial agents and foreign capital shaped border regions in the global south in powerful and enduring ways. The problem is that the imported Western-centric models of state formation and border integration, which are based on idealized examples drawn from Westphalian Europe, do not apply well to regions of the world where the desire of imperial powers to acquire certain raw materials have shaped long-term patterns of production, capital investment, and the development of regional inequalities. In the past century, American involvement in the production of rubber in Brazil and oil in Venezuela, British and Soviet development of petroleum production sites in Persia and other sites in the Middle East, and Chinese investments in mining enterprises in Ghana, the Congo, and other states in Sub-Saharan Africa are all examples of how foreign investment helps create enduring production priorities in resource-rich states in the global south. Excavating the layers of investment and institutions in Xinjiang offers a new way of thinking about patterns of state investment, institutionalization, and economic development as well as a new model for thinking in a more complex, transnational way about the long-term legacies of formal and informal empires.

### Ethnicity, Violence, and the Spatial Contours of the Chinese State

This book seeks to reveal the infrastructures that shaped the socioeconomic and political topography of Xinjiang in the twentieth century. Susan Leigh Star argues that studying infrastructure can help reveal the hidden mechanisms that shape our modern world. She writes, "Study a city and neglect its sewers and power supplies (as many have), and you miss essential aspects of distributional justice and planning power."[28] Following Star, this book asserts that if we want to understand the logics that undergird the formation of Chinese state power in Xinjiang, we must look beyond the nakedly political institutions that serve to establish, enforce, and project that power. Indeed, by focusing on the efforts to stake claims to natural resources, I seek to reveal the infrastructures that have shaped the economic, political, and indeed social geography of the region.

Twentieth-century Xinjiang has been witness to shocking violence and struggle. The region has been the site of battles, massacres, power struggles, and, in more recent years, cycles of violent interethnic strife and state repression. The study of modern Xinjiang has been shaped by a desire to understand these events. Over the last two decades, historians writing in English have focused on the formation of indigenous and particularly Uyghur ethnic identities in the region, seeking to root the escalating tensions in the province in the formation and strengthening of ethnic identity.[29] These efforts have been mirrored in the work of social scientists addressing how this ethnic identity has been used to inform Uyghur resistance to the Chinese state.[30] These important works have aided in our understanding of the ways that ethnicity has shaped contemporary Xinjiang and go a long way toward countering the nation-centered historical narratives about the linear, inexorable expansion of Chinese state power proffered by the People's Republic.[31] But they tell us little about the socioeconomic and political systems that have shaped Chinese state policy in the region. Recently a new generation of twentieth-century Xinjiang scholars, drawing heavily on new sources drawn from underutilized archives in China, Taiwan, Central Asia, and Russia, have sought to understand the formation of these political systems, and in so doing have helped uncover the dynamics that have shaped imperial policies, interethnic tensions, and state power.[32]

Pulling back the layers that have shaped modern Xinjiang, my work complements this new crop of political histories. But also, by revealing the material foundations that undergird the development of political power in Xinjiang, it offers a unique perspective on the logics that support the region's political topography. Perhaps facetiously, Star positions her work as a "call to study boring things," arguing that they can help reveal the "ecology" of the economic, political, and social systems that have allowed for the emergence of presumably more exciting things.[33] While I hesitate before labeling the struggle to control and promote the production of raw materials and local products boring, my work suggests that in Xinjiang her larger point is certainly true. The infrastructures of state power laid over the course of the twentieth century have helped create the conditions that have led to the violence and unrest in the region in more recent years. Focusing on efforts to promote and control the production of raw materials and local products by a wide assortment of state actors, imperial agents, and local and provincial officials, this work reveals the structures that have shaped Xinjiang's socioeconomic and political ecology in powerful ways.

For those familiar with much of the previous work on Xinjiang, it will come as a surprise that Uyghur and other indigenous groups are underrepresented in this work compared to their population in the region. Indeed, the geologists, miners, surveyors, road builders, traders, and truck drivers who serve to drive this book's narrative engine are primarily Han Chinese and other immigrant groups from China-proper, Russian and British subjects, or citizens of the Soviet Union. The stories of these actors were drawn primarily from sources uncovered in national and provincial archives in the People's Republic of China, including the Xinjiang Uyghur Autonomous Region Archive and the National Geological Archives of China, as well as sources from archives in Taiwan, the United Kingdom, and the Russian Federation. As a result, on some level, the underrepresentation of indigenous peoples is a product of what Laura Newby argues, in her work on Qing imperial reports and travelogues focused on Xinjiang, is a "textual apartheid," as Han and Manchu travelers and officials largely wrote these groups out of their work.[34]

The issue, however, is not simply one of a blinkered imperial gaze. Indeed, the meager data that does exist suggests that Uyghurs and other indigenous groups, aside from possibly having discovered several of the more prominent resource sites, played a secondary role in large-scale state-sponsored raw material production, infrastructural development, and local product purchasing and distribution. Beginning in the 1820s, Qing officials saw Han Chinese and other migrants from China-proper as playing a critical role in balancing out the questionable loyalties of indigenous groups.[35] This dynamic continued throughout the twentieth century as, with only brief exceptions, the major political leaders in Xinjiang were almost exclusively Han Chinese and remained devoted to maintaining a Han presence in the region as a counterbalance to the Turkic Muslim demographic majority. As a result, Uyghurs and other indigenous groups did work in large-scale capital-intensive production operations in the region, but their numbers lagged well behind those of their immigrant counterparts.

In the twentieth century, Uyghurs and other Turkic Muslims exerted little control over the resources that have shaped Xinjiang. In this book, there are moments of resistance to Han power in the region, including several substantial uprisings that often targeted production facilities and a few notable but isolated attacks on mining and other enterprises. But these events are an anomaly in this region prioritized for exploitation by larger powers eager for resources. While Uyghur elites in particular sought to influence politics throughout the twentieth century, Chinese and Soviet patrons largely insulated them from resource exploitation efforts and larger economic policies. Indeed, when it came to the large-scale capital-intensive production facilities that served as the layers upon which modern Xinjiang continues to rest, indigenous actors played a largely secondary role. Even when they were present, these groups existed primarily as a pool of unskilled labor, aiding the efforts of Chinese and Russian planners, geological teams, and engineers.[36] They, like subalterns everywhere, are largely silent.

State production priorities and layers of state investment over the course of the twentieth century served to establish northern Xinjiang as the primary locus of large-scale capital-intensive production. As such, this region located north of the Tianshan Mountain range is the setting for most of the action in this book. For much of its history, northern Xinjiang, a region dominated by arid open steppe land and towering mountain ranges in the north and west and long controlled by nomadic Mongols, stood in stark contrast to the south, with its communities of Uyghurs working the rich agricultural land located in oases dotting the edges of the vast Taklimakan Desert. Following the brutal Qing campaigns in northern Xinjiang against the Zunghar Mongols in the mid-eighteenth century and the implementation of a hands-off policy in the southern stretches of the province that was intended to maintain the peace with the large Uyghur population there, the less populated north became the location where much of the region's Han Chinese migrants settled.[37]

The transformation of northern Xinjiang into a raw material production hub in the twentieth century served to create the conditions that would facilitate growing socioeconomic differences between the Han immigrant–dominant north and the agricultural, largely Uyghur south. My work suggests that if we want to understand the ethnocultural tensions in Xinjiang more generally, we need to historicize spatial patterns of institutionalization and economic development more carefully. For this, we need to understand the development of the layers, which are laid thick over northern Xinjiang, and their role in shaping Chinese state investment and institutions of power in this region. Focusing on these layers reveals the uneven, lumpy nature of Chinese state formation in Xinjiang and offers a new perspective on the region's "ecology," to borrow from Star, that has shaped this often restive border region. The recent work on ethnicity, resistance, and the development of political systems offers an important contribution to understanding the emergence of tensions in the region. But they can only go so far in understanding the logics that have helped produce these tensions.

These ethnocultural tensions, the emergence of religious fundamentalism, and indeed the cycles of violence and state repression that have swept across Xinjiang in recent years can be understood only in the context of the development of a list of state priorities that are concentrated in the north at the expense of the south. The lessons that we can take from Xinjiang speak to a larger perspective on the development of state power that applies broadly across Chinese peripheries. Rather than focusing on the impact of the formation of ethnic identities in isolation, this work reveals the value in understanding the ways in which ethnic formation and state economic policies have helped create the conditions for inequality. My work suggests that in Xinjiang but also in other resource-rich ethnic peripheries, these two factors have combined to create a combustible socioeconomic environment.

## Organization of the Book

In Xinjiang, the development of the infrastructure of state and the efforts to find, exploit, process, and transport certain raw materials and local products unfolded hand in hand. In order to highlight this connection, this book is organized around the efforts to gain access to an evolving set of resources and local products. Each chapter focuses on a discrete set of resources as well as the layers laid by a wide assortment of actors seeking to identify, extract, process, and transport those resources. While organized thematically around the resources and the human structures built to facilitate their extraction, it still follows a largely chronological path, as certain economic and political conditions ensured that production priorities changed over time. The text is divided into two parts: the first focuses on the production of high-value minerals and raw materials, many of which are used in commodity products. The second focuses on the production of industrial raw materials. The division reflects a transformation of Xinjiang in the minds of leaders in China and the Soviet Union in the 1930s, from a region largely defined by its wasteland, where officials prioritized the production of resources capable of extracting profit and boosting state revenues, into one defined by its ability to produce the specific raw materials needed to bolster large-scale industrial development.

Chapter 2 begins with a focus on a Chinese imperial border policy that centered around agricultural reclamation in steppe lands. The failure of this policy in northern Xinjiang in the late nineteenth century and the emergence of new ideas about resource production imported from the West prompted a shift toward new ways of thinking about the connections between natural resources, local production, and border policy in the late Qing period. In chapter 3, the discovery of gold in southern Xinjiang and oil in the north by Russian geologists and subsequent efforts by Russian imperial agents to stake claims to these lucrative resources led to more aggressive attempts to exploit these same products by Qing officials and later by their counterparts in the early Republic of China. These surveys and extraction efforts are the earliest layers laid over a handful of sites in northern Xinjiang. Chapter 4 highlights the growing power of the Russian Empire and later the Soviet Union in the region, as they sought greater access to certain commodity products with high values on international markets, including wool, furs, pelts, and other animal products. The desire to exchange these goods for Soviet military and material support prompted provincial officials to exert greater control over their production and distribution in the 1930s.

Part two begins with a shift in priorities in the 1930s, as the Soviet Union increasingly saw Xinjiang as capable of producing a set of raw materials, including tungsten and beryllium as well as petroleum, that were desperately needed by Soviet planners gearing up for a large-scale heavy-industry drive. The demand for industrial minerals critical for military industries in particular prompted a greater push by the Soviet Union to extend their control over production, processing, and transport facilities in this Chinese province. Their investments in surveying, infrastructure, mining, and processing plants, which were undertaken in conjunction with their counterparts in the provincial capital, are the focus of chapter 5. The layering of surveys and investment in the region helped shape long-term production, processing, and infrastructural development plans drawn up by subsequent Chinese regimes. In chapter 6, after the provincial governor cut his ties to the Soviet Union in 1942 and turned to the Chinese Republic, Republican officials, immediately sought to build upon the efforts of their Soviet counterparts to produce industrial minerals. These efforts were duplicated by the Chinese Communist Party after it came to power in 1949. Chapter 7 focuses on CCP industrial campaigns and the efforts to strengthen state control over resource-rich petroleum and nonferrous metal sites, and reconfigure the patterns of investment and development in the region in the late 1950s and 1960s in the face of growing Sino-Soviet tensions.

The book concludes with a reflection on the long-term impact of the patterns of state investment in resource extraction and local production in Xinjiang. This final chapter reveals the legacies of these patterns and seeks to make a connection between them and the growing ethnocultural tensions in the region. The chapter also highlights the portability of the layered model, pointing to its applicability in other border regions in China and beyond.

# PART 1

# Lucrative Products and the Pursuit of Profit

# Grain, Agricultural Reclamation, and a New Perspective on Production

In its section on "taxes and tribute" (*gongfu*), a 1762 Qing dynasty gazetteer details the various taxable products produced in Xinjiang, including copper, sulfur, saltpeter, cotton, grapes, and tin. Other products that were listed as tribute to be delivered to the court in Beijing included black otter pelts and Kazakh horses from Ili, wild geese from Dihua, pears from Aksu, white jade from Khotan, and Hindustani gold thread satin from Kashgar.[1] But well into the nineteenth century, the only product that Qing officials in Xinjiang were willing to promote using vast sums of state resources and attention was grain. Indeed, Qing officials invested heavily in agricultural reclamation campaigns, as they sought to grow the grain needed to feed frontline troops and imperial administrators as well as establish permanent communities of agricultural settlers in the northern steppe. It is only in the late nineteenth century, as a gripping financial crisis forced Qing officials to reconsider the high cost of maintaining irrigation canals, that they began to question the singular focus on grain and turn an eye toward Xinjiang's various other products.

The promotion of agriculture had long been a central component of border policy for expansionistic dynasties stretching back to the Han (206 BCE–220 CE). In their own campaigns in the arid northwest in the first half of the eighteenth century, Qing officials too came to embrace the ability of state-sponsored agricultural reclamation to provide grain for troops and fodder for their mounts.[2] In 1758, one year before the Qing unification of the Zungharian and Tarim basins and the establishment of what was referred to as the "New Frontier," or Xinjiang, the imperial court began aggressively expanding reclamation in the region. Focused primarily on northern Xinjiang, a sparsely populated region dominated by expansive grasslands that seemed suited to the establishment of large-scale farms, the effort was successful in producing substantial amounts of grain and fodder.[3] After little more than a century, however, in 1864 Qing control collapsed, when outsiders from the Kokand khanate (today located within the borders of modern Kyrgyzstan, Uzbekistan, Tajikistan, and Kazakhstan) helped foment a rebellion against Qing authority.

The Qing court tapped the reformist official Zuo Zongtang to head the military campaign to reconquer Xinjiang. By 1878, his New Hunan Army completed the reassertion of Qing control over the region and Zuo was called upon to administer it. Zuo, along with the New Hunan Army officers who governed Xinjiang after his departure, drew inspiration from a set of Han-centric assimilationist border policies developed by adherents of the "statecraft" (*jingshi*) school of imperial administration.[4] Seeking to erase the yawning economic, political, and cultural differences that separated regions located "outside the pass" and those located on the inside (a distinction marked by passage through the Jade Gate [Jiayuguan] in western Gansu province), they prioritized the establishment of Xinjiang as an official province, the importation of the prefecture-county system of local governments adopted throughout the empire, and also called for the aggressive expansion of agricultural reclamation. For them, reclamation could create stable communities of migrants from China-proper who could serve as labor and generate tax revenue and food for the state, serve as an ethnocultural counterbalance to the region's Turkic Muslim majority, and help in the task of transforming unruly, unbounded steppe "wasteland" (*huang*) into ordered, bucolic fields (*tian*).[5]

The Qing court was initially willing to underwrite the costly reclamation campaign with resources from the imperial treasury. Flush with state support in the years immediately following the reconquest, the networks of irrigation canals came to extend deep into northern Xinjiang, transforming arid grassland once populated by pastoral nomads into irrigated agricultural land. The challenge emerged with the late Qing financial crisis that took hold in the late 1880s and continued until the collapse of the dynasty in 1911. As support from the imperial court in Beijing dried up, provincial officials lacked the funds to maintain the irrigation networks, and as a result, vulnerable agricultural communities situated on newly reclaimed land withered on the vine and large numbers of the settlers who had been called upon to populate the steppe fled back to their home villages in China-proper. For Qing officials, by the early twentieth century, the reclamation-centered border policy was an undeniable failure.

This failure, coupled with the ongoing need to settle territory, raise revenues, and protect sovereignty in this distant border region, forced late Qing officials to view landscapes and production in new ways. Expanding beyond an agriculture-centered perspective in which the state was focused primarily on grain production, the first decade of the twentieth century was witness to a transformative shift, as Qing officials came to "see" (in James Scott's sense of the word) their territory's productive potential in new ways.[6] While not discarding grain production, imperial officials increasingly emphasized other forms of production alongside it, whether it was gold, oil, hides, or cotton. Influenced by the specific needs of cash-strapped provincial officials as well as new, Western-inspired discourses about the stewardship of the land that circulated among reformist officials throughout the realm, the waning years of the Qing were witness to aggressive state-sponsored efforts to identify, quantify, and categorize the multitude of resources and local products produced in the diverse landscapes and ecosystems of the empire.

### Emphasizing Agriculture

When the New Hunan Army's supply lines stretched and eventually broke during their campaigns in the northwest in the 1870s, General Zuo Zongtang quickly turned to agricultural reclamation to feed his troops. He sponsored the construction of irrigation networks, established fields, and settled soldiers and displaced civilians on state farms in Shaanxi and Gansu provinces, calling on them to produce grain for devastated local communities and soldiers.[7] On these farms, Zuo wrote, "the harvest will be taxed and given to officials, while excess grain will be sold to the military at market prices; this way public and private both benefit."[8] As his armies marched west toward Xinjiang, Zuo opened "reconstruction bureaus" (*shanhouju*) that distributed agricultural equipment and land to facilitate the resettlement of refugees and immigrants.[9]

Passing through the Jade Gate and into Xinjiang, Zuo and his officers understood that the situation here was far worse than in other places in the northwest. "West of the Jade Gate on the official road you can travel one-thousand *li* without seeing a person or a wisp of smoke," writes the author of a late Qing provincial gazetteer regarding the devastated landscape of Xinjiang that unfolded before Zuo's conquering New Hunan Army.[10] Yet this destruction was not equally distributed. Southern Xinjiang suffered more from neglect: local officials noted that they required state investments in road repair, the development of postal relay stations, and the construction of administrative buildings. Northern Xinjiang, which had served as the administrative and military capital in the High Qing period and had once been the home of large numbers of Han migrant settlers, was witness to some of the fiercest fighting. Imperial reports, as well as travelogues from Western explorers, noted that in this region, cities were largely rubble, roads were potholed and overgrown, and administrative centers almost completely destroyed.

Amidst the general devastation, of arguably greater concern for Zuo and Qing officials was the destruction of the state farms established in northern Xinjiang on reclaimed land in the eighteenth and early nineteenth centuries. Many of these farms had returned to open steppe over the preceding decade through lack of attention to irrigation canals and the absence of laborers working the land. According to official estimates, of the more than one million *mu* (one *mu* is equal to approximately one-sixth of an acre) of farmland that had been reclaimed in the High Qing period in the state farms established around Urumqi and in the Ili River valley, much of it had returned to wasteland by the 1870s. The large population of immigrant settlers who had once worked the northern steppe land had vanished; indeed only around 20 percent remained in the 1870s, most of these being Turkic Muslims from the south who resettled in the region.[11] According to one report, even by the 1880s, 70 to 80 percent of all potentially arable land in northern Xinjiang remained uncultivated.[12]

Inspired by classical examples and High Qing agricultural enterprises, as well as the writings of nineteenth-century statecraft thinkers, Zuo and his successors in Xinjiang saw the aggressive expansion of agricultural reclamation as the key to the transformation of this poor, restive border region into a stable, productive, and fully integrated province of the empire.[13] Reclaiming these lands and opening them to settlement would allow provincial officials to resolve a number of problems simultaneously. The settlers called upon to work the reclaimed steppe land would constitute a stable civilian population that could lower the high cost of labor in the region, help ease the burden of empire by both reducing the need to import grain and increasing land tax revenues, and help facilitate the settlement of vulnerable, underpopulated border regions.[14]

Given the lack of a stable labor pool and the distance from China-centered commodity markets that could inexpensively provide food, equipment, and material, the price tag on reconstruction was extremely high. The labor shortage in the north in particular was a constant concern for Qing officials in the late 1870s and early 1880s. While the use of soldiers to dig and dredge irrigation canals, build city walls, and chop down trees was an adequate short-term solution, the long-term success of Xinjiang depended on the strong backs of immigrant civilians drawn from the overcrowded agricultural lands of China-proper.[15] Without this population, the costs of reconstruction and administration would be substantial. As Liu Jintang, Zuo's second-in-command who would later become the first Qing governor of Xinjiang, worried in 1881, "Goods are expensive and people scarce, the total cost of reconstruction cannot be measured."[16]

These immigrant populations would not only aid short-term reconstruction, but also help alleviate the ongoing burden of empire on the imperial treasury. With Xinjiang's large swaths of arid land, small population, and high military budget, officials had been fully dependent on annual shipments of silver from Beijing to make ends meet since the initial conquest of the region. Known as "interprovincial assistance" (xiexiang), the payments came to be closely associated with the finances of the northwest in general and Xinjiang specifically.[17] Eliminating the fiscal burden of the interprovincial assistance payments was a priority for Qing officials after the reconquest. Yet, Xinjiang's distance from markets in China-proper meant that the cost of grain to support soldiers and administrators was high and its small tax base ensured that revenues were low. As Governor Liu reported, "since grain and grass all must be imported from afar, the cost and effort are double."[18] Agricultural production would serve to shorten the distance that grain and grass (for fodder) imports would have to be shipped, thereby reducing state costs. Furthermore, the new communities established on reclaimed land were also seen as Xinjiang's future fiscal backbone. Qing officials had long sought to maintain relatively low land tax rates in southern Xinjiang in order to shore up the loyalties of the Turkic Muslim "wrapped heads" (chantou, a name referring to Uyghurs) who worked the oases of the south. The establishment of stable communities of agricultural migrants in northern Xinjiang then would help generate tax revenues that could alleviate the province's perennial fiscal shortfall.

The arrival of immigrants from China-proper would not only help boost the pool of cheap labor and facilitate the production of grain and commodities demanded by the imperial administration and its coercive apparatus, but also begin the task of filling out and claiming underpopulated border regions. The expansion of the Russian Empire into Central Asia in the 1860s led to new concerns from Qing officials about defending sovereign territory. A series of subsequent military crises in the mid-nineteenth century spawned a deep-seated Russophobia in Qing officials, who feared that Russia had its mind set on forcefully incorporating Xinjiang into its growing empire. The prominent late Qing diplomat Prince Gong summarized these suspicions when he lamented that "Russia, whose territory is contiguous to ours, having long nourished the intention to bite off our land 'as the silkworm devours mulberry leaves,' is our sickness of body while Great Britain, which seeks to trade, is our sickness of limb."[19] These fears, exacerbated by an ongoing series of threats and border incidents, made it clear to the Qing court that the efforts of delineating the borders of the empire undertaken in the eighteenth and nineteenth centuries were not enough to protect its territory.[20] The settlement of areas along the border with permanent agricultural migrants from China-proper was seen as a critical element of a new Qing policy. Qing officials dubbed the strategy "using migrants to solidify the borderland" (*yimin shibian*).[21]

In addition to the pragmatic considerations, the transformation of nomad-dominated steppe into peaceful farmland was also a central element of a larger campaign of cultural assimilation intended to reinforce Qing control over the region. The so-called "opening of wasteland" (*kai huang*) facilitated the transformation of wild steppe into ordered, delineated field.[22] From the position of governance, this effort was part of a long-standing "emphasize agriculture" (*zhongnong*) policy rooted in a Sinitic belief in the moral superiority of ordered, plowed fields and a dark mistrust of unplowed, unbounded grassland.[23] The policy was one embraced by numerous officials throughout the Qing period, but particularly by those adherents of the reformist statecraft school—a group that included Zuo and his officers—which called for a new imperial border policy bound even more closely to agricultural reclamation. For them, a renewed commitment to the production of grain would transform this region from an unincorporated region made up of uninhabitable wasteland into one made up of ordered, governable fields. These officials believed in the sociocultural civilizing power of agriculture. As Liu Jintang wrote in 1881, "Now the wealth of the earth is being opened daily, the number of families are increasing daily, and all of the tribes [of Xinjiang] (*gezu*) are all coming together to live in villages."[24]

## Opening the Steppe in Late Qing Xinjiang

For late Qing officials it was clear that agricultural reclamation was central to the maintenance of empire in the far west. The flowering of farms all across the northern steppe had the power to resolve the region's fiscal, security, and social issues in one stroke. And when it came to implementation, the success of the agriculture-centered border policy appeared to never be in doubt. There was a relaxed confidence in the memorials to the court written by provincial officials who argued that only a minimal investment would allow the steppe to bloom. In one representative assertion about the unsurpassed fertility of northern Xinjiang, the Board of Revenue (Hubu) claimed that "all along the north road, from the Mulei River west to the Ili the soil is rich and moist to the touch."[25] The statement, along with others like it, was intended to justify the new calls for an aggressive agricultural reclamation campaign in northern Xinjiang.

In addition to making sweeping claims about this massive, nearly one-thousand-mile swath of territory encompassing an extreme variety of climates and ecosystems, Qing officials also relied on complex, often-questionable reasoning to justify their calls to undertake an ambitious reclamation campaign that perhaps we should view as magical thinking. One official argued that the lack of rainfall at many sites in the arid northern steppe rather than being a detriment was in fact a positive attribute, as it ensured that soil retained its fertility.[26] Another claimed that while the harsh winters in eastern Xinjiang make for an extremely short growing season, the high fertility of the soil made up for it. The writer noted that grain around the town of Barkol often grew to maturity in one night and that one *dou* (nearly a third of a bushel) of sown seed yields between forty and fifty *dou* at harvest, a yield-to-seed ratio that exceeds the best harvests in the United States today.[27] Even Zuo Zongtang got into the spirit, arguing that certain indigenous forms of irrigation were capable of producing "irrigation water without end."[28]

Their confidence was inspired by what was seen as a proven track record of agricultural productivity in the region. Late Qing officials continually recited the words of the second-century BCE diplomat to the Han dynasty's "western regions" (*Xiyu*) Zhang Qian, who detailed the production of vines, rice, and other crops at various sites located in modern-day Xinjiang, as if it were a mantra. To add credence to their confident assertions about Xinjiang's productivity—assertions that one might have challenged simply by opening the door in many places in this arid province—officials also frequently cited claims about agricultural production of the far west drawn from Chinese classics including the *Shiji* and the *Hanshu*.[29] The more recent successes by the Qing emperors Qianlong and Jiaqing in the eighteenth and early nineteenth centuries, the evidence for which lay not only in the historical record but also in the abandoned fields, irrigation canals, and dwellings still clearly visible in the 1880s, helped put to rest any nagging worries that late Qing officials may have held onto about widely promoting reclamation in the harsh climate of the northern steppe regions. The case for the agricultural productivity of northern Xinjiang appeared to be largely open and shut: dredge irrigation canals, open the door to migrants, and the long-term transformation of Xinjiang's landscape (and consequently its polity) would take care of itself.

Qing officials beginning with Zuo Zongtang were convinced that investments in reclamation activities would, after a short incubation period, result in stable, taxable agrarian communities. The construction of irrigation canals; loans of equipment, seed, and livestock; and the provision of food were intended to encourage the outflow of not only Han and other migrants from China-proper but also Muslims from oasis communities of southern

Xinjiang. A plan unveiled by Liu Jintang offered new immigrant families (*hu*, though according to the regulations these could be made up of any two adults, including siblings or friends) 60 *mu* of land, 3 *shi* (one *shi* is equal to 160 pounds) of seed, 6 taels worth of agricultural tools, a home worth 8 taels, and two oxen valued at 24 taels. Every month in the first year they were to be given 1.8 taels and 90 *jin* (one *jin* is around 1.3 pounds) of grain. In total, each household received 73.1 taels worth of goods and equipment that would have to be repaid to the state by the end of the second year. In the third year, taxes would be assessed on the previous year's production and levied at half of the usual rate, while in the fourth year, the state would levy full taxes.[30]

At least at first, the strategy of opening wasteland and offering incentives to encourage settlement appeared to work, as Qing officials settled large numbers of migrants in northern Xinjiang. In an 1882 memorial to Beijing, Governor Liu proudly points to growing harvests and dropping grain prices throughout the province, noting that it was only a matter of time before settlement communities in the north grew substantially and grain tax revenues came rolling in.[31] In an 1887 report, he notes that they settled 1,090 *hu* at 9 reclamation sites stretching the length of the northern slopes of the Tianshan Mountains: 306 in Dihua county, 100 in Qitai, 104 in Changji, 53 in Fukang, 320 in Suilai, 66 in Jimusa, 74 in Hutubi, 45 in Hami, and 22 in Jinghe.[32] The settlement cost the provincial government 49,800 taels in loans for equipment and food to settlers.

In addition to the settlements established for hard-up civilian migrants from China-proper and southern Xinjiang, Qing officials also restarted the system of settling those with commuted capital sentences in the region; they also began settling Chinese Green Standard as well as Manchu and Mongol banner troops, and large number of demobilized soldiers from Zuo Zongtang's conquering New Hunan Army on reclaimed land. Things were successful enough that by the late 1880s, provincial officials were growing concerned that the policies of tax forgiveness and the payment of incentives intended to encourage settlement were too generous. In an 1887 memorial, Governor Liu complained that along the north road, many officials had allowed local communities to submit their own harvest reports to local officials. This "tolerance" (*gukuan*), he argued, had cheated the provincial government of 1,340 *shi* of grain that year.[33]

The modest successes were not enough. By the mid-1880s, a decline in the annual shipments of interprovincial assistance to Xinjiang meant that provincial officials found themselves under pressure to expand reclamation policies to generate even more land tax revenue. In 1885, the Qing Ministry of Finance fixed annual interprovincial assistance payments to Xinjiang at 3.6 million taels, the bulk of which provincial officials used to pay soldier and official salaries, to fund construction projects, and to fill the often gaping holes in the provincial budget.[34] The problem was that a series of crises in China-proper and a growing fiscal crisis more generally threatened the annual payments, which by 1886 made up around 85 percent of the province's total revenue.[35] To cite one example, the 1887 flooding and subsequent famine in the region around the Yellow River affected crop yields and thus land tax revenues in North China, and led to a 10 percent drop in interprovincial assistance payments to Xinjiang. "Day after day there are new debts added and so day and night we are terrified that the amount of money for other programs will be insufficient and will have to be disbanded," Governor Liu worried.[36]

The hope for provincial officials like Liu was that the seeds sown in the northern steppe would bear fruit in the form of heightened tax revenues. To facilitate and indeed increase the population of immigrants living on the northern steppe, Liu undertook a policy of aggressively promoting the construction of irrigation networks. In the years immediately following the 1878 reconquest of the region, Qing officials focused their efforts on dredging and repairing existing irrigation canals. Regarding the repair of canals in southern Xinjiang, Liu explained in 1881 that "our most critical duty is to urgently promote irrigation works in order to alleviate the suffering of the people."[37] Late Qing sources are filled with numerous stories about how, as the weather warmed and spring snowmelt flowed out of the mountains in the early 1880s, the decade-long lack of maintenance to the canals ensured that water flowed into the newly opened fields only in a modest trickle.[38] By 1886, the problems at several notable sites were serious enough that the provincial finance secretary (*buzhengshi*) Wei Guangtao called for a complete overhaul of the irrigation network.[39]

The period from 1882 to 1888 saw massive increases in construction on Xinjiang's irrigation canals and on northern Xinjiang's water control network in particular. The high cost of civilian labor in northern Xinjiang, due to its low population and distance from commodity and production networks, ensured that a significant amount of the physical effort expended to construct canals was shouldered by Qing imperial banner troops or demobilized New Hunan Army soldiers. According to one noncomprehensive late Qing source, pushed by new priorities set by provincial officials and the court, civilian laborers and soldiers constructed or repaired forty-four separate irrigation canals during this six-year period, most of which were located in the northern steppes.[40] The construction of these irrigation canals drastically increased the amount of arable land in Xinjiang, which by 1887, had grown to a historic high of 11.2 million *mu*.[41] While the bulk of arable land was centered in the

TABLE 2.1. Length of irrigation canals and area of irrigated land

| Circuit (administrative districts) | Length of irrigation canals (in li) | Area of land irrigated (in mu) |
|---|---|---|
| Zhen-Di (12 in northern Xinjiang) | 15,785 | 1,164,299 |
| Yi-Ta (4 in northern Xinjiang) | 7,479 | 722,229 |
| Aksu (11 in southern Xinjiang) | 16,842 | 3,303,918 |
| Kashgar (12 in southern Xinjiang) | 33,754 | 6,031,455 |
| Totals | 73,860 | 11,221,901 |

Source: Hua Li, Qingdai Xinjiang nongye kaifashi (Harbin: Heilongjiang Jiaoyu Chubanshe, 1998), 254–256. For detail on the dates, and specific lengths county by county, see XJTZ, sections 30, 3–4; XJTZ, sections 73–79.

oases of the south, the aggressive reclamation campaigns of the north led to substantial increases in agricultural production and the growth of communities in the northern steppe (see table 2.1). The figure of 11.2 million *mu* represented the upper limit of agricultural reclamation in Qing Xinjiang. From this high, amounts of arable land in the province declined through the collapse of the dynasty in 1911.

## The Steppe Strikes Back

The tightening hold of a financial crisis in the late Qing period translated into a sharp drop-off in interprovincial payments and resulted in declining state support for migrant communities and their newly constructed irrigation networks. Short growing seasons, a reliance on fickle snowmelt to fill canals, and harsh winters all conspired against settlers seeking to cultivate the steppe regions. By the mid-1880s, these communities dotting the northern steppe were already hanging by only a slim thread. That thread was support from the provincial government in the form of emergency grain, winter clothes, and the waiving of taxes. In one case, local officials in the Zhen-Di circuit, in the northeastern corner of the province, wrote to Governor Liu that "settlers have finished a regretfully weak harvest: they have either been afflicted by drought or by insect infestation, have had their crops affected by freezing, or have been reported to have fled." Noting that in Changji, located just east of the provincial capital, forty-eight families harvested only a paltry 47 *shi* (one *shi* is equal to less than three bushels) of grain, local officials asked that settlers in the circuit be relieved of having to pay taxes on that year's harvest.[42]

Similar cases of low harvests, famine, insect infestations, and late frosts appear regularly throughout Qing-era sources.[43] Despite the efforts to accommodate these communities as much as they could, throughout the 1880s and particularly into the 1890s, local officials were frequently forced to contend with the problem of settlers picking up stakes and fleeing back to China-proper. "On the northern road the land and air are bitter and frozen and of those resettled households more than a few flee," wrote Liu Jintang's successor, Tao Mo, in 1895, echoing a growing chorus of provincial officials.[44] The solution to the problem of declining or at best stagnating populations was greater state spending on water control, transportation infrastructure, and general support for immigrant communities.

By the late 1890s, however, there was little money for provincial officials to undertake these types of programs. From 1899 to 1900, the amount of unpaid interprovincial assistance to Xinjiang exploded from 48,000 taels to 520,000 and increased by over 50 percent in the next year to 790,000 taels (see table 2.2).[45] The situation worsened in the years following the Sino-Japanese War in 1895, as provincial treasuries were called upon by the court to help shoulder the burden of paying a large indemnity to Japan, assist in the payment of a number of foreign loans, help pay off a series of ill-advised investments, and at the same time weather various droughts and famines. Compounding the situation, the Boxer Protocol, signed in September 1901 following the crushing of an antiforeign movement in North China by several imperial powers, imposed a massive 450 million tael indemnity on the Qing court. The fiscal impact of the indemnity rippled into Xinjiang, as provincial officials were obliged to contribute 400,000 taels annually, an amount that

TABLE 2.2. Annual interprovincial assistance shortfalls for Xinjiang (in thousands of ounces of silver or taels)

| | |
|---|---|
| 1899 | 48 |
| 1900 | 520 |
| 1901 | 790 |
| 1902 | 304 |
| 1903 | 302 |
| 1904 | 333 |
| 1905 | 328 |
| 1906 | 339 |
| 1907 | 830 |

Source: Wei Jianhua, "Qingdai xiexiang zhidu gailun," in Wu Fuhuai and Wei Changhong, eds., Xinjiang jinxiandai jingji yanjiu wenji (Urumqi: Xinjiang Daxue Chubanshe, 2002), 234.

was taken directly out of interprovincial assistance payments. On top of these payments, in 1902 provincial officials were also helping repay eight separate loans from various domestic and foreign sources at a total cost of 290,000 taels annually, an amount which was taken directly out of interprovincial assistance payments.[46] In one unusual 1903 effort to make ends meet, provincial officials took out a two million tael loan from the Russo-Asiatic Bank (Hua'E Daosheng Yinhang) in which they used mining rights in Xinjiang's ore fields and potential tax revenues from land reclamation as collateral.[47] By 1908, Xinjiang officials were only taking in 2.58 million taels of interprovincial assistance annually, and this amount was itself cut in 1910 to a meager 1.48 million.[48]

Despite recognizing the importance of settler communities in stabilizing Xinjiang and facilitating Qing control, provincial officials simply did not have the means to support them. By the first decade of the twentieth century, appeals from local officials for material support in even the most promising reclamation sites were largely met with a sympathetic shrug of the shoulders from provincial officials who did not have enough funds to cover the costs of basic provincial security and administration. All across northern Xinjiang, small-scale but seemingly promising reclamation sites were handcuffed by a lack of state support. In the waning years of the dynasty, officials overseeing these sites resorted to begging the provincial government for the funds needed to build irrigation canals, granaries, and public buildings, and pay for basic services. To reveal the difficulties faced by local officials, I will highlight two case studies from two very different regions of northern Xinjiang. In both cases, one in the far north and the other in the fertile Ili River valley the maintenance of promising reclamation sites crashed against fiscal realities (map 2.1).

A state-sponsored reclamation site had existed in the fertile fields abutting the Ulungur Lake in far northern Xinjiang since the reign of the Tongzhi emperor (1861–1873). By the first decade of the twentieth century, settlers at the Burultokay (known in Chinese as Fuhai) reclamation site were producing around 700 *shi* of wheat, barley, and highland barley in the more than 10,000 *mu* of fields in the region.[49] As far as officials were concerned, by the first decade of the twentieth century this operation was drastically underfunded. After negotiating a complex series of loans in 1902, local officials undertook the construction of an irrigation canal critical for harnessing snowmelt in the mountains and thus necessary for the expansion of reclamation activities in the region. Local officials desperately sought state support for the expensive endeavor. Drawing on workers from the Urianghai Mongols as well as a score of skilled craftsmen from the town of Gucheng more than 350 miles to the

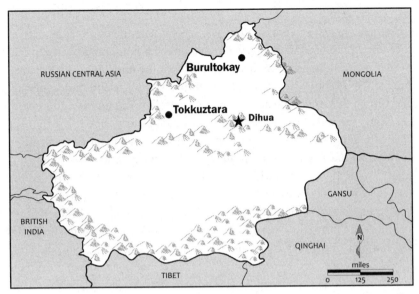

MAP 2.1 The Burultokay (Fuhai) and Tokkuztara (Gongliu) reclamation sites. Map by Debbie Newell.

south, officials broke ground on the project in 1902. The high cost of labor, the task of acquiring sources of the wood and stone that needed to be brought in from long distances, and the sky-high prices being charged for commodities and livestock ratcheted up the price tag on construction. While the project would open up more than 30,000 *mu* of land, it would also cost a substantial 34,000 taels.

In order to ensure the project's success, local officials also called for the construction of a granary, a mill, farmhouses, and public administration buildings on-site. In their reports, they argued that the 40,000 taels requested for this critical site were well below amounts requested in other parts of Xinjiang, including most notably in the border towns of Tacheng and Ili.[50] Facing a litany of more pressing budgetary obligations, provincial officials found themselves unable to help. The lack of funding forced local officials to rely on a complex web of borrowing and repayment with various entities including Mongol banners and an assortment of provinces from China-proper in order to pay for the necessary repairs and upgrades that would ensure the long-term endurance of the site. Officials expressed their frustration with this unsatisfactory state of fiscal affairs, comparing the steady stream of state support the site had received in the years prior to the rebellion in the 1860s with the present. "In earlier days, determining what was true and what false, what was savings and what was expenditure was easy," wrote a Qing local official.[51] Trying to convince his tight-fisted superiors that investment in settler communities was a long-term investment, he argued that "the wealth of all under heaven rested on the promotion of agriculture in border regions." He went on to argue in his 1903 memorial that, if adequately funded, "in twenty years we will have turned arid wasteland into fertile soil and turned this strategic gateway [of the empire] into an interior" (tang'ao).[52]

Nearly 650 miles to the south, in a reclamation site located in the Ili River valley, the situation was largely the same, as local officials in the early twentieth century begged Beijing for more funding. The site at Tokkuztara (Gongliu) traced its origins back to reclaimed fields established in the years prior to the 1864 rebellion. But the more recent iteration was established in 1896, as farmland to support two units of demobilized troops, including two hundred horse armorers and forty rear echelon soldiers. The soldiers each farmed wheat, barley, and highland barley on twenty mu granted them by local officials. They produced around 4,000 shi of grain the first year and were able to meet their targets of providing 15 percent to local officials in taxes. In total, between 1896 and 1903 they produced around 37,000 shi of grain. The harvests were large enough that officials worried they had not constructed enough granaries to prevent rotting.[53]

Despite the successes of the site, the soldiers working the land and the families that they brought with them still depended on state support. Indeed, gaps in allocation ensured that they did not have the money to procure tools, livestock, or the means to construct buildings and fortifications themselves.[54] In the years prior to the rebellion in 1864, the site had relied on three large irrigation canals, and even this was insufficient to fully open adjacent "wasteland." Since 1896, however, due to budgetary constraints, they relied on only two canals, which ensured that the amounts of grain they produced were too small to make them fully self-sufficient. In a series of memorials, local officials requested state support to cover the high cost of construction as well as the cost of basic tools, livestock, and equipment. "If we take advantage of this moment to allocate funds for reclamation, we can achieve the results we hope for," wrote one official around 1904.[55]

Without investment, however, they could expect exactly the opposite. And as funds for local projects dried up in Xinjiang, reclamation sites like Burultokay and Tokkuztara themselves began to wither. Once tilled, the arid grasslands of northern Xinjiang, indeed like grasslands in North America and elsewhere, require almost constant irrigation. The need to construct new canals and maintain old ones was a significant expense in this region where even the most commonplace equipment and commodities were slapped with

high price tags and where the cost of labor widely outstripped court estimates that were calculated based on other places in the empire. Facing severe
budget problems and an ever-lengthening list of pressing spending priorities,
the Qing court in Beijing proved unable to foot the substantial bill. Instead,
the court suggested to officials in Xinjiang and other impoverished border
regions that they raise money from overseas Chinese communities in Southeast Asia to form companies that would undertake large-scale agricultural
reclamation campaigns. Provincial officials dismissed the court's plan as farfetched and unreasonable.[56]

Despite the continuing calls from local officials to support reclamation in
the lands north of the Tianshan, the costs of undertaking these campaigns
proved prohibitive. As a result, irrigation canals were frequently not maintained, the quality of the land declined, and many settlers, facing bitter winters and bleak harvests, chose to flee back to the lands inside the pass. For
the authors of the 1909 *Xinjiang Illustrated Gazetteer*, the region's landscape
was a tragedy in the making. The fabled success of irrigation canals and networks laid out in the High Qing period by notable early nineteenth-century
exiles to Xinjiang like Lin Zexu and Xu Song no longer existed and once-
productive fields sat abandoned. "Fields are many but households few," wrote
the author of the gazetteer. Emphasizing the lack of settlers to demarcate and
work the fields of the northern steppe, the author described a depressingly
open landscape, where "the land is broad and unbounded."[57] According to
official sources, by 1911, the last year of the Qing, arable land had actually
declined since 1887—the high-water mark for land reclamation campaigns in
the province—dropping from nearly 11.5 million *mu* to around 10.5 million.
While the source does not indicate where these declines were concentrated, it
is safe to assume that much of the declines were centered in the harsh newly
opened landscapes of the northern steppe.[58]

## A New Perspective on Xinjiang's Landscape

Qing officials were well aware that Xinjiang sat atop a wide assortment of potentially lucrative products. Gazetteers carefully listed the handful of highly
regulated taxable products as well as those goods reserved as tribute. Yet aside
from warhorses and livestock, as well as a few smaller-scale, periodic efforts
to promote copper, iron, jade, and gold production, into the mid-nineteenth
century there were few sustained, state-sponsored efforts to promote the production of nonagricultural products in Xinjiang.[59] While straitened financial
circumstances in the early nineteenth century prompted a certain amount of

creativity from provincial officials eager to uncover new sources of revenue, when it came to nonagricultural production, their emphasis did not extend much beyond the efforts to control access and extract taxes.[60] It was only the failure of land reclamation and the looming fiscal crisis alongside the import of new, imported ideas about modern state formation that together changed the ways in which imperial officials viewed landscapes and nonagricultural local products.

Faced with a string of military defeats, in the 1860s a faction of Qing reformist officials and elites began a new effort to study the West as part of their larger "self-strengthening" (*ziqiang*) campaign. Among other things, these officials found that the imperial powers placed a clearer priority on industrial production and mining in particular in order to produce the raw materials needed for industry and precious metals needed for wealth. Surveying the small-scale, decentralized mining operations of the empire, these Qing elites worried that they were falling too far behind. The influential official Xue Fucheng complained at the time that "mining policy has not yet been formulated and so wealth is simply being discarded. It is like water drying up, but people do not even realize it."[61] Further, Xue and others called for the expansion of mining enterprises in order to claim ore rich territories and protect them from foreign powers eager to stake their own claims to Qing minerals. "Chinese minerals are plentiful. They are first among the world's nations. If we are careless they will be taken away, but if we manage them well they can definitely be used for profit," Xue argued.[62] Qing officials came to believe that the key to so called "wealth and power" (*fuqiang*) could be found in the way that Western states managed territory and the more active role that they played in promoting the production of various resources. Encouraging the Qing state to play a greater role in producing resources was the means through which the dynasty could return to glory, or at the very least hold off the forces of Western empire.[63]

A series of military failures in the Sino-French War in 1871, the Sino-Japanese War in 1895, the Boxer War in 1900, and various smaller incidents all fueled a growing belief that the Qing empire was falling farther and farther behind the West. This growing urgency prompted a new generation of reformers to more aggressively promote new forms of production. Reformers called for the promotion of "industry and commerce" (*shiye*) and marched under a new slogan: "industry and commerce to save the nation" (*shiye jiuguo*). But the task of "saving the nation" depended on the abilities of Qing elites to identify and promote the extraction of critical products.

Mining in particular was a major focus for Qing reformers in the waning years of the dynasty. As the influential merchant and comprador Zheng Guanying noted, "If we extensively examine how the various countries of the West attain wealth and power, we see that they have tapped the benefits of opening mines."[64] In order to aid in the process of identifying the ore fields that would be used to strengthen the Qing state, by the latter years of the Qing a growing number of students were sent overseas to learn geology and the mining sciences. Returning home, they formed the core of a nascent geological community that saw their efforts at pinpointing minerals in the Qing empire's vast and largely unsurveyed territory as a central element in the broader effort to save the motherland. As *Geographical Magazine*, the publication of the newly formed China Geological Survey, noted in its inaugural issue in 1910, "If one wishes to secretly examine a country's weakness or strength, the state of its industry, then look at the progress of its geological surveys."[65]

The result of this emphasis on identifying and accessing various products was a new way of envisioning landscapes. Inspired by the lessons learned overseas, Chinese geologists brought home what Bruce Braun calls a "geological vision." As Braun argues, this vision abandoned a culturally influenced surface-level "pastoral vision that took delight in the appearance of prospects and open meadows" and replaced it with a new vision focused on uncovering the geological secrets locked away beneath the landscape.[66] The embrace of scientific geology in the late Qing period and the growing number of Chinese students traveling overseas introduced officials and elites to this new vision, thereby transforming their understanding of the relationship between the state and the land. This new vision was not limited to geological substructures. Indeed, the new perspective on the relationship between state power and resources by Qing reformers extended to a wide assortment of products, including wool, furs, camel hair, and animal parts. By the early twentieth century, Qing officials were seeking to much more clearly identify all potentially lucrative products and underwrite their production and dissemination for the good of the state. This effort, James Scott suggests, points to a primary difference between the modern state and its premodern counterpart: while the former sought enough knowledge to simply "keep order, extract taxes, and raise armies, the modern state aspired to 'take in charge' the physical and human resources of the nation and make them more productive."[67]

Qing elites and officials in the late nineteenth century began undertaking the quintessentially modern task of surveying, mapping, and categorizing the products held within the empire's complex landscapes, from the eastern seaboard to the far west. In Xinjiang, to uncover these new products capable of bolstering state power and finances, Qing officials turned to classical texts, tax records, and reports from local officials. The "shiye" section of the 1909 *Xinjiang Illustrated Gazetteer* contains subsections on agriculture, silkworms, forests, herds, minerals, handicrafts (*gong*), and trade (*shang*), as it sought to clearly identify and promote all products capable of generating revenue. Similarly, a series of county-level gazetteers for Xinjiang compiled in the late nineteenth and early twentieth centuries had separate sections listing various products, including livestock, game, medicinal herbs, and minerals.[68] In carefully detailed entries, these publications, which include precise geographic locations of production sites stretching back to the classical period and even rumored sites of potential production, were intended to render Xinjiang's landscape legible to officials seeking to bolster state revenues and strengthen state power.

The reliance on the resource wealth of border regions to support the state was part of a larger "imperial repertoire" embraced by Qing officials in the late years of the dynasty.[69] Drawn from classical Chinese examples but also relying heavily on Western imperial models, Qing officials called for a greater state commitment to the exploitation of Xinjiang's resource wealth, broadly defined. As the last Qing governor of Xinjiang, Yuan Dahua, wrote, Western empire builders "rely on the products of foreign lands (*waidi*) as a source of revenue for the motherland." Directly comparing Xinjiang to foreign imperial holdings, Qing officials urged that the region's lucrative local products be used to alleviate the fiscal burden it had long placed on the imperial coffers. "It is unheard of that the motherland expends its resources to support foreign lands and sits by while its local products (*wuchan*) are not managed," wrote Yuan in a call for greater state attention to Xinjiang's rich local products.[70]

The effort to reassess the landscape of Xinjiang was folded into a new border policy seeking to maximize the production of products beneficial to the state. As the *Xinjiang Illustrated Gazetteer* argued, "The development of industry and commerce to the highest degree possible is the hasp on the lock of a country's wealth and power."[71] Qing officials in Xinjiang in the waning years of the dynasty increasingly sought to actively promote and support new forms of production. These efforts were meant to boost state revenues, facilitate the influx of new settler populations, and also to lay claim to resource-rich territories before other grasping imperial powers did. Indeed, in arid Xinjiang, by the late nineteenth century, mines in particular were seen to play nearly the same role as that of large-scale agricultural reclamation sites, as they allowed for the generation of revenue and the influx of new populations of settlers who would fill out lands located perilously close to the imperial border regions but unfit for large-scale agricultural reclamation (for more on this see chapter 3). While goldfields, herds, and forests may not have resembled the bucolic orderliness of grain fields, as far as Qing officials beginning in the 1890s were concerned, their function for the state was similar.[72]

*

The campaigns to uncover new resources and forms of revenue allowed for a complete reconfiguring of perceptions of this arid border region. According to Yuan Dahua, the compiler of the *Xinjiang Illustrated Gazetteer* and the last Qing governor of Xinjiang, critics had long pegged the southeast coast as the foundation for state revenues while viewing the northwest as an impoverished drain on imperial finances.[73] "Recently, scholars and literati are beginning to realize and change" their evaluations of the western periphery, as they adopted a more expansive approach to evaluating the productivity of Qing landscapes, wrote Yuan in the gazetteer.[74] The key, however, laid in uncovering and tapping into this productive potential.

The shift in the late Qing period, as officials struggled to make the landscapes of the empire more legible, opened the door to a new conception of Xinjiang. No longer would the land be divided between unplowed wasteland and plowed orderly field. Instead, both agricultural and nonagricultural land had the potential to bolster state power. In a 1911 memorial to the imperial court, Governor Yuan noted that in eastern Xinjiang "the bleached bones [of horses and men] lie scattered." He went on to point out, however, that amidst this desolation, "for those who investigate carefully there are substantial quantities of gold and coal."[75] The failures of the ambitious efforts at agricultural reclamation in the late Qing period, coupled with new ideas about modern statecraft, prompted more aggressive efforts to sift the region's arid soils to uncover new resources and promote new forms of production.

Agricultural production played a critical role in the process of state formation and national integration in the region throughout the twentieth century. It is, however, only one part in a much larger story of production. Reclamation will not go away (indeed I will return to a discussion of the connection between reclamation and resource production in the 1960s in chapter 7), but the failure of reclamation as a silver bullet capable of generating revenue, food, and a stable population of settlers in the late nineteenth century and first decade of the twentieth prompted a search for other forms of production that could strengthen the hand of the state and transform this borderland into a component part of the Qing empire. These efforts by the state to promote other forms of production, which began in the Qing period but continued well into that of the People's Republic, is the core around which the rest of this book will revolve. These efforts have shaped the spatial distribution of institutions of power, new communities of settlers, and the development of infrastructure in powerful ways. To put it another way, the initial foundational layers that have shaped the political, economic, and social contours of modern Xinjiang were laid in the wake of the failure of agricultural reclamation and the subsequent shift in the ways in which Qing officials and later their successors came to view landscapes.

# 3

# Gold, Oil, and the Allure of Foreign Capital

Memorials and gazetteers stretching back to the initial conquest of Xinjiang reported that prospectors at various places in the region regularly uncovered gold nuggets as large as a pigeon's egg or a horse's hoof with their bare hands. In certain desolate river valleys, gold veins were said to be so numerous they were "arrayed like chess pieces or stars in the sky."[1] Into the late nineteenth century, however, even as the Qing court promoted the development of centralized, state-sponsored mining enterprises in other places in the realm, provincial officials refused to establish similar operations in Xinjiang. This was partially a product of a long-standing worry about the potential for the emergence of rowdy mining communities in tense border regions.[2] But the main concern for late Qing provincial officials was a lack of capital in the provincial treasury and a fear of investing precious resources into risky mining ventures.

In the waning years of the nineteenth century, a growing interest in the Qing empire's subterranean resource wealth prompted a rising tide of foreign geologists, surveyors, and explorers in Xinjiang. On the one hand, these agents of imperial powers were seen by Qing officials as a threat, as they seemed bent on annexing the region's most lucrative resource sites. On the other, however, the scientific surveys undertaken by these expeditions appeared to confirm Xinjiang's potential as a producer of lucrative resources and pointed toward a handful of sites as low-risk and high-reward options for state support and investment.[3] The presence of the foreign surveying teams, equipped with high-tech equipment and armed with scientific training, hinted at a gilded fiscal future for officials in this impoverished border province that prompted provincial officials to embrace mining's potential.

Despite interest from various regional and international powers, the bulk of those actively pursuing Xinjiang's resource wealth in the late nineteenth

century and early twentieth were agents of the Russian Empire. The completion of the Russian Trans-Caspian railroad in 1899 and the fact that little aside
from open steppe separated Russian Central Asia from northern Xinjiang,
opened the door wide for Russian explorers and investors. For Qing officials,
suspicion about Russian intentions in the region that stretched back to the
mid-nineteenth century never really subsided. But faced with a growing fiscal
crisis and the need for technical expertise, capital, and access to international
markets to make centralized mining enterprises successful, provincial officials
increasingly turned to Russian actors to facilitate the identification, extraction, processing, and transport of the province's lucrative natural resources.

Xinjiang has a number of productive resource sites scattered throughout
the region, from the far south to the north and at many places in between.
Qing officials' reliance on Russian surveys, capital, and technical experts, however, gave Russian investors considerable influence in shaping patterns of resource extraction and capital investment in the province.[4] These investors focused on a small handful of isolated sites located along Xinjiang's northern
borders in the late Qing and early Republican periods. Russian surveys as
well as a number of extraction enterprises that drew on some combination of
Russian capital, equipment, and expertise helped outline a highly delimited
pattern of resource extraction and state investment. Even when provincial
officials established their own enterprises, lacking access to trained geological teams and fearing the risk of investing in unproven out-of-the-way fields,
they tended to establish their extractive operations at sites previously prioritized for development by their Russian counterparts. By the 1920s, shaped by
Russian priorities, the most well surveyed and best capitalized sites in Xinjiang
were those in northern Xinjiang located only a short distance from the Sino-
Russian border.

The role of the Russian Empire in Xinjiang's oil and ore fields reflects a
larger trend at work throughout the realm in the late Qing period, as imperial
powers sought access to lucrative resources, particularly along China's borders. The publication of Ferdinand von Richthofen's account of his travels to
the Qing empire and his estimates of its rich mineral wealth in 1877 prompted
fervent interest from Western powers in gaining access to Qing minerals. At
first, they were most interested in acquiring coal mines, in order to create a
network of coaling stations for steamer ships plying trading routes in Asia. After 1895 and the signing of the Treaty of Shimonoseki following the first Sino-
Japanese War, foreign powers began taking a more active interest in the Qing
empire's mineral wealth. The treaty allowed for the influx of large amounts of
investment capital; as a consequence, significant numbers of geologists and
imperial agents entered Qing territory to discover new ore sites and establish

new concessions that would allow them to have unfettered access to critical resources. In this "great underground race," as Shellen Wu terms it, German geologists actively explored Shandong province, the French undertook significant expeditions in southern Yunnan, and the Russians and Japanese explored much of Manchuria and parts of Mongolia.[5] Just as in Xinjiang, these efforts helped highlight various important resource sites that were later prioritized for exploitation by Qing and Republican officials.

In Xinjiang, the interest and preliminary investment in a small number of gold and later petroleum fields in the late Qing and early Republican periods helped change the impression of the region's landscape, which had long been simply dismissed as being mostly wasteland in the minds of officials. It also began the process of creating a blueprint for long-term state investment that was closely tied to the priorities of Russian state and nonstate actors. It may be tempting to see Russian influence in Xinjiang as simply another case of imperial domination in China's so-called century of humiliation. But this interpretation overstates foreign imperial power and minimizes the agency of Qing- and Republican-era provincial officials, who in many cases actively pursued foreign partnerships and support for their own resource extraction enterprises. Beginning in the late nineteenth century, provincial officials were convinced by the promise of the geological vision brought by Russian geologists as well as the power of Russian investment capital. Far from passive subalterns, provincial officials were active agents in a collaborative process of resource extraction in the late Qing and early Republican periods.

This collaborative process, undertaken by provincial officials and a shifting coterie of Russian explorers, merchants, and government officials helped lay the initial layers of state interest and investment at a handful of resource sites in northern Xinjiang. The region's size, rugged terrain, and difficult climate meant that the early surveys, reports, and maps helped create geographic waypoints in this massive territory that influenced the itineraries of future surveyors and state planners hailing from not only China and Russia but also the United Kingdom, the United States, Japan, and other regional powers. Eager to tap Xinjiang's resource wealth but unsure of where to find it, surveying teams used these sites as hubs and focused their efforts on carefully examining the mountain ranges, river valleys, and steppe lands that surrounded them. The high cost of labor, importing equipment, and constructing new infrastructure in the region likewise prompted state planners, investors, and technical experts who were intent on holding down costs to concentrate their extraction efforts at these well-surveyed, proven sites. The layering of surveys and investment into a handful of sites along northern Xinjiang's border with Russia helped transform these sites from blank spots on the map into oil and ore fields highlighted and prioritized for future surveys, investment, and development.

## Fiscal Crisis and Its Gilded Solution

In 1893, the Qing envoy to the Russian Empire wrote a report to the Qing court that called for a fundamental rethinking of imperial mining policy in Xinjiang. The communique, marked "urgent" was rushed via the Qing post road system to Beijing; in it, the diplomat Xu Jingcheng (figure 3.1) argued that Xinjiang's abundant gold wealth held the key to all of Xinjiang's myriad problems. Based on findings drawn from a covertly obtained translated Russian report, Xu's memorial declared emphatically that "gold ore in the vicinity of Khotan [a city in the southern stretches of Xinjiang province] is abundant," and called for a large-scale extraction campaign using Western methods to realize its financial potential.[6]

The original Russian report was written by the geologist Karl Ivanovich Bogdanovich, who had led a year-long survey of southern Xinjiang's Kunlun Mountains in 1889 and 1890 for the Imperial Geographical Society. The report included detailed maps of the region, laid out a history of the various Russian and British expeditions to the Kunlun Mountains stretching back to the time of Peter the Great (1682–1725), and detailed the gold wealth located at several sites scattered across the mountain range. Bogdanovich's assertion that there was gold in the Kunlun was no news to Qing officials in Xinjiang. Indeed, Chinese classics stretching back to the Han dynasty described the goldfield.[7] Reports from the Qianlong period pointed to the vast gold wealth of the Kunlun, and an assortment of officials stretching back to the original conquest of Xinjiang worried about the presence of illegal prospectors working the region's rich veins. But the fact that the Russians were able to scientifically quantify the region's gold wealth was held up by Xu to convince cautious skeptics, who continued to worry about the high cost of mining. He noted in his report that Russian scientists, at the behest of the Russian foreign office, tested gold ore collected near Khotan and found its quality to be even higher than ore from the famous goldfields at the so-called Old Gold Mountain (the goldfields outside of San Francisco) as well as the New Gold Mountain (the rich Victoria goldfields outside of Melbourne, Australia).

As far as Xu and the Qing court were concerned, the development of the goldfields in the Kunlun as well as other resource-rich sites in this region bordered by two acquisitive imperial powers (the British to the south and the Russian to the north and west) had two major advantages. The first was that gold mining operations could serve as a Qing claim on ore-rich border

庚子辛亥忠烈像贊

第一冊

許景澄

FIGURE 3.1 Xu Jingcheng in the mid to late 1890s. Original image published in Feng Shu, *Gengzi xinhai zhonglie xiangzan* (n.p., n.d.).

regions. Mining operations, officials argued, could help settle underpopulated stretches of border with prospectors loyal to the court who would act as scouts and a first line of defense against imperialist aggression.[8] Secondly, the development of a productive gold mine could help generate the revenue needed to finally make Xinjiang financially self-sufficient. "After several years of official oversight of the ore fields, finances will gradually be abundant," Xu optimistically predicted. And in a conclusion that surely was calculated to

catch the attention of the court, which was perennially seeking a way of ending the annual interprovincial assistance payments to the province, he added,
"This capital can be used as a foundation upon which to eliminate the need
for the Central Plains [China-proper] to continue to support the frontier."[9]

Qing officials in Beijing appeared energized by the scientific endorsement
of Xinjiang's mineral wealth in the Russian report and confidently asserted
in a statement that "the quality of the gold in the area was higher than that
found on any of the five continents." The Ministry of Foreign Affairs (Zongli
Yamen) argued that as soon as Western ore extraction methods were applied,
the flow of gold ore would, without doubt, serve as a lucrative source of revenue for the provincial treasury.[10] In their report, ministry officials called for
the hiring of a mining engineer to undertake extensive surveys in the area
and urged local officials to establish a joint public-private mining enterprise.[11]
Three weeks after Xu's original report, the imperial Grand Council responded
by calling for the opening of the Kunlun Mountain goldfield. They argued
that the fields "are at a critical spot on the frontier, we must take precautions
and so should take the initiative" in developing the ore site.[12]

The model upon which the development of the Kunlun fields was to be
based was a gold mining operation at Mohe, a gold-rich stretch of Heilongjiang province located in the far northeastern corner of the Qing empire. In
1885, the imperial court became aware that large numbers of Russian prospectors were crossing into Qing territory near Mohe, illegally mining gold from
the ore-rich river, and selling their products to Han merchants in the area.
Fearing that these prospectors were the first step in a Russian annexation of
northern Heilongjiang province, officials called for the establishment of state-
sponsored military settlements in the region that mirrored agricultural garrisons in other border areas, where soldiers would set up settlements along the
border and serve as mining labor as well as aid in border defense. "Unless we
establish operations early to set up a long-term occupation [of the area], we
will be sowing seeds of disaster," wrote the Grand Council in 1888.[13]

For Xu Jingcheng and other Qing officials who had long been concerned
about Russian intentions in the Qing empire's western border region and were
tired of continually shipping hard-won tax revenues to Xinjiang, the rich ore
wealth of the Kunlun appeared to serve as a solution to many of their woes.
But for their part, provincial officials were initially resistant to the push from
the court. They feared the impact that careless and uncouth immigrant miners would have on border security and also worried about the high price tag
associated with setting up large-scale mining operations. The problem was
that the province's most potentially lucrative ore fields were tucked away in
rugged mountainous areas, the geographic isolation of which only increased

the already sky-high costs of labor, commodities, and transport (see chapter 2). This meant that the margins for mineral enterprises were razor thin. "If [mining enterprises] do not profit immediately, then the investment will be used up and they have no capital with which to keep going," explained the author of the late Qing *Xinjiang Illustrated Gazetteer*.[14] In response to Xu's and Beijing's excitement, in 1895 the provincial governor Tao Mo wrote a strongly critical memorial to the Qing court in which he starkly pointed out the challenges of opening a state-sponsored gold mine in the Kunlun, "The costs are excessive and are more than the amount we can take in in revenue; either the repeated losses will lead to [the mine] closing as we will be unable to write off expenses, or else we will have to support it begrudgingly."[15]

It was indeed true that with the sharp drop-off in interprovincial assistance (see chapter 2), the province could little afford to invest in expensive and risky mining operations. Little had changed since 1882, when the first Qing governor of Xinjiang, Liu Jintang, poetically compared the province's need for revenue to a man dying of thirst, "for whom every drop of water is a pearl."[16] If anything, things were much worse. When the Qing Ministry of Finance called on provincial officials to undertake a careful audit of the Xinjiang provincial treasury in 1906, the only thing they could find were assorted silver coins, nearly worthless paper money, flecks of gold dust, and scraps of gold bars.[17] In 1903, in a risky attempt to make ends meet, provincial officials took out a two million tael loan from the Russo-Asiatic Bank in which they used mining rights in Xinjiang's ore fields and potential revenues from land reclamation as collateral.[18] By the first decade of the twentieth century, Xinjiang was running an annual deficit of 570,000 taels, and provincial officials were desperate to fill the increasingly yawning fiscal gap that was slowly but surely pushing Xinjiang deeper and deeper into the red.[19] The author of one late Qing report colorfully described the difficult financial choices provincial officials had to make, noting they had to "dig out a piece of flesh [from the body] to patch a boil on the skin."[20]

The options for raising revenues and cutting costs in this often tense, arid border province seemed limited. The numbers of troops stationed in the province had already been slashed back to a total of 31,000 by the mid-1890s, a number that helped cut military costs by 110,000 taels annually but was low enough that provincial officials worried that the cuts threatened border security.[21] In 1897 in Ili, a cost-saving plan was put in place to cut official salaries. After successfully generating a relatively meager 2,817 taels in savings annually, officials adopted the plan province-wide.[22] In addition to slashing expenditures, officials also sought to raise revenues by increasing taxes. Qing officials had long kept the burden of taxes relatively low in order to retain the loyalties of Uyghur farmers working the fertile oases of southern Xinjiang and support the fragile agricultural settlements in the north. But the new pressures prompted officials to expand tax collection in the province. In addition to luxury taxes on opium, oil, and alcohol, taxes were also levied on meltage fees, transportation, and salt, among other things. Existent taxes on agricultural production, herds, and contracts were also increased to generate revenue.[23]

Faced with the intractable fiscal crisis, provincial officials in the late 1890s and early 1900s were willing to entertain various new approaches to raising revenue—strategies that were rejected outright in the 1880s and early 1890s. The depth of the fiscal crisis, combined with the positive assessments of Xinjiang's gold wealth by trained Russian geologists, prompted a shift in provincial officials' approach to mining. In a stark turn from the earlier reticence about establishing state-sponsored mines, the newly appointed governor Rao Yingqi, who was intimately familiar with the province's financial woes having previously served as the province's treasurer (fansi), heartily embraced mining as a revenue raising strategy shortly after coming into office. Drawing on the positive assessment by Bogdanovich, Rao targeted the Kunlun goldfields in particular as he actively sought ways to exploit the province's rich mineral wealth.

## Decentralized Mines and the Pursuit of Profit

In 1896, the Qing court outlined a new mining strategy focused on the development of precious metal mines. "Compared to the profits from coal mines and other things, the profits [in precious metals] are huge and each general, military governor, and governor-general should exert himself with real vigor to pursue" these profits, reads the imperial edict announcing the new strategy.[24] The newly appointed governor of the province, Rao Yingqi, embraced the new strategy and heralded what he saw to be a sea change in the province's revenue raising policy. In a report the same year Rao proclaimed: "At a time like this, when funds in the provincial treasury are lacking, we need to urgently expand ore production."[25] In an 1899 memorial that outlined his new provincial mining strategy, Rao dismissed Xinjiang's substantial caches of copper, iron, and even silver as not valuable enough, too heavy and expensive to transport, and too geographically isolated, respectively. Instead, Rao argued that there was only one possible solution to Xinjiang's financial woes: "There is profit to be found only in gold," he proclaimed.[26]

The problem for Rao and other provincial officials was that the obstacles to mining development in Xinjiang that the previous governor, Tao Mo, had laid out in his rejection of mining only a few years earlier continued to loom. While they may have been willing to overlook the potentially disruptive force of miners operating in sensitive border areas in order to raise revenues, the issues surrounding transportation infrastructure and the lack of capital to invest in the development of mining enterprises continued to stymie local officials. Yet for provincial officials, the Russian confirmation of the gold wealth of the Kunlun appeared to lessen the inherent risks in investing in costly mining ventures. The story of the development of the Kunlun goldfield during this period helps illustrate the delicate line that provincial officials were forced to walk as they sought to use Xinjiang's ores to raise revenues.

Considering the fiscal pressure that had simmered in the province since the early nineteenth century, if not earlier, provincial officials were not in a position to take risks. For increasingly desperate officials, the Bogdanovich report offered a scientific confirmation of the area's gold wealth at a moment when many Qing officials were well inclined to listen to the opinions of Western technical experts. This confirmation seemed to lessen the risk of investing in distant ore fields. Rao stated with the utmost confidence that the gold resources in the Kunlun Mountain goldfields were substantial.[27] The problem was that its distance from China-proper, difficult topography, and potentially uncooperative local population (who were said to worry that mining operations would effectively eliminate an important source of income) made it expensive to set up an operation. He seemed almost wistful when he complained that "if there were not these restrictions set by the land and the local population, we could transport in equipment to crush rock and process ore, and we could begin to extract profits."[28]

Understanding the high costs of developing infrastructure, purchasing equipment, and hiring labor, Rao was primarily concerned with the question of devising the best strategy to support mining ventures. He raised this critical issue in his first memorial to the court on the Kunlun goldfields: "If officials open the mine then I fear that there will not be enough capital and it will be difficult to sustain operations." But, Rao went on, "if citizens begin mining and we simply levy taxes according to the number of prospectors [working the ore fields], then I fear that profits will be limited."[29] Encapsulated within this short statement was a worry that would continue to nag officials in the province not only at the Kunlun Mountain goldfields but at isolated resource-rich spots throughout the province, as they grappled with the choice between expensive but potentially productive centralized mines or cheap but potentially unprofitable decentralized operations.

In his memorials to the court, Rao stated that he wanted to emulate the large-scale centrally organized mines like those in Mohe. To help in the process of pinpointing the region's most productive veins and further reduce risk, Rao called upon those Qing officials in Beijing who had been so supportive of using Xinjiang's ores to raise revenues to help pay for a professional mining engineer from the Kaiping mine in Henan province to come to Xinjiang. He argued that an engineer armed with portable equipment could "help explain the maze of doubts and confusion" that the complex geology of the land presented to untrained officials. The court rejected the request the next year, citing the more than 12,000 taels it would cost to send an engineer to Xinjiang. Fearing the risk of investing precious resources into the Kunlun goldfields, Rao dismissed the potentially more profitable (but riskier) centralized approach and instead adopted the more conservative decentralized development strategy of relying on local miners to extract the region's ores.

The operations established by Rao in the Kunlun mirrored a mining strategy that had been in use in Xinjiang since the early nineteenth century, and were referred to as "the people mine and officials buy" (*mincai guanmai*).[30] Under this model, officials simply allowed mining to commence and then officials stationed in the region purchased the raw gold prospectors produced at a below-market set price in silver or copper currency. Early on, officials like Rao expressed optimism about the revenue raised by the mine, proclaiming with pride in 1901 that the small-scale operations in the region had already resulted in more than 1,000 silver taels in profit for the provincial treasury.[31]

Yet others were frustrated that this amount was so much lower than the amounts being smuggled out by unscrupulous local miners. The problem provincial officials faced was in monitoring the gold prospectors, most of whom were local farmers who worked the veins in the spring and winter off-seasons. In the distant southern stretches of the province, officials could little afford to garrison troops near the field to ensure that prospectors were accounted for and selling their gold back to local officials at the officially mandated price. Officials acknowledged the difficulty of counting the people working the gold veins in the region, noting that many worked in secret and simply hid in the rugged river valleys when officials or military patrols came through.[32] If they were able to avoid the long arm of the provincial yamen, these prospectors could increase their relatively meager daily profits by selling their gold to merchants at higher market prices.[33] One former Qing provincial official noted in a 1913 report that the real amount of gold production vastly exceeded Rao's 1,000 tael figure. He asserted that the amount actually should have been more than 5,000 ounces of gold annually, an amount that equaled a substantial 140,000 silver taels at late Qing market prices in Xinjiang.[34]

It was difficult to discourage these furtive prospectors from selling their gold scraps at market rather than official prices. During this period, the value of silver currency was plummeting in relation to gold throughout the realm, and the fact that officials sought to keep prices low to maximize revenues resulted in large amounts of gold being smuggled out. The smuggled gold would then be sold to merchants willing to buy the ore at rates closer to the market price. At the new enterprise set up in the Kunlun in 1901, officials were paying 25 taels per ounce of gold.[35] The problem, however, was that local merchants were willing to pay amounts closer to the market price in southern Xinjiang of between 32 and 35 taels per ounce of gold.[36] Officials later began paying 28 taels per ounce, an amount that Rao suggested helped rectify the issue. But it is difficult to verify his statement, and reports from travelers suggest that in fact gold smuggling continued.[37]

The Kunlun Mountain goldfields never lived up to the expectations of Xu Jingcheng and the Qing court. In the end, the decentralized nature of the mine served to drag down revenues. The operation was representative of the vast majority of mining enterprises in the province during the waning years of the dynasty. Many, indeed most, of the mines in the province were like those in the Kunlun: relatively small-scale with little state investment.[38] These operations, tucked away in isolated, mountainous corners of the province often had no more than twenty off-season agricultural laborers working local veins. According to the account of one traveler, the local prospectors at these sites typically turned over ores to local village headmen, who in turn sold them to local officials.[39] At these types of enterprises, local officials were only able to reap small amounts of revenue annually (and much of this revenue most likely was sent to lower-level circuit treasuries or stayed in the pockets of local magistrates and other officials). On the more positive side for provincial officials, these operations demanded little official capital.

In the latter years of the Qing dynasty, these decentralized operations were fairly evenly spread around the province. Using gold production as an example, one report from the early Republic, which reflects late Qing operations, reveals that five decentralized mines (this number does not include mines started with Russian capital at two sites that I will address in more detail later in this chapter) of various types were located in counties north of the Tianshan Mountain range and three were situated in the south.[40] This points to a fairly even distribution of mineral extraction operations in the province (see map 3.1) and, in comparison to later patterns influenced by foreign investment, hints at the faint outlines of a map of state-sponsored resource extraction that more clearly reflected the real spread of Xinjiang's resource wealth.

For Qing officials in Xinjiang like Rao Yingqi, the promotion of small-scale mining operations was a relatively safe financial solution to the problem of how to develop ores in the province. These small-scale decentralized operations facilitated a limited settlement of ore-rich regions. And they also

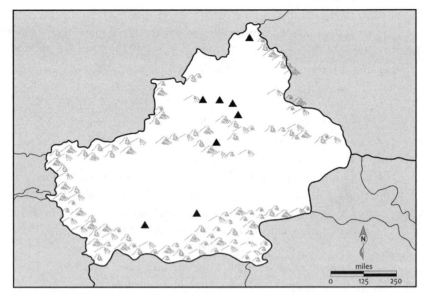

MAP 3.1 Distribution of late Qing dynasty small-scale gold mining operations. Map by Debbie Newell.

ensured that officials were able to reap some amount of revenue from the province's lucrative mineral resources.[41] Yet the revenues from these small-scale mines, worked by only a handful of workers typically using traditional methods to both extract ores and refine them, were severely limited. While they may not have overtaxed the provincial balance sheets, they also did not serve as a major source of provincial revenue. Looking to the example of Mohe, where in the first year of operation the site was regularly taking in more than 1,500 ounces of gold monthly, the small amounts of ore scratched out of the ground in the Kunlun goldfields were insignificant as far as provincial officials in desperate need of a financial windfall were concerned.[42]

These small-scale operations sat lightly on the landscape: they rose and fell with the rhythms of the growing and harvest seasons and with shifts in global gold prices. The growing fiscal crisis in the province, the effort to permanently settle resource-rich border regions, and the presence of deep-pocketed foreign investors to invest in mines formed the context out of which a new type of extraction enterprise emerged in Xinjiang in the late 1890s. These centralized, professionally surveyed, large-scale, and well-capitalized operations shifted long-term patterns of extraction and development away from a fairly even geographic distribution toward one focused on northern Xinjiang generally, and northern regions hugging the Russian border more specifically.

### Foreign Assistance and the Earliest Layers in Northern Xinjiang

In the years following the Sino-Japanese War of 1895, the Western imperial powers became increasingly aggressive in their efforts to stake claims to the Qing empire's resource wealth. The competition to stake claims to minerals prompted a new effort by the Qing imperial court to more clearly protect sovereign territory through the centralization of control over ore fields and mining operations.[43] New regulations unveiled in 1902 were intended to shore up Qing control over ores and mines by regulating the use of Western capital in mining operations and giving the state broad latitude in overseeing mining production. Subsequent revisions of the regulations over the course of the first decade of the twentieth century were clearly based on examples culled from imperial powers and sought to equip the court with the legal standing to resist imperial efforts to claim Qing resources.[44]

The ongoing stream of foreign explorers seeking to discover Xinjiang's most lucrative resource sites prompted provincial officials to establish centralized mining operations that could protect sovereign territory and generate revenue. The problem of funding, however, remained. The Mohe model depended on finding outside investment to fund the risky but potentially high-profit frontier precious metal mines. Under the original Mohe regulations issued in 1888, officials in Heilongjiang province depended on investments from officials, gentry, and wealthy merchants to raise more than 200,000 taels in initial start-up costs. Each 100 tael "share" issued by the officially controlled mining company guaranteed the holder 7 percent interest annually on profits generated by the mine.[45] Officials in Mohe, who were aided by high-level patronage from the powerful Beiyang general Li Hongzhang, successfully raised money by selling shares in large cities like Shanghai and Tianjin, as well as in overseas Chinese communities in Southeast Asia and North America.

For officials in Xinjiang, the idea of raising a similar amount in private investment was an unattainable pipe dream. The fact was that the Han immigrant communities in Xinjiang, which were the closest allies of Qing officials in the waning years of the dynasty, were simply too few and too poor to shoulder much of the burden of investing in mining enterprises. As provincial treasurer Wang Shunan remembered, with only a few exceptions, immigrant Han in Xinjiang "are hooligans and demobilized military stragglers, they own no property and most cannot read."[46] The governor Tao Mo complained that for those lucky few who managed to stumble into money in the province, they typically chose not to reinvest it into the province. "Occasionally, one will get wealthy and he will immediately return through the Jade Gate [to China-proper] singing a song," he wrote bitterly to Beijing.[47]

Compounding the difficulties of provincial officials, wealthy investors from outside the province stayed away from Xinjiang, where costs and risks were higher. Faced with an empty treasury and handcuffed by the inability to raise outside domestic capital, provincial officials were forced to look elsewhere for investment.

The steady drip of geologists, surveyors, and other foreign parties interested in discovering Xinjiang's geological secrets in the late nineteenth century suggested that the answer to the question of financing might lie in reaching out to foreigners. In 1898, provincial governor Rao Yingqi, provincial treasurer Ding Zhenduo, and provincial judge (and future governor of Xinjiang) Pan Xiaosu went to the Russian consul in the provincial capital of Dihua to inquire whether there were any Russians who might be interested in investing in gold mining enterprises in Xinjiang.[48] The outreach to foreign investors was the beginning of a major policy shift, as provincial officials embraced the potential of joint Qing-foreign mining operations. In the first decade of the twentieth century, at a series of resource-rich sites scattered around northern Xinjiang, the first layers of surveys and investments were laid by Russian geological teams and Sino-Russian extraction operations. Relying on Russian technology, geologists, capital, infrastructure, and in many cases markets, these operations typically bowed to the interests and priorities of Russian investors and planners, who focused their efforts primarily on areas located close to the Russian border and to the Russian transport network in Central Asia.

In their 1898 meeting at the Russian consulate, Rao, Ding, and Pan did not specify which ore field they hoped to develop and instead relied on the Russian side to select a location for the enterprise. After some deliberation and the dispatching of a Russian geological team to survey potential ore sites, the consulate informed provincial representatives that a gold merchant named A. G. Moskvin was interested in investing in a gold mining enterprise in the Katu Mountains, located just outside of the northern Xinjiang border town of Tacheng. The site was a long and bumpy four hundred miles northwest of the provincial capital of Dihua but only a short distance from the Russian border.[49] The region had long been known for its gold ore by officials, local off-season prospectors, and Western travelers alike. But the surveys conducted by a mining engineer hired by Moskvin found that gold veins located in river valleys along the nearby Emin River yielded nearly fifteen ounces of gold per ton and a half of ore.[50] The proximity of the site to Russian territory and the Russian transport network was an added advantage as far as Moskvin was concerned, as it would mitigate the high costs of labor, equipment, and transport that would have doomed other sites in Xinjiang.

Requesting and later receiving permission from the Qing Ministry of Foreign Affairs to begin a joint-stock operation, Rao and the other provincial officials began to negotiate with Moskvin and the Russian consul directly. Out of these negotiations came a nineteen-point agreement establishing the Tacheng Katu Gold Mining Company (Tacheng Hatu Jinkuang Ju). The regulations, which were hammered out by the two sides in 1899, established that provincial officials and Moskvin would each provide 30,000 taels of initial investment to set up the mine site, purchase equipment, and hire workers. After dispensing the province's share of the 30,000 tael investment (which officials were able to come up with only after raiding the provincial defense budget), in January 1900, the team marched into the Katu Mountains. After arriving in the goldfields they quickly set up the concentrating mill and grinding equipment, which had been purchased in Russia at a site pinpointed by the Russian mining engineers hired by the enterprise. In late February 1900, the large-scale livestock-powered mill began grinding the region's ore-laden quartz. Rao and other provincial officials optimistically cheered the operation, and in a memorial that first year enthusiastically trumpeted the fact that the enterprise "has already begun to see results." Indeed, from February to September the mine was said to have produced nearly forty-four pounds of gold.[51]

By the beginning of 1901, however, things seemed strikingly less positive. Ongoing mechanical issues hindered ore production. While the enterprise was still taking in gold, the amounts did not appear to be significant enough to justify the sizable expense of the mining operations. To help make back their initial investment, company officials doubled the size and geographic scope of the operation. The new construction at the site cost the joint enterprise an additional 54,450 taels each, an amount that provincial officials again took out of the military budget. Seeking permission from the court to continue operations despite the growing costs of the enterprise, Rao passionately declared that if they were to leave mining operations "half-finished, then we will be laughed at by the intelligent people of the world."[52] Nevertheless, in October 1902, with losses reaching more than 81,000 taels, Moskvin asked provincial officials to dissolve the partnership. Rao Yingqi's successor as governor blamed machinery ill-suited to the local topography, a lack of skilled Chinese miners, and major strategic errors rather than a lack of gold or the incompetence of Russian geologists for the failure of the Katu Mountain operation.[53]

While the joint-stock company was an unquestionable failure, one of the long-term resonances of the operation was that it expanded the surveying footprint in northern Xinjiang. Opening the field to foreign investment ensured that the surrounding mountains and riverbeds were subjected to far more intensive surveys. Eager to get the Katu Mountain operation off on the

right foot, in a series of 1899 expeditions, surveying teams sought to confirm earlier geological reports, rumors, and hearsay about lucrative resource
caches of all types in this largely unexplored region. In these efforts, the geological teams investigated the resource wealth of much of north-central Xinjiang. One of the surveyors, a man named Matantsev, explored as far east
as the provincial capital of Dihua 500 kilometers to the southeast, where he
investigated oil seepages reported by Russian travelers.[54]

Later, as the gold veins pinpointed for extraction by the Katu Mountain
operation failed to generate the hoped-for windfall, the two engineers employed by the mine explored even greater swaths of the surrounding region,
identifying several prominent new gold veins, pointing out potential mineral sites, and in so doing, laid bare the region's largely unstudied geological
substructures.[55] The reports from these explorations, which were published,
distributed, and filed away in libraries and research institutes throughout
the Russian Empire, guided the efforts of subsequent teams called upon to
uncover the most lucrative resource sites in this vast, rugged territory.

The failure of the gold mining operations in 1902 did not shake the
confidence of provincial officials in the possibilities of Xinjiang's subterranean
resources. Late nineteenth-century Qing officials may have seen gold as the
answer to their problems; but by the early twentieth century, with petroleum
prices ticking upward, Qing officials came to see black gold's potential in helping pay the bills, hold off potential competitors in the region, and, as a bonus,
breaking Xinjiang's reliance on petroleum products imported from Russia.
The fact that there were places in the northern steppe lands where raw petroleum pure enough to light camp stoves and lamps collected in sticky black
pools was no secret. The region had a large number of sites with reported oil
seepages. But one oilfield at a place called Dushanzi (which loosely translates
to "Lone Mountain"), in Korkala Wusu prefecture on the southwestern edge
of the Zungharian basin and conveniently located on the provincial east-west
trunk road, seemed particularly promising. The site had been "discovered" by
a Russian consular officer. The officer, named Uspenskiy, was led to Dushanzi
by locals who reported that there were "three or four rather rich petroleum
springs, whence the local inhabitants collect about five buckets per hour from
each spring" (map 3.2).[56]

The reports of oil and the initial interest in the region in the late nineteenth
century prompted Qing provincial officials to establish a small-scale public-
private operation. In eight months of production in 1904, the operation produced around eighty *jin* (nearly ninety pounds) of raw petroleum.[57] A Russian
geologist named Vladimir Obruchev, who was then the chair of the mining
department at Tomsk Institute of Technology, confirmed Dushanzi's vast po-

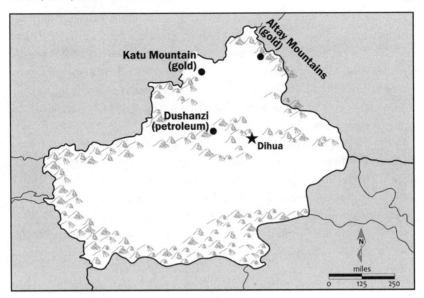

MAP 3.2 Distribution of major resource extraction sites. Map by Debbie Newell.

tential in a 1905 expedition.[58] This confirmation of the region's oil wealth by a Russian expert and a subsequent request by a Russian company to establish an oil drilling operation there helped prompt Qing officials to expand their own enterprise. Provincial officials entertained an offer from their Russian counterparts to either rent the land for forty years or else pay taxes annually on production. But officials in the Qing Ministry of Foreign Affairs, watching the unfolding of the nationalistic "mining rights recovery movement" which sought to buy back foreign shares of mining operations in China-proper, rejected the proposal. Instead the ministry called for raising local capital to establish an operation relying only on investments from Qing subjects.[59]

In 1907, provincial treasurer Wang Shunan dispatched a committee of local officials armed with samples taken from oilfields in the petroleum-rich region of Korkala Wusu to Baku in the Russian Empire to test the purity of the region's oil wealth. Their tests confirmed initial reports, finding that 100 *jin* of raw oil from the region yielded 60 *jin* of refined oil.[60] Wang Shunan crowed about Xinjiang's oil wealth, proclaiming it "even more flourishing and profitable than the Americas!"[61] Armed with proof verified by Western experts and technologies and a growing belief that perhaps it was oil, not gold or other resources, that would be the key to resolving more than a century and a half of financial problems, provincial officials founded a new extraction operation in the northern Xinjiang oilfields.

Provincial officials established their new joint public-private enterprise at Dushanzi in 1909. They intended to first distribute petroleum locally and then later, as production and transport improved, internationally. What made the operation unusual was not only its reliance on Xinjiang's emergent merchant community for capital, but also its use of foreign equipment and even foreign engineers hired by provincial officials. These officials purchased the modern refining equipment in Russia, which was in turn transported overland via the Russian Trans-Caspian Rail line. Russian experts, relying on Russian surveys then set up the equipment. Replacing so-called "native methods" (*tufa*) of extraction, officials purchased a top-of-the-line Russian drill, which was in turn set up by two Russian mining technicians who were hired full-time to run drilling operations and also to teach Chinese employees how to use the equipment.[62] Even if they did not rely on Russian capital investments specifically, the monopoly on expertise and equipment ensured that Russian representatives played a critical role in shaping the enterprise.

The start of drilling at Dushanzi in 1909 seemed auspicious. Drilling down to a depth of around thirty-five feet, flammable oil vapors began wafting out of the shaft. Drilling further, workers heard a rumble that those present described as sounding like waves crashing. The sound was followed by a Texas-style oil gusher that quickly caught fire and burned brightly.[63] Despite this seemingly promising start, operations were never able to get fully off the ground. The records of the mining operations are not available and it is not clear precisely how much oil was produced at Dushanzi or how much profit the site generated for the provincial treasury. According to scholars, the operation eventually fell victim to the Xinhai revolution, as the uprising in Wuchang against the Qing court in 1911 and the subsequent chaos in China-proper ensured that even the meager flow of interprovincial assistance to support Xinjiang's treasury dried up completely. In this context, there was little left over for the enterprise.[64] Contemporary sources seem to confirm this as, in 1912, after the fall of the dynasty and shortly before fleeing the province, the last Qing governor Yuan Dahua shuttered operations at Dushanzi, writing curtly, "Amounts in the treasury are insufficient."[65]

The operation may have closed but the surveys and the capital investments undertaken in the last years of the Qing helped transform Dushanzi in particular from a backwater along the Tianshan North Road into an important point on resource maps and the object of interest for state- and provincial-level planners. Even after the operation closed its doors in 1911, the layers laid over and around Dushanzi by Russian experts and provincial officials ensured that the site was circled on the itineraries of geologists and surveying teams, dog-eared in gazetteers and reports, and highlighted in planning priority lists being drawn up in Moscow, Beijing, and Dihua by officials eager to uncover potentially lucrative resources in this border region.

## Foreign Capital and the New Republic

The collapse of the Qing dynasty following the outbreak of revolution in 1911 did little to fundamentally alter the financial and political challenges facing provincial officials in Xinjiang. Established in 1912, the new government of the Republic of China left Xinjiang largely on its own, as officials focused their state- and nation-building efforts on Han-dominated regions of the former Qing empire in central and eastern China. The new regime in Beijing refused to reinstate the annual interprovincial payments, payments that Yang Zengxin, the first governor of the province in the Republican period, described as Xinjiang's fiscal "lifeblood" (*mingmai*).[66] Compounding the challenges facing provincial officials, the Han-centered rhetoric coming out of Beijing prompted imperial competitors to test the commitment of Republican leaders to the former empire's borderlands. The threat was not merely a rhetorical one, as British backing led Tibet to declare its independence from the Republic in 1913 and later, Soviet influence facilitated Mongolia's independence in 1921.

In Xinjiang, there were well-founded fears that Russians, British, and other foreign powers were actively seeking an opportunity to seize Xinjiang's rich resource wealth, if not the region itself. By the late Qing period, there was plenty of evidence that imperial powers harbored a deep interest in the region's minerals, considering the various geological expeditions to the area, the frequent requests to rent mineral-rich lands, and the attempts to set up joint stock mining operations. In 1913, during a bloody struggle for power in the province following the revolution, holdouts to the ascension of Yang Zengxin based in the border town of Ili received a four million–ruble loan from Russian merchants. The loan used the region's mineral wealth as collateral. After having learned of the agreement, Governor Yang darkly predicted in a report to Beijing that "Russians covet Ili's minerals and when the economy is bad they will seize the rights to the ore."[67] In another incident the next year, a local official was troubled to stumble across an Englishman illegally mining gold outside the ore-rich southern oasis town of Qiemo.[68] Foreigners, it seemed to provincial officials, were already pushing their way into Xinjiang's ore fields.

Like his Qing predecessors, for Yang, the key to securing control over these resource-rich but underpopulated border regions was the establishment of extraction operations. He was well aware that mining can help settle landscapes

and claim territory by introducing semi-permanent communities into contested border regions. "Mining," he explained to Beijing in 1919, "was not
merely for increasing national revenues but was also beneficial in stopping
the foreigners who are lying in wait."[69] He went on to note that mining was
"an essential factor in colonization," as it allowed for the settlement of mine
workers in contested borderlands not suitable for agriculture.[70] Yang was
confident that mining operations could serve as a claim on underpopulated,
contested landscapes and that any profits these operations generated could be
funneled back into the provincial treasury.

The problem, however, was that Yang simply did not have the means to
establish expensive mining operations himself. The elimination of interprovincial assistance payments following the founding of the new Republic immediately put Xinjiang in a deep fiscal spiral. In a frantic 1912 message to the
Republic's new Ministry of Finance, Yang wrote, "Now that provincial assistance payments have dried up we are doing our utmost to make ends meet,
but things are very difficult to handle; we are in crisis."[71] The crisis prompted
Yang to undertake an unprecedented campaign of money printing that severely undercut the value of provincial currency. Additionally, efforts at fiscal
belt tightening gutted Xinjiang's already meager military and administration,
leaving Yang with few options to directly confront threats to China's sovereignty and maintain his own grip on power.[72] Like his Qing predecessors,
Yang saw a solution in encouraging foreign investment and technical assistance in Xinjiang's most lucrative resource sites. The operations Yang established, which relied almost exclusively on private (both domestic and foreign)
capital, tended to follow directly in the wake of Russian geological surveying
teams and Russian merchant requests to establish joint operations.

Officials in Xinjiang knew that the Altay Mountains in the far northern
stretches of the province, a region surrounded on three sides by Russia and
Mongolia, had several sites known to produce gold. But the "discovery" of
several gold rich sites by Obruchev in the late Qing period helped confirm the
region's mining potential for provincial officials and interested Russians alike.
In 1916, a Russian consular officer approached a local official with a request
to open a gold mining operation.[73] The Russian representative argued that an
enterprise would resolve the long-standing problem of illegal mining in the
area, in which furtive Chinese, Russian, and Mongol prospectors worked the
region's rich gold veins without oversight or paying taxes.

Together with Governor Yang, the Republic and Russia agreed upon a plan
to establish a joint Sino-Russian mining operation in the region that abided
strictly by Chinese mining regulations and gave a more than 50 percent interest in the enterprise to Chinese shareholders. Officials in the Republic were

wary of their partners, however, and the head of the Ministry of Foreign Affairs in Beijing cautioned their local counterparts that "if [the Russians] make any requests outside of the specifics of the agreement, they must be rejected in the sternest of terms."[74] The fate of the project is lost in the archival record. But considering the influx of Kazakh refugees who fled to northern Xinjiang from Russian Turkestan and the subsequent unrest in the region in the run-up to the Russian Revolution, in all likelihood the project never got off the ground.[75]

In addition to gold, Russian surveyors were also interested in Xinjiang's petroleum wealth, as global oil prices skyrocketed following the outbreak of World War I and the ramping up of production of new petroleum-swilling war machines like tanks, trucks, and airplanes. The rapidly increasing price of oil fueled a new global effort spearheaded by a handful of international oil companies to discover and tap new oilfields in unexplored regions. The effort led to a number of new discoveries in the Americas and the Middle East.[76] Hoping to tap Xinjiang's oil wealth, Russian officials and investors pored over old maps, government documents, and geological reports.

In November 1915, a delegation of Russian merchants arrived at the provincial governor's office in Dihua asking to finance a Russian surveying team that was hoping to set out the following spring for Suilai and Wusu counties—the heart of northern Xinjiang's richest oilfields. Their plans centered around Dushanzi, the site pinpointed by Obruchev as being the most potentially productive site in northern Xinjiang. In a report to the Ministry of Foreign Affairs in Beijing, Governor Yang worried, "Russian merchants and officials constantly covet Xinjiang's mineral wealth . . . I fear that this time the Russians coming to survey Xinjiang's oil are harboring bad intentions."[77] During his meeting with provincial officials, the Russian consular officer asked for a six-month "pass" (huzhao, here the term is related to the modern concept of a visa) that would allow expedition members to work in Xinjiang. While Yang pointed out in his communication with Beijing that he was inclined to deny the request, he also knew that the team could easily gain illegal passes from the masses of largely unmonitored Russian merchants who were able to slip into Xinjiang every month to trade. As a result, he asked the ministry to offer three-month passes to the expedition members and confidentially informed the ministry that "we will order local officials to join [the Russian expedition] under the pretense of offering them official protection and use [these officials] to monitor and observe their activities."[78]

In addition to his cloak-and-dagger tactics, Yang also called on the Ministry of Foreign Affairs and the Ministry of Commerce and Agriculture to approve plans to start up an oil drilling operation funded with Chinese capital.

He pointed out that only through the exploitation of the province's mineral wealth would they be able to hold off the Russian advance in the region. Yang proposed the establishment of a 30,000 tael joint stock operation.[79] In a pointed appeal to the protection of China's sovereignty and a deft use of nationalistic rhetoric, Yang argued that "words alone cannot block [Russian intentions] and ensure that Xinjiang's oil wealth is used to support the nation."[80]

Despite his rhetoric, which we should see as at least partially representing a strategy intended to convince the central government of the need to provide the province with more financial support, Yang also understood the potential that the Russian teams represented.[81] Unlike their counterparts in the Russian Empire, officials in Xinjiang lacked the capital and technical expertise to establish profitable extraction operations. Also, considering the proximity of Dushanzi to Russian territory, it would be cheaper to ship in refining and mining equipment along the Russian rail network and ship raw oil produced at Dushanzi into international markets the same way. With these considerations, Yang delicately suggested to the Chinese Ministry of Foreign Affairs that his new enterprise accept Russian merchant capital as well as Chinese. Swayed by Yang's argument and mindful that a successful mining operation, even a jointly operated one, would begin the process of finally generating the revenues needed to make the province a contributor to the national coffers, officials in the ministry approved Yang's plan in December 1915. The seemingly sure prospect of receiving funds from Russia to open Xinjiang's oil wells crashed and burned with the unrest wracking the Russian Empire and the eventual collapse of the tsarist government in 1917.

The reliance on foreign capital and expertise ensured that the sites selected for exploitation by these joint enterprises tended to be ones prioritized for production by the foreign partners. Beginning in the late 1890s, Russian agents began exerting a significant amount of influence over the placement of mines and drilling operations. They tended to place sites near the border and near the regional rail transport network in Russian Central Asia. Indeed, of the three sites focused on in these two sections: the Katu Mountain goldfields, the Altay Mountain goldfields, and the Dushanzi oilfield, the latter is located the farthest from the border, a mere 150 miles to the west. With agreements in hand, these operations served as the institutional conduits through which much more extensive surveying occurred. Further, the subsequent surveys and reports served as the foundational layers upon which future extraction operations would be negotiated and established.

It is important to recognize that there is no evidence to suggest that the decisions made by provincial leaders to orient patterns of extraction and spending toward a Russian blueprint is a product of threats. Quite the contrary, without dismissing the power of unuttered, implicit threats, all of the available evidence suggests that it was a desire for capital and a need for revenue that prompted provincial leaders to invest in sites of production that conformed to Russian interests. With a limited quantity of capital to draw on, provincial officials had to prioritize their investments, and Russian confirmation of resource sites appeared to lessen the risks posed by extraction operations. As a result, even when they did not rely on foreign capital, those sites Russians explored, surveyed, and exploited in the late nineteenth century and early twentieth remained the focus of provincial officials desperate to generate lucrative resources at low expense.

The result was a network of integrated resource production sites that lined the eastern and northern borders of the province. Future geological expeditions and surveying teams would continue, as their predecessors did, to study provincial government reports about potential resources, and rely on local informants including both local officials as well as indigenous Uyghurs, Kazakhs, and Mongols. But none of these potential sources could match the power of Russian investments and scientific surveys in attracting the interests of provincial leaders. The backing of capital and the symbolic power of science helped tilt patterns of spending in the region inexorably away from historically productive sites in the southern stretches of the province and toward sites prioritized by Russian actors in the north and west.

## The Power of Layers

In 1917, the Russian Empire collapsed and civil war spread across Central Asia and Siberia. At the same time, chaos was also sweeping across China-proper, as the death of the first president of the Chinese Republic, Yuan Shikai, led to a swirling political struggle among various regional power holders. A fear that the churning political chaos in Central Asia and China would engulf the province prompted Yang to worry in a quiet conversation with a Chinese visitor that, without vigilance, "Xinjiang will be thrown into the whirlpool."[82] Fearing the whirlpool, Yang steered a policy of de facto autonomy for Xinjiang, in which he asserted the region's legal status as a province of the Republic of China but sealed the region from the influence of the factional fights and party politics of the Republic. When it came to the production of gold and petroleum Yang effectively closed the door to outside surveying and capital investment from China and the Soviet Union alike.

The result was that by the 1920s Xinjiang's resource map was effectively frozen in amber. During a period in which China's nascent geological community began to rapidly expand its reach, surveying much of the vast territory of the Republic and compiling and publishing extensive resource maps and geological reports, the territory of Xinjiang remained as largely a blank spot, aside from the well-established foreign-supported sites in the northern parts of the province. Even as late as 1932, the geological map for Xinjiang compiled by the National Geological Survey of China was one of only a few provincial geological maps of the Republic that remained incomplete.[83] Similarly, before 1942 there was not a single stand-alone article on the mineral wealth of Xinjiang published in the flagship journal of China's geological community, the *Bulletin of the Geological Survey of China*.

The lack of access to Xinjiang during this critical period meant that planners or investors interested in staking a claim to the region's lucrative resources, whether in Beijing or some imperial capital, had to rely on little more than outdated reports, hearsay, and the physical evidence of Russian operations. In his highly influential 1919 report *The Mineral Resources of China*, the prominent geologist and future Minister of Finance for the Republic of China, Weng Wenhao, leaned on secondhand reports of Xinjiang's most promising resource sites that were provided by provincial officials.[84] Not surprisingly, these sites, particularly petroleum wells, tended to track those prioritized for production by Russian officials. Likewise, in a 1926 follow-up to Weng's report, an analysis of Xinjiang's oil wealth by geologist Xie Jiarong drew almost exclusively on Weng's 1919 report and an English-language publication that itself was explicitly based on secondhand reports on Russian activity in the region.[85]

Provincial officials in the post-1917 period, who lacked the economic means or the technical expertise to undertake large-scale geological surveys in the province, established a series of small-scale operations built directly upon those sites identified and funded with Russian capital in the previous decade. Hoping to exert clearer provincial claims to the Altay goldfields, in 1919 Yang established a decentralized "people mine, officials buy" mining operation that was supported by the provincial government and worked by laborers recruited in the provincial capital of Dihua. The operations Yang set up in Dushanzi to take advantage of still-climbing global oil prices consisted of only a handful of fairly shallow wells that were producing a meager 14,500 catties (19,000 pounds or around 63 modern barrels) of oil annually at a profit of only around 7,000 or 8,000 provincial taels.[86]

The focus on both of these sites in the years following the collapse of the Russian Empire suggests the power of Russian capital and surveys. The fact is that there were known goldfields in the Tianshan Mountain range located far closer to the provincial capital of Dihua and Xinjiang's provincial transport network. Similarly, earlier reports and even a few smaller-scale Russian surveys identified several oilfields located within 10 kilometers of Dihua, a major market for petroleum products, the center of government, and the primary hub on the provincial transport network. At this site, located in the foothills of the Tianshan Mountain range, Obruchev noted that "petroleum springs flow abundantly from the soil."[87] But these sites were not included on the production priority lists emerging from Yang's provincial yamen in the early 1920s. The focus on Dushanzi, which was located 250 kilometers west of Dihua on the road toward the Russian border, suggests the resonant power of Russian interest and capital in shaping investment priorities in Xinjiang.

The Russian surveys and the initial investment in Dushanzi resonated well beyond provincial government offices. Indeed, the collapse of the Russian Empire in 1918 prompted the British government to try to take over the central role that Russian investors and surveyors had played in Xinjiang. In 1920, the British government signed an agreement with the government in Beijing to establish the Joint Sino-British Xinjiang Oil Company. The company, which was to be capitalized at 1 million British pounds, was focused specifically on exploiting the oil wealth of Dushanzi and its oil-rich surroundings. The problem, however, was that the Chinese government did not first inform Governor Yang in Dihua, who found out about the establishment of the operation from an article in the *Shuntian Times*.[88] In a series of lengthy telegrams to the Ministry of Foreign Affairs in Beijing beginning in December 1920 and ending in late February the next year, Yang, through his mouthpiece in the provincial assembly, demanded that the agreement be cancelled. He angrily denounced the agreement, arguing that it threatened the Republic's hold in Xinjiang.[89] The strenuous opposition of provincial leaders and the inability and unwillingness of leaders in Beijing (who were beset by a series of internal political problems of their own) to enforce the agreement ensured that in the end it would be cancelled.

By the mid-1920s, lacking any meaningful source of revenue, Yang felt compelled to embrace an "empty citadel" (*kongcheng*) small government ruling philosophy. He slashed his bureaucracy and cut military expenditures to the bone. Chinese visitors marveled at his success in gutting the provincial bureaucracy, and foreign visitors were appalled by the ragtag qualities of his military. Before dying from an assassin's bullet in 1928, Yang even subjected mining to his bureaucratic knife. Yang ended decentralized operations in the Kunlun Mountain goldfields first highlighted by Bogdanovich and embraced by officials in Beijing in the 1890s. He ended any pretense of profiting off of these ore fields by withdrawing bureaucratic and military oversight, allowing prospectors to dig for gold without paying taxes to the provincial government and without requiring them to sell gold chipped out of the quartz veins back to the government at fixed prices.[90] Despite the decision to withdraw provincial support or oversight, the layers placed in the form of surveys, maps, and extraction operations continued to cast these isolated sites in northern Xinjiang in a sharp, distinct relief against the unmapped, unsurveyed territories surrounding them.

*

The unwillingness of the Qing empire and later the Chinese Republic to invest in Xinjiang effectively opened the door to foreign capital. Working closely with officials in the provincial administration, Russian agents in particular worked to tap Xinjiang's lucrative resource wealth at a handful of sites mostly concentrated in the northern stretches of the province near the Russian border. The discovery of lucrative resources in places like the Katu Mountains or at Dushanzi helped establish these sites as geological waypoints for future teams charged with uncovering Xinjiang's resource sites. In 1911, the geologist Obruchev published a map of western Xinjiang that traced in red the routes his three expeditions in 1905, 1906, and 1909 took in the province. They show dense nests of red lines circulating around proven ore sites near the border, as his teams traced and retraced their steps in the ridges and valleys surrounding them.[91] The result is an accumulation of data on a handful of sites and a relative lack of information on others.

The reports, resource maps, and priority lists compiled by geological teams, provincial officials, foreign investors, and state planners were published, distributed among formal and informal networks of professional societies, translated into multiple languages, and filed away in libraries and reading rooms throughout China, Europe, Russian Central Asia, and British India. These were the initial layers that would guide later decisions made by provincial officials, Chinese and foreign governments, and private investors, all of whom were eager to quickly recover lucrative ores without breaking the bank. The reports and investments in these out-of-the-way resource sites helped establish a list of production priorities that had a surprising endurance over the course of the twentieth century, no matter which regime held sway in the region.

The afterlives of the expeditions extend deep into the twentieth century, as operations in the Altay Mountain goldfields in the first decade of the century helped reveal the presence of various critical rare minerals that later would be prioritized for production for military purposes by the Soviet Union (see chapters 5 and 6). The oil operations at Dushanzi became a major site of oil production beginning in the early 1940s, and surveys that were focused on the site led to the discovery of nearby oilfields, some of which would come online only under the Chinese Communist Party several decades later (see chapter 7). These operations in turn would spawn new surveying teams, who would continue to layer investment and interest into these highly delimited spaces located in northern Xinjiang. In this way, these regions would become ever more visible to surveyors, state planners, and investors eager to uncover the region's most lucrative and important resource sites.

In the end, the Qing and early Republican mining operations sat lightly on the landscape. Every successive mining gang brought in to open its respective fields was forced to grapple with the ghosts of its predecessors. The historical record is littered with an accounting of the relics of mining operations past: abandoned equipment, old dug-outs used as living spaces, mounds of ore tailings and empty drill shafts, and, in one grisly case, the green-stained corpse of a former miner who fell into a pit in the Katu Mountains and was mummified by the high copper content of the water supply.[92] The detritus speaks to the forlorn quality of the sites, but also to the power of the layers that continued to draw surveying teams, officials, and investors back. These layers, however, did not only draw investors and state agents back to mines and oilfields. Rather, they also helped shape larger patterns of production. In the early twentieth century, new global markets for various products produced in Xinjiang including most notably furs, pelts, and other animal parts created a renewed interest in the region. The pursuit of these products and efforts to facilitate their distribution into international markets helped strengthen and even reinforce the earlier layers laid in northern Xinjiang.

# Furs, Pelts, Wool, and the Power of Global Markets

Xinjiang's resource wealth was not restricted to oil and precious metals. According to an eighteenth-century Qing gazetteer, the northern half of the province, an area long defined by grasslands that connected Outer Mongolia with the Central Asian steppe, produced large amounts of horse, ox, and sheep pelts, as well as various furs. Supplementing this was a collection of various medicinal plants, from rhubarb, licorice root, ephedra, and wormwood to more exotic species such as siler root, asafetida, and *Rubia tinctorum* (madder). The agricultural oases of southern Xinjiang produced textiles, including cotton, coarse cloth (*tubu*), and silk piece goods.[1] The Qing court had long been focused primarily on taxing and regulating the production of these products. But just as with the subterranean resources covered in the previous chapter, the expansion of international markets and the arrival of growing numbers of foreigners seeking access to products in the late nineteenth century prompted officials to play a more active role in promoting the production and distribution of Xinjiang's so-called local products (*tuchan*).[2]

There were three primary trade conduits that bound Xinjiang and its commodities to global markets in the late Qing period. A long 2,000-mile trek across Outer Mongolia bound the region to markets along the China coast, a route across the towering Kunlun Mountains connected it to markets in British India, and a third across the Central Asian steppe linked the region to markets in the Russian Empire. By all accounts, the connections to Russia were the smoothest. According to British documents, transport costs from the Russian Empire were one-quarter of those from India, as the Muslim and Hindu traders were forced by the difficult terrain to carry substantial amounts of food and fodder for their pack animals.[3] While the pack trails across Outer Mongolia had no lack of fodder, the problem on the Chinese side was distance, as the caravan trails crossing the grasslands took a long and arduous three months to complete a one-way journey well into the Republican period. The author of the *Xinjiang Illustrated Gazetteer* connected Xinjiang's poverty with the difficulty of the journey from China-proper: "Why has [Xinjiang's] wealth been exhausted? Because commodity transport takes several months and it still does not arrive."[4]

The favorable topography as well as a series of preferential trade agreements (later included within the category of "unequal treaties" imposed by imperial powers on the Qing court) led to growing numbers of Russian merchants plying the trading routes into Xinjiang in the late nineteenth century. Driven by high values on international markets, Russian merchants pursued a series of goods produced in abundance in northern Xinjiang in particular, including livestock, wool, lamb hide, lamb intestines, cotton, pelts, medicinal products such as rhubarb, and fabric piece goods.[5] The earlier layers developed along the Russo-Xinjiang border by geologists and planners seeking gold and oil shaped the itineraries of these traders, guiding them to sites of production located around the Ili River valley as well as to sites outside of Tacheng and deep in the Altay Mountains. Their efforts were supported by the development of the Russian rail network in the region, as the extension of rails into Siberia and Central Asia in the late 1890s allowed Russian merchants to mainline huge volumes of manufactured products into Xinjiang's markets, including textiles, resold brick tea, sugar, thread, oil, tobacco, matches, and iron products in exchange for the province's raw materials.

Qing officials in Xinjiang ominously noted the more than 150,000 camels crisscrossing the Russo-Chinese border annually in the 1890s.[6] In reports to Beijing, provincial officials noted that Russian dominance of the export market was so extensive that, in some cases, Chinese merchants seeking products produced in Xinjiang for export back to China-proper often had little choice but to buy them from Russian traders. In a memorial to the court, Governor Tao Mo sounded the alarm, noting that the profusion of Russian products was allowing Xinjiang to "quietly slip into the grasp of Russian merchants."[7] The emergence of the foreign threat and a new discourse about a global "commerce war" (*shangzhan*), for which the Qing empire seemed woefully unprepared, prompted Qing officials in the late nineteenth century to try to exert more state control over trade to both generate tax revenue and also protect Qing sovereignty. They sought to do this through the development of new public-private ventures, infrastructure, and tax policies favorable to merchants working the long trade routes to eastern and central China.[8]

But just as the late Qing financial crisis handcuffed the abilities of provincial officials to profit off of gold and oil fields, the unwillingness of the Qing and Republican central governments to invest their resources in Xinjiang limited the options of provincial officials. Indeed, lacking capital and all but the most rudimentary infrastructural connections to China-proper, officials in Xinjiang, who were eager to profit from the growing demand for the region's lucrative commodity products, had little choice but to reach out to their Russian and, after 1917, Soviet counterparts. The problem was not unique to this single border province. In the tumultuous early years of the Chinese Republic, central government officials lacked the resources and the political will to assert their authority over other wayward peripheries like Manchuria, Mongolia, and Tibet. As a result, leaders in these regions had only the most tenuous political connections to the newly established Republic of China. In Xinjiang, by the late 1920s, while provincial officials continued to express their allegiances to the new government at Nanjing, their connections to China-proper were weak. Desperate for some type of material support, these officials signed a series of agreements with the Soviet Union beginning in the late 1920s in which they bartered Xinjiang's lucrative local products for Soviet aid. To facilitate the exchange of local products for manufactured goods, provincial officials worked directly with Soviet advisers to develop a new transportation infrastructure capable of handling the growing volume of goods traveling from northern Xinjiang into the Soviet Union. Supplementing these infrastructural connections, they also developed new institutions of control and oversight that sought to facilitate the production, processing, and transport of local products. These new institutions led to increasingly intensive campaigns to survey and categorize local populations and local products in northern Xinjiang. This effort, alongside the new infrastructural networks, served to bind Xinjiang's hides, furs, and pelts to Soviet industrial centers and global markets. The subsequent collaborative efforts between Soviet agents and their provincial counterparts to deliver local products to the Soviet Union helped reinforce the layers placed earlier in northern Xinjiang in pursuit of lucrative subterranean resources (see chapter 3).

## Merchants and the State

The ability of Russian merchants to "barge into every nomadic camp, using cheap goods to exchange for livestock and furs," as one Qing official put it, was due in large part to support from Moscow.[9] Indeed, throughout the late Qing and Republican eras, Russian merchants operating in Xinjiang were aided by strong advocacy from government officials, who worked hand in hand with them to uncover new commercial opportunities in Xinjiang, whether they were gold mines, oil wells (as noted in chapter 3), or the production of various furs, pelts, or wool. These efforts were reinforced by the willingness of Moscow to use state funds to construct a regional transport network that gave Russian merchants significant economic advantages in the province.

The staggering growth in the number of Russian merchants in the late nineteenth century prompted late Qing officials to increase their support for Chinese merchants plying the trade routes to China (while many of these merchants were ethnically Han Chinese, not all were). In order to protect the region from the economic and political power of their neighbors, Qing officials created new public-private enterprises, developed preferential tax laws, and advocated on merchants' behalf in disputes with foreigners. But provincial officials also prioritized the development of new transportation connections binding Xinjiang to markets in China-proper. As the last Qing governor of Xinjiang asked, "In 10,000 *li* of poor wasteland, where transportation is not convenient and where there are no funds and no population, what method do we have" to strengthen the hand of the state? He looked to the West for the answer to this question: "foreigners depend on the railroad to swallow territory and open new frontiers."[10] In the first decade of the twentieth century, Qing officials drew up ambitious plans for a rail line connecting Xinjiang to China-proper that would cost a staggering 140 million taels to construct. In the end, faced with the necessity of taking on foreign loans to pay for the line, the payments for which would be shouldered primarily by the cash-poor northwestern provinces, the Qing court scrapped the plan.[11]

This failure to build a rail line or even an improved highway connecting Xinjiang to the lands "inside the pass" stood in stark contrast to the significant investments in a regional transport network undertaken by Russian officials in the late nineteenth century. Throughout the 1890s, Russian officials extended their rail network east across Central Asia, until the Trans-Caspian rail line reached its terminus at Andijon, not far from Qing territory. Completed in 1899, the line facilitated the large-scale, inexpensive transport of Russian goods into Xinjiang and also allowed for a commensurate export of Xinjiang's local products back to Russian and European markets. The new line, as well as the gradual extension of the Trans-Siberian line stretching just north of the province during the same period, troubled Qing officials. "Xinjiang is besieged by Russian railroads to the north and to the west," wrote provincial treasurer Wang Shunan.[12] In addition to rail development, Russian engineers were also developing the region's rivers, and by the first decade of the twentieth century, Russian steamships were plying the Ili River in western Xinjiang as well as the Irtysh in the north. Comparing Russian transport into Xinjiang with transport from China, the first Republican governor Yang Zengxin, noted with irritation that Russian imports "are shipped into [the province] by trucks and steamers rather than carts and camels; therefore they are extremely numerous."[13]

There was no shortage of bold developmentalist rhetoric about the creation of a new nationally integrated infrastructural network from the modernizing reformers who came to power with the founding of the new Republic of China in 1912. But when it came to a rail network that could counter Russian infrastructural power in the region, these plans, ambitious as they were, never came to fruition. Sun Yatsen's 1912 plan for the construction of a 67,000-mile rail network with a line that extended the width of Xinjiang never got off the ground. And neither did a 1921 plan in which he proposed a 100,000-mile rail network that connected Xinjiang to China-proper with a dense web of rail lines binding even the most out-of-the-way backwater in the province into a larger national network (see figure 4.1).[14] While not as ambitious as Sun, another Chinese surveyor who crisscrossed Xinjiang and Outer Mongolia in the early Republic laid out his own, more conservative plan, which consisted of a nearly 2,000-mile rail line that would connect Xinjiang to China via Outer Mongolia. But even this plan which he estimated would cost 165 million Chinese yuan, was deemed too expensive for the cash-strapped new Republic and too risky to attract potential investors.[15] Outer Mongolia's declaration of independence and the closing of the border to Chinese merchants in 1922 effectively closed the most accessible route to Xinjiang and ended the dreams of a rail line for the foreseeable future. Alongside the lack of financial support from Beijing since the 1911 revolution, the closing of the most accessible route connecting Xinjiang to China-proper served to reinforce Yang's growing autonomy and insulate the province from the dangerous factional politics of the Republic of China in the 1920s.

Without a transport network binding Xinjiang to markets in the east, provincial officials became fully dependent on Russian and later Soviet merchants to deliver critical industrial and manufactured products like sugar, matches, and iron goods into this distant border region. As a consequence, throughout the early years of the Republic, inexpensive Russian manufactured goods dominated Xinjiang's markets and, in exchange, products produced in the province flowed west in a steady stream. The Russian presence dried up in the years immediately following the 1917 Russian Revolution and the ensuing civil war that ranged across Central Asia. But the power of Russian rails and markets meant that despite signing a new, more restrictive trade agreement a few years later in 1920, cross-border trade was once again rapidly expanding. In 1923, the total volume of trade between Xinjiang and the Soviet Union was nearly seven times higher that of 1922, it tripled from 1923 to 1924, and then doubled from 1924 to 1925 (see table 4.1).

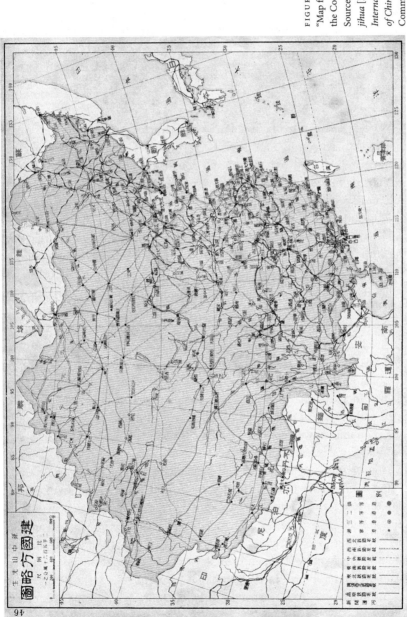

FIGURE 4.1 Sun Yatsen's "Map for the General Plan of the Construction of China." Source: Sun Yatsen, *Shiye jihua* [English title: *The International Development of China*] (Shanghai: Commercial Press, 1920).

TABLE 4.1. Trade between Xinjiang and the Soviet Union (in thousands of rubles)

| Year | Exports to the Soviet Union | Imports from the Soviet Union | Total trade volume |
|---|---|---|---|
| 1922 | 177 | 197 | 374 |
| 1923 | 2,198 | 413 | 2,581 |
| 1924 | 4,357 | 2,683 | 7,040 |
| 1925 | 7,971 | 6,069 | 14,040 |
| 1926 | 10,294 | 10,232 | 20,526 |

Source: Li Sheng, Xinjiang dui Su (E) maoyishi, 1600–1990 (Urumqi: Xinjiang Renmin Chubanshe, 1992), 324.

Soviet traders were interested in a wide assortment of products including wool, livestock, cotton, and pelts. Furs were a particularly profitable commodity, and Soviet merchants actively sought to corner the markets in furs in Xinjiang to profit from the lucrative European markets.[16] Led by the large volume of products flowing into the Soviet Union from Xinjiang, by 1926 the total volume of trade between the Chinese province and the Soviet Union topped out at 20.5 million rubles (see table 4.1).[17] In addition to the strength of the Soviet rail network, much of this growth in trade volume was a product of Soviet state-centered trade policies that picked up momentum following the founding of five Soviet consulates in Xinjiang in October 1924. The consulates served as advocates for local merchants, as informal trade and commercial affairs organs, and even as banks, providing the capital needed to purchase large volumes of local products.[18]

The connection between the consulates and Soviet merchants operating in Xinjiang helped ensure, as one official in the border town of Aksu complained in a report to Governor Yang Zengxin, that "a large quantity of exports and the sale of [Soviet] goods remained within the grasp of the state."[19] The economic power mustered by the consulates allowed Soviet citizens to dominate local markets and threaten Chinese merchants. As one local official in Xinjiang asked as he watched Soviet merchants control Xinjiang's tea trade: "Chinese merchants transporting tea are individuals, how can they compete with the power of a country?"[20] In addition to the deft use of loans in order to create relations of dependency between local producers in Xinjiang and Soviet purchasers, the consulates also spearheaded the purchase of cotton, pelts, and wool in quantities large enough that it allowed them to outbid other merchants.[21] They also instituted a ubiquitous barter policy, in which Soviet sellers insisted on the direct exchange of Soviet exports for Xinjiang products.

The Soviet trading tactics ensured that many merchants in Xinjiang viewed the growth in trade with real concern. When Soviet and provincial officials convened in 1926 to renegotiate the restrictive 1920 trade agreement, a delegation of merchants sent a message to Yang requesting that he proceed with caution. "International trade relations must first ensure that the economic rights of both are protected and that profit is balanced with harm," they wrote. Expressing an underlying fear about the Soviet Union's rapidly expanding position in Xinjiang, Chinese merchants identified the province's local products as the ammunition that would be used in the looming "economic war" with other imperial powers, and asked for protection using nationalistic rhetoric that they knew would resonate. "We ask that the governor undertake negotiations according to the popular will, to protect the profits of Chinese merchants [*Zhongshang*] and defend the nation's sovereign rights."[22] Despite convincing provincial officials to retain the restrictive terms of the 1920s treaty, waves of Russian merchants, both legal traders and illegal smugglers, continued to break on Xinjiang's shores in the late 1920s. The growing economic power of the Soviet Union also elicited concern from provincial officials who feared that Soviet ambitions would doom Chinese control of Xinjiang. Watching the growth of Soviet economic power, one local official worried, "How will our 'New Frontier' [Xinjiang] not turn into the Russian 'new frontier' [*xinjiang*]?" he asked, playing on the name of the province.[23]

After Yang's death in 1928, his successor Jin Shuren issued a report that restated the restrictive terms of the 1920 treaty and called for a crackdown on violations of the treaty. "Before completing a formal Sino-Soviet trade agreement, free trade within the borders of Xinjiang is not permitted," Jin stated in the 1929 report, insisting that trade be confined to the town of Ili, as stipulated in the 1920 treaty. To hammer the point home, when provincial officials caught a Russian trader making an illegal purchase of 54,000 kilos of cotton in the eastern town of Turfan that same year, the Xinjiang government was unwilling to simply let him off the hook. "We have irrefutable proof of the transaction. If we do not strictly punish him, how can we protect our sovereignty and our laws?" the provincial government asked unequivocally.[24] Jin's larger policy was one of mustering provincial government support for commerce to both reassert control but also generate precious revenue for the treasury. He noted that while Soviet traders were operating under the aegis of centralized, governmental-owned trading companies that were supported by aggressive consulates, and aided by a centralized transport network, traders in Xinjiang were largely on their own. "The Soviet Union has a national trading policy, while our country has a trading policy made up of an assortment of individuals," he wrote in a report. "Comparing the capital of an individual with that of a government, how can the Soviet Union not be fully in control?"[25]

Local merchants and officials who were direct witnesses to the Soviet Union's growing power in local markets echoed Jin's concerns. The historical record from the late 1920s is filled with reports from Chinese merchants and provincial officials calling for greater provincial government control over trade in order to level the economic playing field. A local official in the border town of Tacheng noted that, given the Soviets' abilities to muster heavy capital investments for bulk purchases of commodities, it was difficult for traders in Xinjiang to compete. Therefore, he called for a rapid centralization of government control over trade. Jin received numerous proposals from local merchants and officials laying out the framework for a new trading regime with the heft needed to compete with the Soviet trade machine. Their proposals called for a state-operated trading warehouse through which all goods must flow, the establishment of a monopoly on certain lucrative products like furs and pelts, the creation of a protective tariff, and the expansion of the trade monitoring apparatus. "When [a policy of heightened monitoring and taxation] is established, although the initial costs will be high, the revenues in the future will be even more substantial," argued a local official in Tacheng. It will, he said, "be like giving bricks in exchange for jade."[26] Supplementing these reforms, in 1930 Jin proposed the establishment of a provincial Local Product Transport and Sales Company as well as a provincial bank that would be capable of providing the capital that local merchants and transport companies needed to compete. The company received lucrative monopolies on the sale of lamb skins and sheep intestines and was called upon to move furs and cotton, along with various types of skins and animal horns, into international markets via harbors in Tianjin and Shanghai.[27]

The growing fears from many throughout China that the Soviet Union not only sought profit but territory in the Republic's vulnerable border regions exploded with the Zhongdong railroad incident in July 1929. The incident, in which Soviet forces were sent into Manchuria to protect Soviet control over the East Manchurian Railway, inspired a wave of anti-Soviet nationalism in the Chinese Republic. It seemed to confirm officials' and many local merchants' fears about what they called a "Soviet secret plot with intentions to control" Xinjiang.[28] A radical proposal from a merchant in Altay, which called for a full ban on Soviet imports, even reached Jin's desk in 1930. Referencing the illegality of Soviet entities operating outside of the trade entrepot of Ili, Jin proclaimed in March 1930 that Soviet "transport and trading companies are squatting on our land and exploiting our profits."[29] He undertook an aggressive campaign of shuttering illegal Soviet trading companies in the border towns of Kashgar, Tacheng, and Altay.[30]

Jin's hard-line policies that sought to control Soviet trade had a momentary impact, as Soviet-Xinjiang trade volumes for 1929 fell by more than 1 million rubles over the previous year. This decline was noted by Soviet trade officials who experienced a severe lack of capital. As one such official stationed in Kashgar wrote to Moscow in 1930, "We should warn you that if we do not receive help, we will be in desperate circumstances bordering on catastrophe." The result of their lack of capital, this official argued, was that much of the trade that had once been dominated by Soviet merchants was floating into the hands of Hindu traders connected to the British Empire.[31] Overall, however, Jin's hard-line policies did little to undercut the long-term upward trajectory of cross-border trade.

### The Turk-Sib Line and the Long Road to China

The rebirth of Soviet industry in the mid to late 1920s ensured that trade volumes in both legal and smuggled goods continued to grow from the mid-1920s into the early 1930s. According to Soviet documents, the total trade volume in 1929 was more than five and a half times larger than 1923.[32] But the real factor that saved the Soviet trading position and ultimately the force that transformed the contours of trade in the region more generally, was the completion of the Turkestan-Siberian rail line in 1929. The Turk-Sib, as it was known, served to connect the Trans-Caspian and Trans-Siberian lines with a line that ran parallel to the Xinjiang border in the northern part of the province (see map 4.1).

The construction of a rail line connecting the Trans-Caspian and Trans-Siberian Lines had been discussed by Russian officials since the nineteenth century. After a number of stops and starts, the Turk-Sib was once again prioritized in the early 1920s. Soviet planners surveyed the area in 1925, fast-tracked it as a component of the First Five Year Plan, and earmarked the funds needed for the construction of its 870-mile length in 1928. While certainly not the only factor in driving its construction, the ability of the rail line to siphon out lucrative raw materials and deliver large volumes of light industrial products into Xinjiang helped convince Soviet leaders to move forward with their plans.[33] Proponents estimated that the construction of the line would increase the total annual trade volume in and out of Xinjiang to 57 million poods of goods (around 916,000 tons), of which 51 percent would consist of exports into the province, the rest being made up of various raw material imports into Soviet Turkestan.[34] Perhaps hoping to convince budget-conscious members

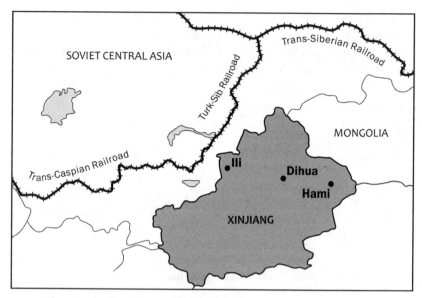

MAP 4.1 Trans-Caspian, Trans-Siberian, and Turk-Sib rail lines. Map by Debbie Newell.

of the Soviet Politburo, the report noted that the 14 million ruble annual cost of operating the line would be more than compensated for by the estimated 18 million rubles in annual revenue.[35] While Soviet geologists and surveyors had long been primarily interested in the resource wealth of northern Xinjiang, the new line allowed for even greater Soviet penetration of the region and helped set the contours for future patterns of trade and extraction that focused ever more closely on the northern half of the province in regions along the border.

In 1927, the Chinese consul stationed in Irkutsk was able to obtain a copy of plans for the Turk-Sib project from the Soviet Ministry of Transport along with a detailed map that revealed just how close the new line was from Xinjiang's western border. "I fear that [Xinjiang's] provincial economy will be completely monopolized by Soviet Russia and that afterwards disasters will surely multiply," the consul worried in a communiqué to the Chinese Ministry of Foreign Affairs.[36] For him, the economic benefits cited in the report seemed to conceal a darker purpose. "On the surface they have stated that the [rail line is being built] for the economic purpose of developing commerce in border regions," the Chinese consul wrote in his report. "But in reality their plans contain a political end," he said referring to the potential domination and ultimate annexation of the province.[37] Governor Yang, who received the reports a year before his death, responded bitterly to the alarmed messages:

"Since the establishment of the Republic, there has not been one day that has not been witness to internal fighting. It seems that if [China] had diverted one-third of the amounts we spend paying back foreign loans or on military expenditures to the construction of railroads, then we surely would have already announced the completion of a line linking Shaanxi, Gansu, and Xinjiang." He went on, "How can we make foreigners not build a rail line surrounding us on all four sides, when we do not have the desire to build a railroad ourselves?"[38]

The growing Soviet presence in Xinjiang's markets following the completion of the line in 1929 prompted local officials and merchants to seek out ways to more aggressively counterbalance Soviet commercial power. As far as both sides were concerned, the way forward was clear: open new transport routes that would allow merchants direct access to markets in Europe and North America.[39] To undertake this ambitious strategy, Jin sought to improve the infrastructural and institutional connections binding the province to international trade depots in China-proper.[40] Indeed, after 1929, in a major reversal of Yang's policy of holding China at arm's length out of fear of being swept into the country's so-called political "whirlpool" (see chapter 3), Jin actively courted trade with China. He sought to underwrite a massive campaign of infrastructural and institutional development in order to solidify links to the east and replace tax revenues on Soviet imports with taxes on goods coming from China-proper. Jin's decision to underwrite the substantial cost of surveying and paving an auto road connecting the provincial capital of Dihua to the major transport hub of Gucheng (modern-day Qitai) in eastern Xinjiang in 1929 reflected an effort to shift the province's orientation away from the Soviet Union.

Gucheng was the western terminus of the east-west caravan road to and from China-proper, a city described by Owen Lattimore as the "gate of Inner Asia."[41] In a telegram to China's Executive Yuan (Xingzhengyuan) in Nanjing, Jin laid out a construction plan that relied on soldiers for construction, and four steamrollers purchased from Germany to pave the road. The road, which it was estimated would cost 500,000 provincial taels to complete, ended up costing 2 million and after beginning construction in 1929 was finally finished in 1931.[42] Further solidifying the connections to markets in the east, the Gucheng road was extended south through Turfan to the town of Hami and ended at the Xingxingxia pass on the border with Gansu province to the east.

The shift underway in Xinjiang must have been music to the ears of officials in the new capital of the Chinese Republic in Nanjing. The 1926–1927 "Northern Expedition" undertaken by Sun Yatsen's political heir Chiang Kaishek and the Guomindang Party (GMD) seemed to herald a new era in China's modern history. Indeed, the founding of the new national capital in Nanjing seemed to augur the end of decentralized warlord control that had characterized much of the period since the 1911 revolution. The "Nanjing Decade," which began in 1927 with the extension of central government control over much of central and eastern China and only ended with the Japanese invasion in 1937, is typically seen as a period of centralized bureaucratic control of China. Taking a page from Sun Yatsen's bold, developmentalist vision, GMD leaders hoped to reexert control over wayward provinces like Xinjiang and extract their resources for use in ambitious industrialization plans. Jin's proclamation in December 1930 that "railroads in the strong nations of England, France, America, and Japan spread out like a spider web facilitating communication," made with reference to the need for greater transportation infrastructure linking Xinjiang to the rest of China, could just as easily have been uttered by countless state builders peppered throughout any number of government offices in Nanjing.

To carry out this integrationist vision, officials in Xinjiang and China spearheaded a campaign to open a trade conduit to China-proper. In a 1930 report to the government in Nanjing, the governor of Suiyuan, Li Peiji, pushed a plan to open a tamped earth road across the Inner Mongolian grasslands and the wastes of Ningxia and Gansu and into Xinjiang. Li noted, "Now there is a desperate need to open the profits of the northwest and develop the national commercial economy; we plan to quickly complete the Suiyuan-Xinjiang auto road in order to improve transport."[43] From the other side in Xinjiang, Jin was enthusiastic about the plan, and dispatched representatives to Tianjin to purchase nine trucks that could ply the route and would be able to ship approximately 500 pounds of goods per trip.

Despite their enthusiasm for integration, when it came to building the road, GMD officials in Xinjiang were less than willing to open their wallets. Surveyors would later estimate that the cost of constructing such a road would run nearly 3 million Chinese yuan.[44] The price tag forced officials to reconsider their investment priorities. "Because the finances of the central government are impoverished, we ask that the costs of the road be covered by those provinces through which the road travels," declared the Ministry of Railroads in September 1931. The financial situation was no better in Xinjiang, however. And in a terse reply, Jin grimly stated, "We ask that the Ministry draw up a concrete plan for how to do this."[45] The exchange foreshadowed a gloomy future for the mutual desire to strengthen Sino-Xinjiang connections. Unable and unwilling to underwrite the costs of constructing transport links to the east that could compete with the Turk-Sib railroad on the Soviet side of the border, the total volume of trade with China remained relatively flat. Without improved infra-

structure or a hardline policy against their neighbor to the west, Xinjiang and
its local products were completely at the mercy of Soviet traders.

## Exchanging Wool for Guns

The period following Governor Yang's 1928 assassination was a tense one for
his successor Jin, who feared that the warlord general Feng Yuxiang intended
to take advantage of the political instability and invade Xinjiang.[46] As a result,
one of Jin's first acts as governor was to rapidly increase the size of the province's standing army. He increased the number of troops by more than three
times after coming to power in 1928 and a few years later, he doubled it. The
military expansion, which came to occupy 74 percent of the provincial budget, pushed Xinjiang's financial ledgers to the breaking point, as Jin failed to
recover enough in revenues from land, customs, and transport taxes to make
up the difference.[47] As a result, when a large-scale rebellion broke out in the
eastern Xinjiang city of Hami in 1930 and quickly spread through the east and
south, Jin simply did not have the economic resources to deal with the crisis.
Compounding the problem, he also lacked the transport and purchasing networks capable of importing the military hardware he needed to crush the rebellion. In desperation, Jin turned to the Soviet Union.

In the past, Jin had relied on the British government to provide weapons
for his growing army. In 1929, he purchased four thousand machine guns
and four million bullets from the British consulate in the town of Kashgar in
southern Xinjiang.[48] Later, Jin hoped that Germany might be able to provide
the weapons needed and dispatched the future leader of the province, Burhan
Shahidi, to Berlin to establish connections with manufacturers.[49] But these efforts proved insufficient to meet Jin's growing needs. With Nanjing's unwillingness to offer any material support, Jin had little choice but to reach out to
the Soviet Union. In August 1931, the Xinjiang provincial government ordered
the Chinese consul stationed in the city of Semipalatinsk to contact Soviet officials about the possibility of purchasing weapons and allowing third-party
imports of weapons and equipment through Soviet territory. The consul was
instructed to hold up the possibility of renegotiating the restrictive 1920 temporary treaty as an incentive.[50] Jin followed this outreach with a September 1931
communique to the representative of the Soviet Ministry of Foreign Affairs in
Dihua requesting the sale of military aid to the province.[51] For their part, rapidly escalating regional tensions with the British in the late 1920s made Soviet
officials eager to purchase and stockpile goods produced in Xinjiang.[52]

The provincial government and Soviet officials had wrangled over the te-
nets of the highly restrictive original 1920 trade accord for more than a decade

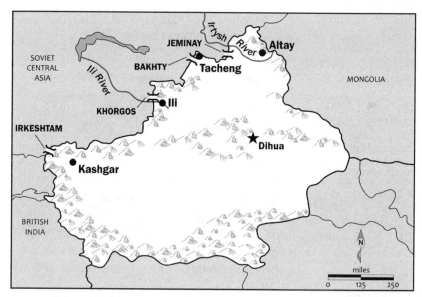

MAP 4.2 Cities and border crossings opened to trade with the Soviet Union in 1931. Map by Debbie Newell.

without being able to arrive at an agreement. But within a month after opening negotiations with the Soviet representatives in September 1931, Jin signed off on a new agreement that drastically transformed the province's relationship to the Soviet Union. The agreement, which was signed on October 1, 1931, opened up trade substantially and reversed Jin's (and earlier Yang Zengxin's) policy of holding the Soviets at arm's length. The agreement opened four new cross-border trading sites, one at Irkeshtam on the southern border of Soviet Central Asia, outside of Kashgar, and three in northern Xinjiang at Khorgos outside of Ili, Bakhty outside of Tacheng, and at Jeminay in the far northern region of Altay. The agreement also mandated that the provincial government could offer no restriction whatsoever on the trade and transport of Xinjiang's resources, it limited the amount of customs taxes that could be levied on cross-border trade, and it opened the towns of Kashgar, Ili, Tacheng, Altay, and Dihua to trade. In exchange, Xinjiang received a Soviet pledge to consider sending experts to the province and the permission to transship goods via Soviet territory. Perhaps most importantly for Jin, the agreement seemed to repair tensions in Xinjiang-Soviet relations and appeared to open the door for the sale of weapons to the province.

The 1931 accord was not revealed to GMD officials in Nanjing and neither was it announced to interested parties inside the province, including some departments within the provincial government.[53] For their part, Soviet officials explicitly agreed to not publicize the agreement and urged officials not to talk about it. The reason for the secrecy was that Jin feared not only a backlash in Nanjing, but also one among the local (mostly Han) merchant community, which was one of his most ardent blocs of supporters within the province.[54] Merchants had long been an important source of support for provincial governors and had wildly cheered Jin's enforcement of hardline policies toward the Soviet Union in the period immediately following the Zhongdong railroad incident. Jin knew that the 1931 accord would be a difficult pill for them to swallow, but his need to import weapons to crush the simmering rebellion trumped his need to firm up his political and economic base in the province.

The result was a complex dance, as Jin sought to allow the new trade freedom guaranteed by Soviet traders under the agreement and also pander to the province's merchant community, which was increasingly frustrated with the dramatic increase in Soviet traders in Xinjiang. A 1932 report sent to the provincial government by ten of the most prominent commercial firms in the province complained about the growing prominence of the Soviet Union in areas once sealed off from trade. "Recent investigations have found that Soviet traders are willfully and freely penetrating into local villages to trade; if we do not aggressively forbid this, in the future it will be detrimental for local officials and for the people," they wrote.[55] Unable to inform them of the reason for the increasing prominence of Soviet traders, Jin lamely urged merchants to work collectively, improve their products, and lower prices in order to be able to compete.[56] At the same time, he also begged his Soviet counterparts to operate less aggressively in the province so as not to completely alienate Xinjiang's merchant community.[57]

In November 1931, Jin was given two Soviet military planes in exchange for an equivalent value in wool, camel hair, and marmot pelts, as well as fox and wolf fur. After these initial purchases, provincial officials issued a long list of military equipment that they hoped to purchase, and readied 15,000 poods of processed wool and other products in Ili to exchange for weapons. But Soviet officials seemed hesitant to produce all of the weapons desired and as the time ticked by without a Soviet response, Jin and his officials began to worry. After sending a series of self-righteous and later flattering communiqués to their Soviet counterparts, Jin returned to the negotiation table, hoping to open the flow of weapons sales more completely. Eager for an agreement, provincial officials caved to Soviet demands for increased prices for weapons and happily signed away even larger quantities of furs, pelts, and wool.[58]

Pressed to provide the local products needed to foot the bill for Soviet deliveries, the provincial government issued money from a special fund that was used to purchase local products demanded by the Soviet Union.[59] In

Kucha, where officials took charge of purchasing and shipping 15,000 poods of washed wool bales, local officials were tasked with the difficult task of acquiring wool at below market prices. To track down the wool needed from merchants unwilling to sell at such low prices, they were forced to fan out throughout southern Xinjiang, extending as far as Ruoqiang county in the east and Yarkand in the far south. Provincial officials borrowed 500 civilian mules in order to tackle the substantial logistical task of moving the more than 540,000 pounds of wool to the Ili border crossing.[60]

In September 1932, nearly a year after signing the 1931 agreement, Jin informed the Nanjing government of the trade accord.[61] It was quickly denounced by GMD officials, and any shred of hope that Jin might have held that the government in Nanjing would ride to his aid evaporated overnight. By 1933, unable to quell the ever growing rebellion and facing down a provincial balance sheet that was sinking further and further into the red, Jin fled the province. The situation facing his ultimate successor, an ethnically Han Chinese military man from Manchuria named Sheng Shicai seemed equally bleak. Lacking allies and any foreseeable form of material aid, Sheng turned desperately to the Soviet Union. He was well aware that Xinjiang would be asked to pay for that support with substantial quantities of local products.

Soviet officials were divided on the question of whether to support Sheng's Han Chinese administration of the province or to support what some were suggesting were the forces of Turkic Muslim–based revolution in Xinjiang.[62] While some supported the uprising, others feared that its pan-Turkic and pan-Muslim ideals suggested that it was being supported by regional competitors (most notably Japan or the British Empire) and could threaten the stability of Soviet Central Asia. Equally disconcerting, the uprising appeared to threaten the Soviet Union's hard-fought economic interests in Xinjiang. As one official based in Uzbekistan bluntly pointed out in a report, the uprising "threatens our raw material bases in neighboring countries to the east." Noting that "Xinjiang is one of the most important commodity markets for our industry," the official concluded by saying that the uprising "undermines the long period of relative stability in Xinjiang, and we have interests in maintaining the status quo."[63]

Assessing the chaos sweeping across Xinjiang, in an August 3, 1933, meeting of the Central Political Office of the Soviet Union, Soviet officials stated their new position. First and foremost, they proclaimed that "the slogan and policy of separating Xinjiang from China is not desirable." Further, the group asserted its willingness to support Sheng in exchange for his willingness to first take on various enemies in the province who were opposed to the Soviet Union, including Sheng's most powerful opponent, the ethnically Hui general

Ma Zhongying, and second to "develop and strengthen" trade relations with the Soviets.[64] To encourage Sheng's compliance, they reopened the spigot of Soviet aid shipments into the province. According to archival records kept in the Xinjiang Uyghur Autonomous Region archives, the first eighteen truck convoy, each truck filled to the brim with oil needed to ship troops to the front and keep planes in the air, arrived at the border crossing outside the town of Tacheng on July 11, 1933. Throughout the late summer and fall of 1933, trucks continued to deliver the material and weapons needed to keep Sheng Shicai in power.[65]

In exchange for the support, Xinjiang's resource wealth began to hemorrhage out of the northern border crossings of Tacheng and Ili. The ground shook with the rumblings of horse carts, trucks, and airplanes loaded down with wool, furs, silver ingots, and gold dust all bound for Russian representatives overseeing the transactions. The archival record for 1933 is filled with log books and reports about the arrival of these vehicles packed down with goods. In one case, 20,000 poods of furs were shipped to the Soviet border in payment for oil shipments.[66] A September 21, 1933, letter from a Soviet bank to the provincial government confirms that sixty-six deposits were made that year by the Xinjiang government's representative Kong Qingde.[67]

In January 1934, Sheng sent his Foreign Relations Office head Chen Deli to the Soviet Union asking for an even greater degree of military support to crush the ongoing uprisings in the province. In response, two brigades of Red Army troops entered the province through the two northern towns of Ili and Tacheng. The troops dealt an initial blow to Sheng's opponents in February in a series of battles. Later that spring, Sheng's troops, supported by the Red Army and a squadron of Soviet fighter planes, administered a killing blow to the opposition. While Sheng continued to express his allegiance to the Nanjing government in word, in deed he drifted into the Soviet orbit. In January 1934 he was already making intimations about a new policy toward the Soviet Union and in an April 17 meeting of the Xinjiang Provincial Nationalities Representative Congress, he publically proclaimed the province's new policy of "closeness with the Soviet Union" (qin-Su).

To seal this relationship and prop up the provincial government, in May 1935 the Soviet government offered Sheng a major loan of five million gold rubles at 4 percent interest. According to the terms, the loan was to be repaid not in currency but in commodity exports like wool, cotton, hides, and furs. The loan was the first bulk influx of foreign currency into the province since the abrupt end of interprovincial assistance payments in 1911 and signified a shift in Xinjiang's orientation that would last for the next eight years and resonate for much longer. Seeking to head off any criticism from Nanjing, Sheng assured Chiang Kaishek that the loan "was only of a commercial nature and is in no way political," and optimistically continued, "after this the border region will be wealthy and without poverty."[68] Chiang Kaishek was not buying Sheng's saccharine rhetoric and publicly responded to the events of 1934 with scorn. Chiang was quoted in a newspaper report as saying, "No matter what country it is, not one soldier can be stationed in Xinjiang, not one inch of land can be occupied by foreign powers, and even more, not one government organ can disobey an order from the central government."[69]

Chiang's self-righteously nationalistic proclamations must have been hard for Sheng to stomach. The archival record reveals that before accepting Soviet rubles, on at least two occasions Sheng begged the Nanjing government for financial assistance. In an April 29, 1934, telegram to Nanjing, he requested a loan of two million silver dollars to offset military costs. "I hope to recover land lost [in the uprising] in a short amount of time and reunite Xinjiang. After this is completed the entire amount will be returned."[70] After the Nanjing government ignored his urgent request, Sheng felt he had no choice but to turn to the Soviet Union. As he himself explained, "In a situation in which the central government could not give us any assistance, we firmly accepted the hand of friendship offered by a friendly nation, we did not sell one inch of our territory, and this nation [the Soviet Union] did not impose any conditions on its assistance."[71] Located more than two thousand rugged miles to the west of Nanjing, Sheng Shicai could not have felt that he owed any more to Chiang's government than the simple expression of allegiance that he had already offered.

The fact was that a succession of governments since the late Qing period had barely acknowledged the difficulties faced by provincial leaders grappling with an unrelenting fiscal crisis. Instead, Chinese planners simply drew up ambitious plans backed up with little more than the paper they were written on. True to form, in December 1934 the Executive Yuan of the GMD government, in their cozy offices in Nanjing, put together a new plan to connect Xinjiang to China-proper. The plan, referred to as the "Draft Outline for Construction Planning in Xinjiang," was ambitious in its scope. It called for a highway bisecting the province from east to west, the improvement of Xinjiang's internal road network, and a new railroad line connecting Dihua to Lanzhou, the capital of Gansu province. The plan was big on dreams and short on cash, offering a vague financing plan that called for the "mobilization of the people in the provinces all along the line to work together cooperatively."[72] It did not include a penny's worth of aid from Nanjing to cover the 2.65 million yuan price tag for a fully integrated highway network or the 269 million yuan price tag for constructing a rail line.[73] In stark contrast to the toothless reports from Nanjing, in 1934, the same year that the central government had put out its "Draft Outline," the Xinjiang provincial government, working closely with Soviet technicians and planners, set up a Dihua-Tacheng Long-Distance Automobile Road Planning Office. Unlike agreements with Nanjing, this one was backed with action and cash. The office invited in twenty-six surveyors from the Soviet Union, who undertook a four-month survey of the route, which ended at Xinjiang's western border with the Soviet Union (these plans are addressed in greater detail in the following section).[74]

The willingness of Soviet officials to respond to the desperate requests for aid and support from provincial officials helped steer Xinjiang's allegiance along with its resource wealth to the west. In October 1936, the provincial government requested a new infusion of funds from their Soviet partners. "Now Xinjiang is in an unusually difficult financial position. For example, this year fabric for military uniforms all needs to be bought from the Soviet Union, and other commodities for various organs all need to be bought from the Soviets," reads a provincial government communique. It went on, "For the purpose of putting our finances in order, we plan to ask the Soviet Union to disburse a loan of two million rubles, to be paid over five years and to be repaid in local products."[75] Not four months later, on January 27, 1937 provincial officials and their Soviet counterparts finalized an agreement for a loan of 2.5 million gold rubles to be repaid in local products.

The Nanjing government offered the government of Xinjiang nothing but political machinations and empty promises. The Soviet Union on the other hand offered precious military aid, financial assistance, and ongoing technical help for the foreseeable future. Whether he admitted it publically or not, Chiang Kaishek also understood this calculation. In a private conversation with a Soviet official about the 5 million ruble loan to Xinjiang, Chiang noted that he "had no objection to the loan, provided that it is used for the economic reconstruction of the province."[76] Chiang, busy with a series of military campaigns against the Chinese Communist Party, had little excess revenue to shower on a poor, isolated border province like Xinjiang. For him, as long as provincial officials were willing to continue expressing their allegiance to the Republic and not split off like Manchuria had been by Japan only three years earlier in 1931, he was willing to tolerate the shift. Chiang's choice had a lasting resonance as it ensured that Soviet planners, rather than their Chinese counterparts, were able to influence developmental priorities in Xinjiang. Indeed, the growing volume of local products being exchanged for military goods helped shape the erstwhile province's connections to the Soviet Union in powerful, lasting ways while connections to China-proper withered.

Soviet officials spearheaded the construction of a system that facilitated the large-scale extraction of various Xinjiang commodity goods and transported them to the Soviet Union. The power imbalance in the region suggests that the Soviet role in Xinjiang was "imperial." Indeed, the period from 1934 to 1942 (a period addressed in greater detail in chapter 5) is in many respects a textbook example of what scholars have referred to as "informal empire," as the Soviet Union actively resisted shouldering the additional expense of political annexing Xinjiang, even as it sought to monopolize the region's raw materials. But it is important to note the active role of provincial officials in this wider process—indeed, they were no passive subalterns. Rather, seeking cash along with desperately needed military and industrial hardware, they aggressively bartered Xinjiang's commodities in exchange for Soviet material support.

### Centralizing Control over Resources

The desperate need to guarantee a steady inflow of aid and military hardware prompted Sheng Shicai to centralize control over Xinjiang's local products. At the center of Sheng's efforts was the creation of a centralized institution that could coordinate the acquisition, sale, and transport of local products. Provincial officials established the Bountiful Xinjiang Local Product Company (Yu-Xin Tuchan Gongsi) in August 1934 to facilitate the process of purchasing local products and funneling them into the Soviet Union. Sheng and his underlings exerted direct control over the operation, funding it with an initial outlay of 500,000 provincial yuan and retaining the rights to appoint all company leaders. Considering the relatively high value of Xinjiang's furs, hides, and wool on global markets, Sheng and other officials saw the company as capable of generating substantial revenues for the fragile provincial treasury. After the first loan, however, it began to operate as the primary channel through which Xinjiang's lucrative local products were funneled into the Soviet Union.[77]

While the company relied on private investment as well as public, it acted as an arm of the provincial government, and its financial success was a product of substantial government support. Pointing to the heavy loans hanging over their heads, company managers pushed the government to award them several lucrative monopolies. "How can we protect our credit without having anything to repay [the loans]?" Burhan Shahidi, the company's first manager, asked in a request to the provincial government to grant the company monopolies on furs, pelts, and lamb intestines (for sausage casings).[78] Swayed by the argument, provincial officials issued several monopolies on the most highly valued local products, including smooth fetal lamb skins, marmot and colt pelts, lamb intestines, and silk. The strength of their economic position and their ability to draw upon the coercive power of the provincial government allowed it significant price advantages that extended even beyond those goods that it held monopolies on. In the town of Hami in eastern Xinjiang, the company was paying only one-quarter of the market price for sheep skins (five jiao versus two yuan). The low prices being paid for sheep skins and other such products ensured substantial profits.[79]

Their state-derived commercial advantages extended beyond monopolies and low prices, as officials even went so far as to occasionally withdraw money directly from local tax revenues. The company also enjoyed the right to freely take money from any branch of the provincial bank in order to quickly raise capital for bulk purchases. The borrowing was so rampant and unregulated that in 1940 officials felt the need to issue regulations limiting free withdrawals by managers to only up to one million Chinese yuan. In addition to also enjoying virtual exemption from all taxes, the company was the beneficiary of various unexpected cash infusions, as provincial officials funneled the assets acquired in a series of extractive taxes and asset seizure campaigns conducted by Sheng's government in the late 1930s and early 1940s directly into the company coffers.[80]

To coordinate the purchase and transport of the pelts, furs, cotton, and medicinal products that served as the foundation of loan repayment, the company set up branch offices in Altay, Ili, and Tacheng in northern Xinjiang and Yanqi, Aksu, and Kashgar in the south; officials also set up two additional sub-branch offices at Wusu and Kucha. From these branches, officials drew upon the supply networks of local merchants to acquire products. Managers signed agreements with merchants that specified the time frame and amounts of money that would be advanced, and capped the amounts of profit. To highlight one example, a merchant named An Fuchen signed an agreement in August 1936 in which the company agreed to pay him a sum of thirty million provincial taels (half in cash and half in trade) quarterly over a year in exchange for the procurement and transport of lamb intestines directly to the Soviet-run Soviet-Xinjiang Trading Company (Sovsintorg). The Soviet company would determine the market price paid for the goods.[81] In other cases, officials in local offices themselves oversaw the purchase and delivery of goods to Soviet border crossings.

From 1934 into the early 1940s, the Bountiful Xinjiang Company facilitated the mass outflow of the province's lucrative products. The majority of these products (with the sole exception of cotton and silk) were goods produced in pastoral regions of the province. Indeed, the high value of hides, furs, animal horn, and wool ensured that the company's presence was stronger in the north, a region that specialized in the production of these goods (for a full

TABLE 4.2. Bountiful Xinjiang local product shop purchases in 1940

| | |
|---|---|
| Goat skins | 356,000 pelts |
| Sheep pelts | 1.5 million pelts |
| Ox hides | 130,000 pelts |
| Horse pelts | 39,000 pelts |
| Camel pelts | 3,000 pelts |
| Mule pelts | 4,000 pelts |
| Horse tails | 26,500 kilograms |
| Colt hides | 19,000 pelts |
| Lamb pelts | 298,000 pelts |
| Goat-kid pelts | 69,000 pelts |
| Fetal lamb skins | 41,000 skins |
| Wool | 5 million kilos |
| Camel hair | 137,000 kilos |
| Cashmere | 64,000 kilos |
| Cotton | 3.87 million kilos |
| Silk | 117,000 kilos |
| Marmot pelts | 164,000 pelts |
| Fox furs | 17,000 pelts |

Source: Xinjiang Weiwu'er zizhiqu difang zhi bianzuan weiyuanhui, ed. *Xinjiang tongzhi: shangye* (vol. 61) (Urumqi: Xinjiang Renmin Chubanshe, 1999), 81.

list of the company's purchases in 1940, see table 4.2). Indeed, in the initial capital outlays for the company (excluding the capital distributed to the main office in Dihua), over half was allocated toward Tacheng, Altay, and Ili, those sparsely populated regions of northern Xinjiang that specialized in nomadic products.[82]

As much as capital investments, these institutions served as important layers being laid over northern Xinjiang. The institutionalization of commodity exchanges and creation of vertically integrated networks of exchange bound to the provincial capital helped strengthen the control of the provincial government over the pastoral products produced in northern Xinjiang. The efforts to institutionalize greater state control over these products and their distribution paralleled a broader campaign in the second half of the 1930s to disarm, pacify, and settle nomadic groups, particularly those in the far north.[83] The networks of exchange formed through the Bountiful Xinjiang Company and its agents served to bind pastoral regions and their inhabitants across much of northern Xinjiang into a more clearly integrated raw material hinterland connected to regional and international markets in the Soviet Union.

In order to facilitate the outflow of goods, provincial leaders, working with their Soviet counterparts, established a network of processing facilities that would create a seamless link from raw material production to export. In the early 1930s, Soviet technicians helped construct four factories to process the raw silk, leather, cotton, and textiles produced in Xinjiang. The initial startup costs for these factories were to be paid by Soviet accounts and repaid by provincial officials in the form of local products. Of the four, Soviet capital constituted 92 percent of the total capitalization for the silk factory, 79 percent for the leather tanning factory, 94 percent for the textile factory, and 100 percent for the cotton refinery.[84] The operations helped ensure a unified, vertically integrated system of production and processing that transformed local products into commodities ready for export into global markets.

Eager to strengthen their access to sites of production in northern Xinjiang and facilitate trade, Soviet policy reports on Xinjiang included lengthy addenda outlining plans to develop the transportation infrastructure connecting the province to Soviet territory. A network of highways stretching across Soviet Central Asia were extended to the border with Xinjiang in the mid-1930s. A plan was unveiled in December 1934 to connect rail hubs on the Turk-Sib line to four border crossing points: Kashgar in southern Xinjiang and Altay, Ili, and Tacheng in the north using military labor. The plan cost four million rubles and was to be completed by the end of 1935.[85] Further underscoring the transport connections, the Soviet Union oversaw the strengthening of riverine shipping, which allowed for the bulk import of goods into Xinjiang. In particular, they focused on the Irtysh and Ili Rivers, which served as a critical trade conduit for the northern Xinjiang towns of Ili and Altay.[86]

The main problem, however, was the development of Xinjiang's internal transport network. As one Soviet report from 1934 noted, "There is no transport in Xinjiang; it has been destroyed as a result of the war and there is a need to develop automobile transport on as wide a scale as possible and as quickly as possible."[87] Soviet officials (for a price to be repaid in commodities) dispatched technicians to aid in surveying and building paved roads capable of accommodating large, fully laden trucks. Working in close collaboration with Soviet experts and relying on Soviet loans, the provincial government headed up the construction of a new, modern highway network. In particular, they called for new roads connecting Dihua to Ili and also to Kashgar and Wusu (which was to continue on to Tacheng in the north). A paved automobile

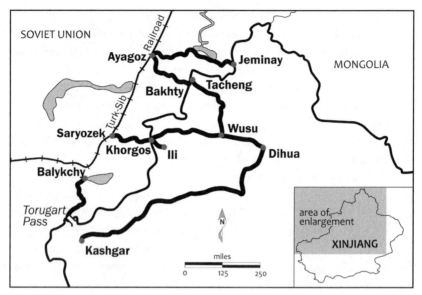

SOVIET UNION

Railroad

Ayagoz

Jeminay

MONGOLIA

Bakhty

Tacheng

Turk-Sib

Saryozek

Wusu

Khorgos

Ili

Dihua

Balykchy

Torugart
Pass

N

area of
enlargement

XINJIANG

Kashgar

miles

0          125        250

MAP 4.3 Soviet transport development plans for Xinjiang. Map by Debbie Newell.

road stretching from Dihua to Khorgos, the border crossing outside of Ili, was a major priority for provincial and Soviet planners, and they called for a joint Soviet-Xinjiang road building team (the surveying and technical work for which would be headed up by Soviet technicians) to complete the road by January 1936.[88] To pay for the ambitious plans, Soviet officials sought promises in the initial agreement laying out the five million ruble loan to Sheng that more than half of the total amount—2.8 million—be used to develop internal transportation infrastructure.[89]

The construction of transportation infrastructure was a central component of Sheng's first Three Year Plan for Xinjiang. The plan, which was sketched out with a Soviet-style Five Year Plan model in mind and undertaken with a substantial amount of Soviet technical assistance, was set to begin in June 1937 and end in June 1940. It laid the framework for a road system connecting the provincial capital to all corners of the province with a total price tag of 160 million provincial taels. The price tag on road construction grew considerably, however, and the sum for bridge construction alone amounted to 3 billion provincial taels under the plan.[90] The high cost of labor and construction meant that Sheng came to rely on the efforts of local officials to underwrite the costs of construction and also to draw on civilian corvée labor. The burden frequently fell on local merchants who were asked to contribute funds, food, and equipment and also on the peasants drafted into labor teams.[91]

The development of these institutional and infrastructural networks in the early 1930s combined to facilitate greater provincial government control over the production, processing, and distribution of the region's lucrative local products. The need for military and industrial goods ensured that Xinjiang's local products flowed in a steady stream toward Soviet light industrial enterprises in the Soviet East and beyond throughout the 1930s and early 1940s. The growing commitment to investing in a regional transport network and the development of new institutions designed to exert greater control over local production in Xinjiang over the course of the first three decades of the twentieth century, helped create networks of producers, transporters, and buyers that bound pastoral northern Xinjiang and its products to global markets. These efforts at both institutional and infrastructural development reinforced earlier layers and connected northern Xinjiang firmly to the provincial capital of Dihua and also, perhaps more importantly, to Soviet transport hubs and markets.

*

The new institutions and the miles and miles of paved bitumen helped physically transform Xinjiang in enduring ways. They not only facilitated the outflow of larger and larger volumes of local products, but also served to consolidate state interest and oversight over resource production in the northern stretches of the province. These interests, strengthened over the course of the 1930s, led to new surveys, maps, and state planning that sought to more clearly quantify the region's most lucrative products and sites of production. This infrastructure and these institutions served to consolidate and strengthen the fragmentary layers laid over the resource production sites of northern Xinjiang in the early twentieth century and knit them together into one regional network bound to the Soviet Union. In the end, the roads, surveys, and new institutions that formed these new layers served as a gleaming beacon beckoning investors, surveyors, and state planners who were eager to uncover and cheaply exploit Xinjiang's resource wealth. Equally importantly, the network also laid out a framework for much more aggressive extraction beginning in the late 1930s, as the roads facilitated the easy import of heavy machinery and the cheaper transport of finished goods.

The trade of local products for industrial goods and military hardware continued to flourish into the early 1940s, and only fell with the souring of Sino-Soviet relations and the closing of cross-border trade in the mid-1940s.[92]

But Soviet interest in Xinjiang's natural resource wealth had already begun to shift by the mid-1930s from the raw materials needed to fuel light industry to those needed to fuel heavy industry. The Soviet Union's prewar military buildup throughout the period and the consequent desire to uncover new sources of critical raw materials pushed Soviet state planners to focus their efforts on facilitating the outflow of various mineral resources present in northern Xinjiang. Hoping to rapidly and inexpensively profit from this demand, provincial officials, working in collaboration with their Soviet patrons, relied upon the earlier layers of infrastructure and institutional networks to facilitate production and transport.

# PART 2

# Industrial Minerals and the Transformation of Xinjiang

# Industrial Raw Materials and
# the Construction of Informal Empire

In an April 1938 letter to his older brother Mao Zedong, Xinjiang's newly appointed provincial treasurer, Mao Zemin, described an economy that had been upended in the years since Sheng Shicai's consolidation of power in 1934. Noting Sheng's reliance on the printing press and his willingness to take on massive Soviet loans, Mao Zemin, who served until 1942, groaned, "We still do not even know how many other outrages to both heaven and earth he has committed."[1] The conflict that wracked the province in the years from 1931 to early 1934 destroyed the agricultural tax base of the province, and Sheng's decision to take on the large loans served to channel Xinjiang's rich local products away from taxable trade and toward the repayment of the province's debts. As the previous two chapters have shown, for provincial officials facing down fiscal crisis, the problem was not a lack of taxable products and lucrative natural resources. Rather, the issue was the lack of capital, technical assistance, and access to international markets that they needed to profit off of these products.

To remedy this, provincial officials sought an outside patron who would be willing to invest in Xinjiang. For their part, planners in the Republic of China had proven themselves unwilling to spend any money or political capital on the province since the 1911 revolution and the abrupt ending of the interprovincial assistance payments that had kept Xinjiang fiscally afloat since the conquest of the region in 1759 (see chapter 2). In stark contrast, Soviet officials had been willing to offer support to desperate provincial officials since the time of Sheng's predecessor Jin Shuren, and it was Soviet military and financial support that allowed Sheng himself to consolidate his hold over the province in 1934 (see chapter 4). This willingness prompted Sheng to unveil his "closeness with the Soviet Union" policy in 1934 as well as a new effort to aggressively increase the exchange of Xinjiang's local products and natural resources for Soviet loans, equipment, and technical assistance.

At first, Soviet planners continued to focus their efforts on acquiring the raw materials needed to fuel their light industry sector (see chapter 4). This priority was reflected in the terms of the 1934 loan, which explicitly stated that repayments were to be made in kind with pelts, gold, silk products, cotton, hides, livestock, and sausage casings. In addition to these products, however, Soviet officials were also interested in Xinjiang's mineral and oil wealth. Tin ore, for example, was also included on the list of goods to be used for repayment. But so little tin was produced in the province that it was not even included in the official pricing list.[2] Later, in a 1938 conversation in Moscow, Stalin asked Sheng about Xinjiang's tin resources. Sheng replied simply that there was tin in Xinjiang. But when pressed about mineral production more generally he replied that he "does not have a big plan" to promote extraction.[3]

When it came to increasing the production of tin and other resources critical for heavy industry, Soviet planners were happy to provide Sheng with a plan, and to this end, in the latter half of the 1930s, they dispatched large numbers of geological teams to Xinjiang. The efforts of these teams were shaped by the layers laid in the province in the early twentieth century, as the geological reports, planning priority lists, and transport infrastructure directed these expeditions to explore the areas around proven ore and petroleum fields close to important Soviet border crossings and transport networks in northern Xinjiang. Using sites identified by earlier expeditions as waypoints, they uncovered a series of important and potentially lucrative new fields in a few select areas. These discoveries and the subsequent efforts to expand production at these sites helped fundamentally transform Xinjiang in the eyes of Soviet state planners, provincial officials, and leaders in the Chinese Republic alike into a region with vast potential as a producer of raw materials essential for heavy industry.

A series of new geopolitical threats to the Soviet Union first from Japan and later from Germany in the late 1930s elevated the importance of Xinjiang, as Soviet planners sought access to essential raw materials located far away from German and Japanese armies. The result was an even greater influx of geological teams into the erstwhile Chinese province in the early 1940s, larger capital investments in extraction and processing operations, and new efforts to develop transportation infrastructure binding the region more clearly to Soviet industries in the east. In this case, war or at least the threat of war drove a broad-based effort to exert greater control over the region and its resource wealth as well as an increase in capital investments in extraction, processing, and transport.

At the same time that Soviet geologists, technicians, and planners were transforming Xinjiang, something similar was happening in Manchuria. In 1931 the Japanese Kwantung Army engineered the so-called Mukden incident, which led to the establishment of the puppet state of Manchukuo on formerly sovereign Chinese territory. The government of Manchukuo depended on Japan for economic investment, security, and foreign policy advice and in exchange offered Japanese geologists and planners nearly unfettered access to the region's resource wealth. As a result, in the years after 1931, Japanese surveying teams fanned out deep into the region. Their efforts and the subsequent investment from private companies and the Japanese government helped uncover a series of important ore fields that would be prioritized for production not only by Japan's imperial government, but also after 1945 by the Republic of China, and after 1949 the People's Republic.[4] The parallels between Manchuria and Xinjiang point to the existence of a larger trend, in which foreign powers seeking the raw materials needed to fuel industrialization campaigns and large-scale military buildups shaped long-term patterns of economic development and institutionalization in Chinese border regions.

In Xinjiang, the sizable Soviet investments in extractive operations and the initial productivity of these sites served to transform the impressions of the region more generally in the minds of Soviet, Chinese, and provincial officials alike. This chapter begins the final part of the book, and highlights a fundamental shift in Xinjiang in the 1930s and 1940s. The efforts of Soviet geologists, planners, and technicians helped transform this Chinese province once and for all, from a region formerly dismissed as wasteland that happened to sit atop a few resources capable of generating revenue for the state, into one notable for its vast quantities of raw materials essential for heavy industry and the production of military hardware. Precious metals and commodity goods continued to be exploited, but it was the pursuit of beryllium and tantalum, as well as petroleum and other resources, that helped define the province's role in the Soviet hinterland, and later its place within the Chinese nation-state. The sizable Soviet investments in surveys, extraction and processing facilities, and transportation infrastructure in pursuit of these resources in the late 1930s and early 1940s served to reinforce the layers laid in the first half of the twentieth century and lock in long-term patterns of economic development at a handful of sites in the northern stretches of the province.

## Putting Xinjiang's Finances in Order

Mao Zemin's top priority after being appointed provincial treasurer was to correct the damage that financial malfeasance, war, and unrest had wrought in Xinjiang in the early 1930s. But the need to pay back the large Soviet loans and the high cost of administration and defense in the province all conspired against Mao's efforts to put the province's account books into the black.[5] By 1933, Xinjiang was already running an annual deficit of 3.06 million provincial taels, a number that quickly grew to 4.26 million the next year.[6] The struggle throughout the mid-1930s for provincial officials was to find a way to make their fiscal ends meet and place the province on a sounder economic footing.

At least at first, provincial officials adopted a series of ad hoc economic strategies to relieve the fiscal pressure on the provincial treasury. In addition to reducing the size of the provincial military, provincial officials also sought to reduce administrative expenses through a vicious campaign against corrupt officials, as well as an aggressive effort to promote government austerity that, among other things, called on government offices to conserve paper and promote the drinking of hot water instead of tea.[7] The larger fiscal strategy in the years immediately following Sheng's consolidation of power, however, relied on the printing press. According to archival sources, in 1935, Xinjiang's treasury was often printing eighteen million provincial taels worth of fifty-tael notes per day. The demand for the fifty-tael bill was said to be so high that sheets of bills were frequently ripped off the printing presses before the ink was dry and immediately put into circulation.[8] Not surprisingly, the flow of bills into the provincial economy caused the value of the provincial tael to drop precipitously. In order to match the growing inflation, bills of higher and higher denominations were printed. While officials had second thoughts about the decision to issue a 10,000-tael note in late 1934, the growing inflationary pressures meant that 3,000- and 4,000-tael notes were a common denomination throughout 1935.[9]

The only long-term solution, as far as provincial officials were concerned, was to uncover new sources of revenue that were capable of floating the provincial government. The problem, however, was that substantial amounts of the province's monthly tax receipts were taken not in currency, but in kind, in the form of grain or livestock. For provincial administrators hoping to balance the province's books, tax revenues in sheep or winter wheat were simply not acceptable. As Mao Zemin pointed out in the letter to Mao Zedong, the population of forty thousand living in the Communist wartime base area of Yan'an in arid northern Shaanxi province were producing more in tax revenue than the four million people of Xinjiang province.[10] To boost revenues, Sheng unveiled a new land reclamation plan that focused on the resettlement of impoverished Han and Hui refugees from Gansu and eastern Xinjiang on open steppe land in the north. Provincial officials also undertook a series of ambitious fiscal strategies intended to channel what Mao Zemin called "floating capital," which existed in the strongboxes of the province's wealthy merchants, the storage chests of officials, and the pockets of local peasants and herders, into the provincial treasury. To get their hands on this capital, officials established the Xinjiang Commercial Bank in 1939, sold government-issued "construction bonds" in denominations of fifty, twenty-five, ten, five, and one yuan, seized property from an expanding network of wealthy citizens accused of various crimes, and encouraged contributions to China and the Soviet Union's war effort that would then be kept in the provincial capital of Dihua.[11]

Like his predecessors, Sheng also focused a substantial amount of energy on tapping Xinjiang's natural resource wealth in order to firm up the province's fiscal base. The GMD agent Wu Aichen, who was dispatched to the province in 1934, argued that at the core of any developmental plan in Xinjiang must be the development of its natural resources, which he listed as "herds, reclaimed land, gold, and oil."[12] Gold mining as a revenue-raising strategy had already been attempted in the late Qing period, and the failure of various operations continued to leave a bad taste in the mouths of provincial officials (see chapter 3). As the compiler of the late Qing *Xinjiang Illustrated Gazetteer* noted in 1909, "After many setbacks, the spirit of those who talk about profiting from mining has been deflated." The author concludes his discussion on mining in Xinjiang by declaring, "Their [provincial officials'] minds are so burdened that they clamp their mouth closed, knot their tongue, and do not dare lightly suggest trying again."[13] But the situation seemed different in the early 1930s. Indeed, the rapidly increasing price of gold, which was prominently listed on the front page of the *Xinjiang Daily* newspaper; the seemingly imminent prospects of a massive gold strike in the Altay Mountains, which had been surveyed by Russian geologists and which no provincial official ever failed to point out meant "gold mountain" in Mongol; and the potential capital infusion from the Soviet Union all seemed to suggest that gold mining might be the answer to the province's fiscal woes.

Noting the ineffectiveness of the strategy of money printing in doing anything more than simply "maintaining the status quo by alleviating the symptoms of the [financial] illness," the Mining and Agriculture Office in Dihua called for a focus on gold mining to solve Xinjiang's problems. "Emphasizing gold mining production is an effective strategy," asserted the March 1935 report, which called for opening the Altay Mountains to gold mining to generate revenue.[14] The development of the region's goldfields was a prominent component of Sheng Shicai's first Three Year Plan, which authorized a detailed survey of the Altay and the establishment of a large-scale government mining operation that was equipped with the newest gold mining technology, and staffed by teams of miners who were fed, clothed, and equipped by provincial government agencies. The plan called for a gradual ramping up of operations, growing from 1,000 workers the first year, to 2,500 by the end of the second, to 5,000 by 1938.[15]

The operation in the Altay Mountains was undertaken with a 6 million-tael loan from the Soviet Union, an amount substantial enough that the operation ran a heavy surplus of at least 300,000 taels for each of the next six months (the only period for which records are available).[16] In addition to a cash infusion, the Soviet Union also provided (for a fee of course) twenty mining specialists who came equipped with five trucks that would also be sold to the mine.[17] Additional supplies for the operations arrived at the mine by transport along the Irtysh River, which connected the isolated mountain range to the Soviet border. In one July 1935 shipment to the goldfields, the Soviets shipped three thousand *shi* (around 480,000 pounds) of wheat, four large trucks, and electrical poles and lines. A separate shipment of forty lamps, telephones, and a number of generators also purchased with a loan from the Soviet Union was shipped in by truck from Dihua.[18]

When the enterprise came on line in 1935, the operation was decidedly small-scale. The mine relied on the labor of the around two hundred mostly ethnic Hui, but also Han and Mongol, workers who had been working the veins since the failure of an operation sponsored by Sheng's predecessor Jin Shuren in 1931. The workers, most of whom lived with their dependents in caves, earthen homes, or lean-tos dug into the sides of cliffs in the area, undertook the arduous task of digging gold-laden sand out of small streams in the area, washing it in wooden sloughs, and picking out the gold flakes. In order to fill out the ranks of these workers, Sheng turned to refugees displaced by the four years of unrest in the province and who seemed more than willing to grab the grain, clothing, and equipment provided by the government as well as the two- to three-tael monthly salary.[19] Despite the investment and attention, the operation remained small and the amounts of gold produced were too insignificant to resolve the province's perennial financial woes. During a 1938 conversation in Moscow between Soviet General Secretary Josef Stalin, Soviet Foreign Minister Vyacheslav Molotov, and Governor Sheng, when Sheng was asked about gold mining in the province, he responded with a sigh that operations were small-scale and located in "several minority areas."[20]

In the short term, Mao Zemin's wider economic and currency policies appeared to have had their intended effect. In a report in 1939, Mao bragged that the price of gold in local currency, a good indicator of fiscal stability, was nearly half the price of the year before and that monthly gold prices had remained relatively stable since the provincial government undertook a series of currency reforms. But finance officials were not able to fundamentally alter the long-term fiscal dynamic that had dominated Xinjiang since the end of interprovincial assistance payments to the province thirty years earlier. The lack of a steady inflow of convertible currency or specie continued to undermine Xinjiang's markets, and while Soviet rubles had once acted to prop up the provincial tael's downward spiral, the last Soviet loan had been issued a long two years earlier in 1937. While gold and other commodity prices stayed relatively stable throughout 1939, they once again began increasing in 1940. Provincial sources indicate that the price for rice climbed steadily, growing by more than four times from 1940 to 1941.[21]

To help counter the troubling shift, Mao and Sheng called for a greater focus on natural resource exploitation and mining in particular. Drawing on the enthusiasm for gold mining, the Second Three Year Plan called for a 560,613 yuan investment in gold mining in the Altay, which, according to Soviet geologists, contained 48 million ounces of untapped gold ore.[22] A Kazakh uprising in 1940 undercut operations in the region, but the wealth of the region's gold reserves and its potential for floating Xinjiang's economy prompted a return to the region shortly thereafter in 1942, as Soviet mining specialists alongside three thousand Chinese workers, who were permitted to keep 30 percent of the ore that they mined, once again set up shop in the Altay. These operations yielded few gold strikes, and the operations devolved into small-scale decentralized prospecting by that first summer.[23]

Mao and Sheng's plans for expanding mining operations, however, were not limited to gold mining. In the mid to late 1930s, the global demand for a number of minerals critical for armament production, including beryllium, molybdenum, tungsten, tantalum, and tin grew substantially, as war appeared to loom low on the horizon. By chance, various surveys undertaken primarily by Russian geologists had identified several sites in northern Xinjiang that were rich in these nonferrous metals. As Soviet demands for these minerals increased and as the price of these ores began to climb on global markets, provincial officials began working closely with Soviet planners to sketch out new strategies to develop these ores as well as a larger system capable of generating a steady stream of revenue-producing resources.

## Pinpointing Critical Industrial Resources

The emerging tensions with Japan and Germany in the mid to late 1930s and the Soviet Union's subsequent efforts to aggressively boost the production of armaments prompted planners to prioritize heavy industry over light. Under the Soviet Union's First Five Year Plan, which was adopted in 1929 at the Sixteenth Party Congress, heavy industry production targets were aggressively scaled upward, with targets for pig iron, for example, being increased from ten million tons annually to between fifteen and seventeen million.[24] The problem that quickly became apparent to many Soviet planners, however, was the desperate need to uncover new sources of raw materials. As Stephen Kotkin notes in his work on the massive steel plant constructed at Magnitogorsk deep in the Ural Mountains in the 1930s, "one of the most surprising phenomena of the emerging planned economy was the rise of an unlimited demand for raw materials and inputs."[25] To secure access to a steady stream of these raw materials, Soviet geologists turned to Xinjiang and, in order to uncover these resources quickly, they relied heavily on the surveys, resource maps, and planning reports compiled by their predecessors stretching back to the late nineteenth century.

The sharp declines in the Soviet production targets for light industry resulted in lower demand for the raw materials produced in Xinjiang that had long served as the cornerstone for cross-border trade. The decline in demand for wool, cotton, and furs was offset, however, by growing demands for other raw materials, most notably nonferrous metals like tin, tungsten, and beryllium, the latter two being relatively rare metals essential for the production of high-tech armaments. Traces of these ores had been discovered by earlier Soviet geological expeditions in northern Xinjiang. While raw materials demanded by light industry continued to flow into the Soviet Union, the emphasis shifted in the mid-1930s, as Soviet economic planners sought larger and larger amounts of the raw materials needed to fuel heavy industry.

Provincial officials asked their Soviet counterparts for technical help in developing Xinjiang's nonferrous ore wealth in 1933. Despite their shared interest in gaining access to these resources, the political instability in the province undercut surveying and extraction efforts. Indeed, various competitors for power continued to operate in both northern and southern Xinjiang into 1934, resisting Sheng's efforts to consolidate his control over the province. As a result, Soviet planners were forced to get creative in their quest to identify Xinjiang's most promising nonferrous metal ore production sites. In addition to blowing the dust off of old geological and planning reports, they also mobilized geological teams. In 1933, noting the ongoing political unrest in Xinjiang, a deputy in the People's Commissariat for Foreign Affairs recommended that the Geological Administration start "immediately investigating the territory of the USSR that borders Xinjiang so that the work can be broadened into the territory of Xinjiang as soon as the situation is more favorable." The surveys explored a region of the border that extended from Zaysan, just opposite of the border crossing in Altay in the far north, south to the Khan Tengri peak northwest of the Xinjiang town of Aksu (map 5.1).[26] These op-

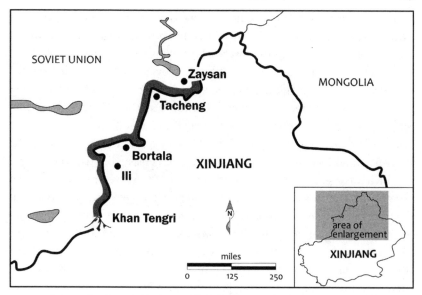

MAP 5.1 Soviet exploration priorities in 1933. Highlighted areas indicate regions prioritized for surveying. Map by Debbie Newell.

erations sought to identify larger geological substructures that might extend across the border. Soviet planners hoped that by identifying these substructures in Soviet territory, they could then target regions in Xinjiang for exploration when the political situation stabilized. The geological expeditions undertaken in 1933 along the border uncovered evidence of several promising ore fields. Officials specifically pointed to the discovery of molybdenum and beryllium in the Zungharian Alatau, just opposite Xinjiang's Bortala prefecture. The site was around one hundred miles north of the Ili River and conveniently hugged the Soviet border.

Not long after the defeat of Sheng's opponents with the help of the Soviet Red Army in early 1934 and his subsequent consolidation of control over northern Xinjiang (he would not be able to extend his control over the south until 1937), provincial officials immediately reached out to the Soviet Union for help in pinpointing resource sites prioritized for exploitation by Soviet surveying teams. "For the purpose of broadening and strengthening trade relations between the two states and also for the purpose of developing the industry of the region, the Xinjiang government decided in 1934 to begin operations," reads one Soviet report.[27] Eager to help facilitate the delivery of essential minerals, the Soviet-run Soviet-Xinjiang Trade Company agreed to provide engineers and technicians specializing in exploration and prospecting as well as to deliver technical equipment and machinery for prospect mining, extraction, and processing. For their part, the provincial government would provide the land, as well as the cost of labor, equipment, and basic tools.[28]

A March 22, 1935, decree issued by the Soviet Politburo called for the organization of a geological expedition to Xinjiang "at Soviet expense" that was to focus on minerals in general, but tin in particular. The expedition, officially named the Xinjiang Special Geological Expedition (Sin'tszyanskaya Geologicheskaya Ekspeditsiya Osobogo Naznacheniya) was organized by the People's Commissariat for Heavy Industry and consisted of ten teams, eight of which were geological prospecting groups. The surveying teams, which began work that summer, relied heavily on previous geological reports, what the team referred to as "Chinese sources," and local agents to direct their expeditions. Their reports pinpointed one specific ore field in the Borohoro Mountain range north of Ili, a range that extended to the Zungharian Alatau (the region prioritized for surveying in 1933) and the Soviet border, where surveyors discovered ores containing more than 20 percent tin. For surveyors, in addition to its ore richness, one of the major advantages of the region was its relative proximity to the Soviet border and Soviet transport network. "Economically, this region is of great importance because it is situated directly next to our border," wrote the leader of the Xinjiang Special Survey in a December 1935 report that called for additional surveying in the region. Furthermore, he noted, the navigable Ili River and the Dzharkent-Khorgos-Alma-Ata road were both nearby.[29]

Despite its official focus on tin, the Special Geological Survey also prioritized oil surveying. As early as 1933, researchers in the Soviet Union's newly formed Oil Exploration Institute were combing through old surveys of Xinjiang, most notably Obruchev's early twentieth-century surveys, seeking confirmation of its oil wealth. Officials came away from their inquiry optimistic about the region's petroleum reserves. Equally importantly, they also praised northern Xinjiang's favorable topography and its proximity to the Soviet border and the Turk-Sib rail line in their reports calling for more aggressive investigations in the region.[30] The Special Geological Survey sent surveying teams to the oil-rich region of Korkala Wusu (known to Russian geologists by its Uyghur name "Shiho") and Dushanzi in particular, which had been first identified by Russian geologists in the late Qing period. One member of an early Xinjiang provincial expeditionary team recalled that in the summer of 1935 a Soviet team led by a geologist named Saidov arrived at one oilfield not far from Dushanzi.[31] The Soviet team, which surveyed various sites between Wusu and the provincial capital, found twenty sites with "oil lakes and springs," many of which they stated had a purity that exceeded that of oil production in important Soviet sites in the Caucasus, most notably at Grozny and Baku.[32]

Considering the relative distance from the Soviet border crossing and the Turk-Sib rail line, the Special Expedition suggested that these fields in particular should be developed at the provincial government's expense in order to feed Xinjiang's domestic oil market. In addition to the stated intention of developing a new generation of petroleum engineers and drilling technicians in Xinjiang, opening oilfields to meet domestic demand would also reduce the amount of oil being imported into the province from petroleum processing facilities in the Soviet Union. That does not mean, however, that the Special Expedition was uninterested in uncovering oil sites that could be exploited to meet Soviet needs. Indeed, it also called for aggressive petroleum exploration in more accessible areas along the border in order to discover new fields located closer to the Soviet Union and thereby better positioned to supply petroleum needed by Soviet industries. Confident that Xinjiang's oilfields extended to much of the northern border region, the expedition called for "detailed geological surveys and prospecting next to the Soviet border in the region of Chuguchak [Tacheng] and Gulja [Ili] districts," sites that could more easily produce petroleum for Soviet markets.[33]

For Soviet planners, the 1935 surveys helped in the process of creating a list of exploitation priorities in Xinjiang. The plans for 1936 centered around the development of the tungsten and tin fields north of Ili; oil wells in Korkala Wusu; the exploration of various nonferrous ore fields in the Altay; surveys intended to confirm reports of piezoelectric quartz crystals, which were used in sonar and other devices, in the southern slopes of the Tianshan; and plans to conduct general geological surveys in Gucheng, Hami, Barkol, and Turfan, all in underexplored eastern Xinjiang (map 5.2).[34] In general, these priorities reflected a larger focus on northern Xinjiang. Despite interest in resources located in regions south of the Tianshan Mountain range, the fact was that these sites were more inconvenient from the perspective of Soviet officials.[35] On the one hand, the south remained outside of Sheng's political orbit in 1934, as the short-lived first East Turkestan Republic and later Ma Zhongying's oversight of the region held out against Sheng's consolidation efforts until 1937. But on the other hand, southern Xinjiang was simply located farther from extant transport networks and remained comparatively unexplored. As a result, Soviet officials chose to concentrate their efforts in northern Xinjiang in resource sites located close to their border. Between 1934 and 1942, as Soviet demand for industrial minerals and for petroleum boomed, twenty separate Soviet geological surveying expeditions operated in Xinjiang. Of these, sixteen were focused specifically on uncovering fields in regions north

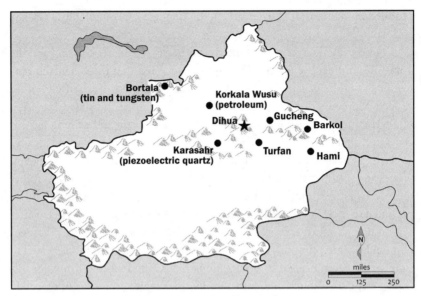

MAP 5.2 Soviet exploration priorities in 1936. Map by Debbie Newell.

of the Tianshan Mountain range.[36] These efforts helped fill in geological maps of northern Xinjiang and, by reinforcing the layers laid in the early twentieth century, helped shine a spotlight on the region for future geologists and economic planners to follow.

As far as the development of the tin and tungsten ores north of Ili in Bortala were concerned, Soviet planners in the Xinjiang Special Expedition targeted 1937 as the year to complete preparations for production. In order to facilitate the incorporation of these critical minerals into Soviet industrial planning as well as exert greater control over the operation, planners decided to build the concentrating plant, electric power station, and various workshops in Soviet territory. Only the mine itself would be situated on the Xinjiang side of the border. The total cost for the factory was to be 10 million rubles with an additional US $200,000 to prepare the ore field for large-scale exploitation. Soviet planners called for the surveying and construction of a network of roads that would bind the plant, located in the Soviet border town of Khorgos, to the Dzharkent highway, which in turn connected to the Turk-Sib rail line at Saryozek. Aiding the transport networks in extracting ore, the People's Commissariat for Foreign Trade was called upon to sign an agreement with Sheng in which "the Xinjiang government would sell ore exclusively to the Soviet Union for the purpose of covering debts under the loan."[37] Additionally, with an eye toward future expansion, money was also allocated to aggressively survey nearby ore fields, which previous expeditions had identified as being potentially resource rich.

Like tin and tungsten processing, the oil production facility in the region around Dushanzi was scheduled to be completed by 1937. By then, Soviet technicians would make decisions about the placement of the site, construct the factory, and build a pipeline network. In addition to the factory and pipeline, the plans also called for the construction of electric power stations, workshops, warehouses, a ten-kilometer highway spur connecting the site to the province's main east-west trunk road, and housing, which included three houses for Soviet technicians, six dormitories for local workers, and two dormitories for workers with families. The Xinjiang side was responsible for providing construction materials, and the Soviets for most of the technical equipment. By May 1939, a decision was made to focus efforts on Dushanzi over other potentially productive oil sites in the area around Wusu. That spring, 1.2 million tons of red brick, 70 tons of lime, 500 cubic meters of wood, 750 cubic meters of sand, and 1,000 cubic meters of gravel had already been delivered to Dushanzi. At the rail hub of Saryozek, 2,500 tons of technical equipment and supplies had been delivered by Soviet agencies and were simply waiting to be delivered to the oilfield by truck.[38]

The problem, however, was that Dushanzi was not immediately productive. Despite high hopes, none of the fifteen wells drilled during the late 1930s and the handful of visually spectacular gushers lived up to their promise. In fact, most quickly petered out, as the imported Soviet drills could only tap into oil pockets between 120 and 360 meters deep, depths that proved too shallow to produce a sustained supply of crude to fuel the refineries.[39] While the first successful wells produced a not-insignificant ten tons of oil per day, these amounts quickly fell to one to two tons daily at most. As one Chinese geologist pointed out a few years later, "Some of these wells produced a certain quantity of oil at first, but ceased to do so one or two years later."[40] According to Soviet officials, the obstacles to production appeared to be surmountable and they largely chalked them up to human error and the lack of drills that could drill deep enough.

The failure to discover oil in regions directly along the Soviet-Xinjiang border, the growing optimism about Xinjiang's potential as a petroleum production site, and new fears about a looming German invasion of the Soviet Union that seemed to threaten the major oil producing sites in the Caucasus prompted a shift in orientation in Soviet policy in Xinjiang. This policy called for greater attention to the proven oil wealth at Dushanzi and a new campaign to tap its oil wealth for use in Soviet industry. In April 1938, the People's Commissariat for Heavy Industry noted that it had "materials concerning this region that allow us to be absolutely confident of its industrial significance and that it [has large enough petroleum reserves] for us to start immediately organizing oil production."[41] Noting its favorable topography and its proximity to the Tianshan North road, a group of oil engineers from the Caucasus dispatched to review reports on the oilfields around Dushanzi seconded the potential of the region. By 1940, Soviet officials called for the construction of a facility capable of producing 50,000 tons annually, a figure twenty-five times higher than the plans only four years earlier.[42]

Similar factors likewise helped drive a greater desire to invest heavily in the exploitation of ores essential in the production of armaments, including tungsten, molybdenum, and beryllium. Tungsten was particularly sought in the years after World War I. The hardness of the element made it useful in high-speed cutting tools critical for armament production. In addition, the invention of tungsten-carbide armor-piercing projectiles helped further boost the value of tungsten on global mineral markets in the 1930s. Japan's 1937 invasion of China, the major producer of tungsten worldwide, fueled a massive scramble for untapped sources of the ore. War with Germany or Japan or both loomed in the minds of Soviet leaders in the late 1930s and early 1940s and the fears of war necessitated an aggressive effort to acquire unfettered access to large quantities of strategic raw materials. Far from Germany, Italy, or Japan, Xinjiang, with its vast reserves of oil, tungsten, beryllium, and molybdenum, found itself being pulled into the Soviet war effort.

### Strengthening Informal Empire

Growing tensions with Japan and Germany in the late 1930s prompted even greater Soviet investments in armament production and heavy industry more generally. The actual outbreak of hostilities in 1939 with the Winter War against Finland and the looming threat of war with Germany following the failed negotiations with Germany's representative Ribbentrop in November 1940 prompted an all-out effort by Soviet planners to stake claims to a wide assortment of raw materials critical for heavy industry. The growing tensions, which culminated with the German invasion of the Soviet Union in 1941, served to strengthen Xinjiang's connections to Soviet industrial centers and prompted more aggressive efforts by Soviet planners to extract, process, and transport the erstwhile Chinese province's resource wealth.

Beginning in late 1940, Soviet geologists began aggressively surveying the Soviet East in particular, as planners sought to uncover resource sites capable of meeting new heavy industry demand but also which were located beyond the reach of the Wehrmacht. New oilfields were discovered south of Kazan that were optimistically deemed the "second Baku," and new aluminum ore sites uncovered beyond the Ural Mountains were seen to be a critical pillar supporting the motherland's Great Patriotic War.[43] Later, in 1941 after the German invasion, over a thousand Soviet factories were relocated east of the Urals as well. As the Soviet Union's economic center of gravity lurched east, Xinjiang's role in Soviet planning increased alongside of it. The distances from Soviet industrial centers, which had once have served as an obstacle to the integration of Xinjiang's resources into central government industrial planning, shrunk overnight. Facing wartime pressures to secure a steady supply of the raw materials needed for industrial production, Soviet officials in late 1940 sought to make a much more direct claim to Xinjiang's mineral and petroleum wealth. Once willing to engage in cooperative agreements with Sheng's government for access to Xinjiang's rich natural resources, after 1940, Soviet officials demanded unfettered access to them.

Inspired by a proposal from the People's Commissariat for Non-ferrous Metals, the Soviet Politburo pushed for a new agreement with Xinjiang that effectively opened the province to unrestricted surveying for minerals vital for heavy industry and the production of armaments. In November 1940, two trusted Soviet Xinjiang hands arrived at Sheng's office in Dihua with an offer they did not allow him to refuse.[44] Sheng later reported that it was Stalin himself who ordered the delegation to impose on the province a new agreement that gave the Soviets direct and unrestricted access to Xinjiang's mineral wealth, with a particular focus on tin and other critical war-related minerals. The proposal granted Soviet geologists unrestricted access to Xinjiang's landscape, allowed for the construction of transportation infrastructure and of buildings and structures deemed necessary for the enterprise, and enabled the mass export of Xinjiang's natural resource wealth.[45] Under the new agreement, Soviet geologists and technicians sought to cut out the provincial middlemen and begin surveying and extracting the ores themselves. Aside from allowing the Soviet Union access to Xinjiang's territory and the provision of cheap labor, provincial officials would play almost no role in production or transport.

The agreement was to last for fifty years and Stalin's handpicked delegates insisted that it was fundamentally nonnegotiable. Sheng reported later that when he protested against the aggressive nature of the agreement, suggesting it smacked of imperial occupation, the delegates rebuffed him, pointing to the Soviet blood spilled in the battles to bolster Sheng's position in the province in 1934. They proclaimed definitively, "This is not a debate over ideology, we came here to fix a problem."[46] Later, Soviet officials would justify foisting the agreement on Sheng, who had joined the Communist Party on a trip to

Moscow in 1938, by saying that it was necessary for the Soviet Union to gain access to minerals needed in the fight against fascism. They claimed that as a member of the party, it was his duty to participate in the fight by providing raw materials for the war effort.[47] They gave him one day to sign without negotiation and did not allow him to consult with anyone before he did so. According to Sheng's own nakedly self-serving account published much later, he felt compelled to agree, fearing that not doing so would have risked a war with the Soviet Union that would have resulted in China's loss of the province once and for all.[48] For Sheng and other officials in Xinjiang, the presence of two Red Army military installations, one at Hami in the eastern stretches of the province and the other near the capital of Dihua, helped ensure their compliance to Soviet demands.

Sheng's memory of the signing of the "Secret Agreement for the Leasing of Xinjiang's Tin Mines" on November 26, 1940, emphasized the threats and an unsubstantiated claim that Stalin desired to sever Xinjiang's connections to the Chinese nation-state. But there were also financial incentives that helped make the bitter taste of the agreement go down a bit more smoothly for Sheng and provincial officials. According to the agreement, with no investment from the provincial treasury, in the first five years the Soviet Union would pay 5 percent of the total value of the "tin and ancillary minerals" (in this case almost certainly tungsten ore) extracted and transported out of Xinjiang annually. After that five-year period, the payment would increase to 6 percent.[49] While these payments would be made primarily in kind through the provision of Soviet commodities, considering the financial difficulties facing the provincial regime in the 1930s and early 1940s, the potential influx of any goods that could be sold in state shops and which would not tax the treasury would have been a boon. The fact that Xinjiang itself was largely powerless to oversee the extraction and transport of these minerals during this period meant that the agreement, for all of its glaring flaws, was an important source of revenue for cash-strapped provincial officials desperately grasping at any potential fiscal lifeline.

After the signing of the agreement in November 1940, Xinjiang's status changed, as it came to be viewed as an integral producer of raw materials for the new Soviet industrial center in the East. As a result, Xinjiang was targeted for new surveys. In addition to dispatching over 260 engineers and technicians to Xinjiang, Soviet officials also equipped two aircraft for aerial surveying, provided surveyors the rights to acquire weapons and ammunition, gave officials the authority to ship freight on the Irtysh River, and offered a virtual blank check to the People's Commissariat for Non-ferrous Metals to fund operations in Xinjiang.[50] Plans called for an aggressive surveying campaign in

TABLE 5.1. Regional groups organized to exploit Xinjiang's nonferrous metals

| Groups | Soviet workers | Local workers | Total |
|---|---|---|---|
| Altai | 40 | 166 | 206 |
| Borohoro | 4 | 18 | 22 |
| Bortala | 76 | 731 | 807 |
| Sayram Lake | 3 | 21 | 24 |
| Southern | 14 | 15 | 29 |

Source: Nachal'nik Planovo-proizvodstvennogo otdeleniya Monin, ekonomist-planovik Banenko, "Plan po trudu Altayskoy gruppy na 1942 g" (no date), file number 9176-19, RGAE, 3; Nachal'nik planovo-proizvodstvennogo otdela upravleniya Monin and ekonomist-planovik Banenko, "Plan po trudu partii Sayram-Nur na 1942 god" (May 13, 1942), file number 9176-19, RGAE, 11; Nachal'nik planovo-proizvodstvennogo otdela upravleniya Monin, ekonomist-planovik Banenko, "Plan po trudu yuzhnoy gruppy na 1942 god" (May 13, 1942), file number 9176-19, RGAE, 17; Nachal'nik planovo-proizvodstvennogo otdela upravleniya Monin, ekonomist-planovik Banenko, "Plan po trudu partii Boro-Khoro na 1942 god" (May 13, 1942), file number 9176-19, RGAE, 25; Nachal'nik planovo-proizvodstvennogo otdela upravleniya Monin, ekonomist-planovik Banenko, "Plan po trudu Borotalinskoy gruppy na 1942 god" (May 13, 1942), file number: 9176-19, RGAE, 31.

the region that focused primarily on already discovered tin, tungsten, beryllium, and molybdenum fields in the Bortala River valley in eastern Xinjiang near the Soviet border, in the far north near Kanas Lake, and at Koktokay (Keketuohai in Chinese) in the foothills of the Altay Mountains in the northern stretches of the province.[51]

Soviet officials in the Geological Administration organized five regionally focused teams to oversee the surveying and initial production. Of the five groups, three were centered around Ili: at Bortala, the Borohoro Mountains, and Sayram Lake; one was focused in the far north at Altay; and one group was assigned to investigate all of the lands south of the Tianshan Mountain range. The main sites of production were in Bortala and the Altay, which employed 807 and 206 people, respectively. None of the other three groups employed more than 30 total people, including that of the "southern group," which covered the largest amount of territory by far (table 5.1).[52] The plans for 1941 alone called for geological surveys of more than 21,050 square kilometers of the province's potentially ore-rich territory, the taking of thousands of samples, and the sinking of multiple thousands of meters of pits, trenches, and core drilling sample wells.[53]

The main focus of Soviet planners was on the production of beryllium and highly valued tantalum in the Altay and tungsten and tin production in Bortala. Plans for 1942 called for the production of 100 tons of beryllium and a single ton of tantalum in the Altay and 70 tons of tungsten and 15 tons of tin in Bortala. Soviet officials clearly had high expectations for the Altay in particular, as they called for a fifty-fold increase in beryllium production by early 1943.[54] Supplementing the extractive operations, the groups were called upon to undertake extensive surveys in the regions under their control, construct buildings, and build roads binding these often out-of-the-way ore fields to the provincial transport network. Both sites had large-scale extraction operations, housing, mineral processing sites, road networks, and even armed guards.[55] Extraction began at Bortala in April 1941, and by the next year the enterprise had already produced more than 5,000 tons of precious tungsten ore.[56] While the data on beryllium production at Koktokay is less clear, so-called pilot mining at Koktokay in 1941 was expected to yield 150 tons of beryllium ore.[57]

The extensive plans laid out for the exploration of the area around the ore-rich tin and tungsten fields in the Bortala River valley called for the sinking of more than 17,000 square meters' worth of pits, trenches, and boreholes. These efforts uncovered three main ore fields in the area. Extraction operations began in earnest in 1941, and at its height, the site had a substantial presence in this region, with more than 3,000 technicians, geologists, and laborers working the ore-laden rock.[58] At Koktokay in far northern Xinjiang, not far from the border with Outer Mongolia, geological plans called for the digging of nearly 5,000 square meters' worth of exploratory pits and trenches.[59] In a series of geological expeditions in 1941 and 1942 undertaken by the People's Commissariat for Non-ferrous Metals, the Number 5 Talas-Altay Work Group helped reveal the 10,000 square mile ore field at Koktokay, which had twenty-five significant ore-bearing pegmatite veins, including its famed Number 3 vein, which was 131 feet wide and reached more than half a mile into the earth. The group began undertaking extraction operations in the spring of 1941 using the gold mining equipment left over from the operations of the mid-1930s. Only a few years later the site had dormitories and offices, a repair shop, a power plant, a wireless station, and guards armed with machine guns.[60]

Soviet officials were no less ambitious in their efforts to uncover Xinjiang's petroleum wealth. While not explicitly covered by the tin agreement, petroleum geologists fanned out throughout the province in the early 1940s. Previously unwilling to promote petroleum production for export to the Soviet Union out of fears about the high cost of transporting it, the threat to fields in the Caucasus and the eastward shift of Soviet industry made oil production in Xinjiang more attractive to Soviet planners. They discovered substantial evidence of petroleum scattered throughout both northern and southern Xinjiang. One report noted that "geological prospecting and scholarly research have found the existence of large numbers of natural oil seepages in the Zungharian and Taklimakan basins."[61] Yet this report also suggested that they concentrate their efforts around Dushanzi, given its proximity to transport networks and the substantial amount of energy already devoted to surveying and prospect drilling in the region. The report went on to call for much more aggressive prospect drilling in order to fully understand the region's oil geology. Rectifying the problems with the drills used in the mid-1930s, in 1941, five steam-powered oil drills imported from the Soviet Union and capable of running at 300 horsepower facilitated substantial increases in oil production.[62] That year, teams drilled eight wells in Dushanzi, which reached depths ranging from 560 meters to 1,107 meters, with one nonproducing prospecting well reaching a depth of 1,453 meters. By 1941, the operation had drilled a total of seventeen operating wells in the area; a total of thirty-three wells had been drilled since 1936.[63]

The Soviet Union extended its control over the region's oil wealth by controlling the refinery operation. Under a 1942 agreement, the two sides established a refinery that was jointly funded, though Xinjiang's portion of the investment was to be covered by Soviet credits that the provincial government was required to repay at an annual interest rate of 4.5 percent.[64] Additionally, under the agreement, "The government of Xinjiang is obligated to set aside the necessary plots of land for prospecting, the commercial production of oil, and exploration free of charge."[65] Further strengthening Soviet control over the operation, the director and chief engineer of the operation were to be appointed by the Soviet side with the deputy director appointed by the Xinjiang side. Provincial officials were entitled to half of the petroleum produced on site.[66]

In January 1942, Soviet technicians installed a top-of-the-line 55,000-gallon crude oil atmospheric distillation unit capable of producing high-octane gasoline. The refining operation had access to freshwater from the Kuitun River, eight kilometers away, through a network of water pipes and a pumping station, while crude oil flowed unimpeded into the distillation unit via a network of 2,500 meters of six-inch pipe, capable of transporting 6,000 tons of crude daily.[67] The joint enterprise was to operate for a period of twenty-five years, after which the Xinjiang government would be given the option to buy back the Soviet portion, though, the agreement noted, they were "obligated not to sell and not to yield its right of redemption to foreigners."[68] According to Chinese sources, in the first half of 1942, the Dushanzi oilfield was said to have produced 100,000 gallons of gasoline and 100,000 gallons of lamp oil.[69]

The growing priority placed on petroleum production in the years after 1941 helped place Dushanzi on the Soviet Union's planning map and the operations expanded quickly. By 1941, Dushanzi employed 158 Soviet engineers on site. These workers, who lived with 160 or 170 family members in four barracks constructed not far from the oilfields, were said to enjoy average wages of between US $80 and US $300 per month, a relatively high salary based on the fact that most had experience in the Soviet oilfields at Baku.[70] The government in Dihua appointed the so-called plant manager (*changzhang*). But according to Chinese official reports, this position, which appears to have been held by a succession of Sheng's cronies also hailing from China's northeast, was largely symbolic.[71] Instead, according to one high-ranking Chinese official who made a personal investigation of the site at Chiang Kaishek's request in July 1942, the real power was held by the Soviet chief engineer, who was appointed by Moscow.[72] In addition to the Soviet experts employed at Dushanzi, in a July 1942 investigation, GMD officials reported that there were 1,000 Han and Uyghur laborers also working in the oilfields, each of whom earned fifty Xinjiang yuan monthly not including the forty or fifty yuan worth of food provided in the mess hall.[73]

The heavy investment in Dushanzi in the late 1930s and early 1940s helped create what Timothy Mitchell refers to as an integrated oil "apparatus," complete with drilling facilities, refinery operations, pipeline networks, and road systems.[74] The expensive, unwieldly refinery equipment helped concentrate extraction operations around the site, as the difficulty and expense of transporting raw oil ensured that drilling tended to focus on potential oilfields located nearby. Further strengthening this geographical focus, Soviet leaders and provincial officials also extended regional infrastructural networks to the refinery in order to facilitate the outflow of petroleum products to urban centers in Xinjiang and the Soviet Union. These efforts helped pave a layer of state investment that subsequent officials and planners could not break without a substantial investment of their own resources in surveying, construction, and transport.

The main east-west trunk road that stretched from Hami in the east all the way to Ili and the Soviet border in the west had undergone substantial upgrades throughout the 1930s. A 1936 plan held the Soviet Union's Central Directorate for Roads and Transportation responsible for aiding the provincial government in constructing this road. To pay for it, they required that 800,000 rubles be drawn from the Soviet loans to Xinjiang and be used for road construction.[75] Later, an agreement reached between the Republic of China in Nanjing and the Soviet Union following Japan's invasion of China in 1937, was the starting point for the exchange of Soviet military equipment for Chinese cash and raw materials. In order to facilitate this exchange, substantial improvements were made to Xinjiang's east-west trunk road in the late 1930s. These improvements were largely paid for by Sheng's government, which was said to have spent three million yuan on a wide assortment of infrastructural upgrades.[76] The agreement between Chiang Kaishek and Stalin collapsed in 1941, following the signing of the Soviet-Japanese Neutrality Pact, but the east-west trunk road retained its utility, as it continued to serve as a conduit for delivering Xinjiang's raw materials to the Soviet Union.

Despite the ongoing improvements made to Xinjiang's transport networks more generally, the importance of the three mineral extraction sites to Soviet planning prompted an emphasis on connecting these far-flung, isolated regions into provincial and regional transport and communication networks. The main east-west trunk road, which would end up becoming the most traveled and best-maintained route in the province, was connected very directly into Soviet transport networks. The road had a paved nine-kilometer spur that connected it to the Dushanzi drilling operation as well as another connecting it to the ore fields in Bortala. While transport to and from Koktokay was undertaken largely by riverine traffic along the Irtysh, a series of new highways and roads were likewise constructed in the Altay region that were intended to help facilitate the transport of raw materials directly into the Soviet Union.

*

It is easy to overlook the institutional power of geological surveys and geological reports. But the Soviet geologists who fanned out into Xinjiang in the 1930s and early 1940s helped place many of the province's most prominent ore caches and oilfields on China's resource maps once and for all. The opening of the province allowed for a much greater concentration of surveying around these known sites. With clear evidence of the presence of valuable resources, surveyors tended to use these extant sites as the jump-off points for their inquiries. As a result, surveying tended to reproduce itself in highly defined patterns, oriented around very specific waypoints. The ghosts of these Soviet geological teams continued to swirl around Chinese geologists operating in Xinjiang, as later Chinese reports filed in the 1960s and even 1970s remain filled with references to previous Soviet geological teams and their findings in the province. Given Xinjiang's distance, size, and the cost of fielding large-scale geological teams for extended amounts of time, the fact that Soviet geologists pinpointed substantial and important resource sites served to convince later generations of economic planners about where they should be focusing their efforts.

Perhaps more tangibly, Soviet capital investments made in the 1930s and particularly in the early 1940s served as the layers that would help set long-term patterns of extraction and development. The presence of oil refineries, ore concentrating mills, drilling rigs, and pipeline networks all became tangible points of focus for future extraction enterprises. The cost of the expensive equipment, the difficulty of moving it, and, in many cases, the necessity of retaining trained personnel to install and operate it prompted future planners to try to work with existing capital investments rather than relocate to other potentially productive areas. Similarly, the cost of constructing paved roads capable of conveying trucks loaded down with petroleum or ores likewise helped set patterns of development. Cash-strapped provincial officials and Chinese state economic planners were unwilling or unable to underwrite the construction of a more comprehensive road network or rail line binding the province to China. But even beyond the borders of the province, the strength of the Soviet transport network made it far more cost effective for a future generation of economic planners in Xinjiang and China to seek out markets to the west rather than to try to undertake the costly task of shipping the region's lucrative industrial resources into China-centered transport networks.

By early 1942, the Soviet Union appeared to be on the verge of being devoured alive by the German offensive in the western half of the country. Chafing at growing Soviet burdens placed on Xinjiang, as well as a parallel slow-down in aid to the province, Sheng began exploring ways to begin loosening Soviet control over the province and its resource wealth. His efforts, which included the purge of Soviet supporters in the bureaucracy and accusations against high-ranking Soviet officials, prompted an ominous June 27 letter from Minister of Foreign Affairs Molotov, who told Sheng that Soviet Vice Commissar for Foreign Affairs Vladimir Dekanozov, a known member of Stalin's feared secret police force the NKVD, would soon arrive in Dihua "in order to resolve the Dushanzi oilfield issue and other important problems." According to Sheng Shicai's biography, which is based on many still-classified Chinese sources, Dekanozov would come bearing a new written agreement for the exploitation of Dushanzi that would replace the 1935 oral agreement and, paralleling the tin agreement's focus on nonferrous metals, would grant the Soviet Union wide latitude to exploit the region's petroleum wealth.[77]

The prospect prompted Sheng to rethink his relationship with the Soviet Union and begin a search for new potential patrons. Turning away from the Soviets, Sheng leapt into the arms of Chiang Kaishek and the Republic of China. The problem that Chinese officials faced, however, was breaking the Soviet economic hold on Xinjiang and its mineral wealth without undercutting their own abilities to access and profit off of those natural resources. The enduring power of the Soviet capital investments and surveys that were layered in northern Xinjiang in the 1930s is the subject of the next chapter, which seeks to understand the resonance of Soviet exploration and investment in Xinjiang, revealing it to be a nearly indelible stamp on the region that Chiang and planners in China were largely powerless to eliminate.

# Oil, Tungsten, Beryllium, and the Resonances of Soviet Planning

At a July 3, 1942, banquet in Dihua for an eighteen-person delegation from Chiang Kaishek's wartime capital of Chongqing, Sheng Shicai recited an emotional poem for his visitors that pointed to his decision to strengthen Xinjiang's ties to the Chinese Republic. "Rearing up my horse on Wu Mountain, I think of the old days / when the areas outside of the Great Wall were connected [to the center] like strands of hair on one's temples / I hope that my life's work [of national reunification] will not be in vain / it is excellent when all of the territories shield and sustain one another," he intoned.[1] GMD officials enthusiastically applauded Sheng's switch. As Chiang Kaishek gushed, "This is our greatest achievement since the founding of the Republic." After five years of war with Japan, the acquisition of Xinjiang offered not only a major morale boost, but it also appeared to resolve numerous obstacles simultaneously including, most notably, the severe shortages in various natural resources critical for the war effort.[2]

By 1942, leaders in Chongqing were desperate for new sources of the oil and nonferrous metals needed to maintain their war effort. Lacking domestic sources of petroleum, Chinese officials had become fully dependent on fickle shipments delivered by American planes flying the so-called Hump route over the Himalayan Mountains from British India. In addition, nonferrous metals, particularly tungsten, were one of China's most important exports to the United States, as planners relied heavily on the ores to repay American economic and military aid. With its proven oil reserves and substantial quantities of nonferrous metals, the acquisition of Xinjiang could not have been more timely. The problem for Chinese planners, however, was in accessing these resources. They had not set foot in the province in nearly a decade, the province lacked all but the most rudimentary infrastructural connections binding it to China-proper, and the pressures of wartime brought about an economic crisis for the government that precluded large-scale capital investments in distant border regions far from the front.

The solution to these challenges seemed to lie in the Soviet Union. While they were aware of the aggressive extraction campaigns embraced by Soviet planners in the 1930s, Chinese geologists and surveyors entering Xinjiang in 1942 and 1943 were clearly taken aback by the scale of the Soviet extraction efforts in the province. Flying in from war-torn Chongqing, they were impressed by the top-of-the-line Soviet oil drilling rigs and the refinery at Dushanzi, the large-scale mineral production sites at Koktokay and Bortala, and the network of roads binding the province to the Soviet rail network. Lacking in both capital and time, the thick layers of Soviet state interest and investment appeared as an opportunity for Chinese planners, who wasted no time in reaching out to their Soviet counterparts for help in profiting from Xinjiang's resource wealth. They turned not only to Soviet development blueprints in the province, but also to Soviet capital, markets, and technical expertise.

Yet, this cooperative approach to the Soviet Union was tempered by a simmering mistrust of Stalin's intentions in Xinjiang and a desire by Chinese officials to tilt this long-wayward province toward China once and for all. To this end, in the weeks and months following Sheng's 1942 switch, Chinese officials established new GMD institutions across Xinjiang; not far behind, a flood of party cadres, teachers, and functionaries washed over the province. They were energized by new slogans such as "open the great northwest" and "establish the foundations of the nation in the northwest" as well as patriotic appeals to ethnocultural Han pride through the employment of well-known historical figures like Zhang Qian and Ban Chao, who had played central roles in the Han dynasty's efforts to assert control over the northwest 2000 years earlier.[3] Republican officials were driven by a desire to roll back the substantial Soviet presence in the region and reestablish central government authority. Portraits of Lenin and Stalin were ripped from the walls of classrooms, government buildings, and private homes throughout the province, and books of Marxist writings were seized and destroyed. These were replaced with portraits of Sun Yatsen and Chiang Kaishek and volumes of Sun's *Three Principles of the People*.[4] Fearing retribution for his perceived betrayal during the Soviet Union's darkest hour, Sheng was an enthusiastic participant in this larger effort to politically and culturally reorient Xinjiang. And throughout 1942 and 1943 he helped spearhead a desperate and often violent campaign to eliminate the Soviet presence and influence in the province root and branch.

Chinese government officials after 1942 were thus caught between two seemingly contradictory policies, as they sought to drive out Soviet influence from the province in order to shore up their political position and at the same time to reach out for Soviet help in facilitating the extraction of resources in Xinjiang. Highlighting these contradictory policies, less than one week after a tense July 1942 conversation between Chiang Kaishek and the Soviet ambassador to China, during which Chiang Kaishek tersely declared that Xinjiang answered not to Moscow but to Chongqing, Chiang floated the possibility of establishing a Sino-Soviet oil drilling operation at Dushanzi. In contrast to his firm tone in the conversation a week earlier, Chiang cajoled the ambassador, explaining that "extracting Xinjiang's oil wealth could have benefits for both of our countries."[5]

For those interested in Xinjiang's resource wealth, the Soviet investments made over the course of much of the 1930s and early 1940s were an inescapable presence in this border region. Eager to quickly and cheaply exploit Xinjiang's resource wealth, Chinese planners, into the post-1949 People's Republic, continued to use the earlier Soviet layers as the foundation for their own extractive efforts in Xinjiang. The enduring resonance of these layers speaks to the material power of capital investments. The large-scale oil apparatus constructed at Dushanzi, with its modern refinery, legion of drilling rigs, and comprehensive infrastructural network, helped concentrate state interest in petroleum at this single site at the expense of other equally oil-rich sites scattered throughout Xinjiang. While to some extent petroleum is unique in its need for large-scale, costly refining equipment, the facilities established to extract, process, and transport tungsten, beryllium, lithium, and other nonferrous ores also served as powerful layers that helped set long-term patterns of state investment and economic development in Xinjiang. The surveys, extraction operations, transport infrastructure, and processing plants built in the 1930s and early 1940s helped create a blueprint for investment that future regimes, who were eager to facilitate the extraction of lucrative resources without investing heavily in this border province, were loath to reject.

### Surveying the Republic's New Frontier

One day in October 1942, the geologist Huang Jiqing recalled, he received an order from his superior: "Go to Xinjiang. The quicker you leave the better."[6] For Huang and indeed nearly everyone in China's geological community, Xinjiang was largely unknown. The region's isolation, distance, and historic resistance to Chinese state integration throughout the Republican period ensured that planners were unclear exactly what resources it held and where they might be able to find them (see chapter 3). Facing this blank spot on the map, in preparing for his expedition, Huang was forced to rely on old unverified reports, the most up to date of which was over a decade old and the oldest a provincial gazetteer published in the Qing dynasty.[7] Hoping to update these old reports, officials in Chongqing established a provincial geological survey in 1943. Shortly thereafter, twenty-one geological teams were formed to survey Xinjiang's minerals.[8] Additional teams from the Ministry of Economic Affairs, the National Resources Commission, the Academia Sinica, and the Salt Production Industry Administration likewise conducted surveys within the newly acquired territory. As one geologist remembered a few years later, "every type of investigative group was organized and sent out to Xinjiang to undertake on-the-ground surveys."[9]

Government planners also began drawing up the outlines of new plans that would bind Xinjiang and its mineral wealth to China through deep and permanent infrastructural connections. In 1943 alone, five surveying teams were dispatched to outline a new northwestern transport network that would link Xinjiang into an infrastructural network binding the province to China-proper and wrench it out of the grasp of the Soviet Union. The rail line, or at the very least a highway, was to begin in western Shaanxi province, cross Gansu via the major northwestern transport hub of Lanzhou, cross the rock-strewn deserts (*gebi*) of eastern Xinjiang, pass through the provincial capital of Dihua, cross the oilfields and refinery at Dushanzi and then end at the major Sino-Soviet border crossing at Tacheng. The plans also included lines connecting Xinjiang to a broader northwestern transport network with lines to Baotou in Inner Mongolia, Xining in Qinghai, and Chengdu in western Sichuan province.[10]

Chinese officials from Chiang Kaishek on down issued stridently nationalistic calls to "open the northwest."[11] These calls, however, were not backed up with money. Pinpointing Xinjiang's subterranean resource wealth necessitated a substantial financial commitment, as it required the dispatching of large numbers of geologists to the province on a semipermanent basis. As Huang recognized in a report to Chongqing, "Sinkiang is too large a province for a score of field geologists to handle."[12] The calls to aggressively survey the province ran up against financial realities and competing priorities in regions located closer to China's wartime industries in the southwest. Constructing the infrastructure to import equipment and transport finished resources back to China-proper was an even more expensive proposition. The cost of constructing the northwestern rail network in particular was so substantial that in its ten-year construction plan issued in October 1942, the Ministry of Transport chose to calculate only the first year, which itself would cost a staggering 657 million yuan. Additional lines crossing southern Xinjiang were estimated to cost 444 million and would not even be completed until 1953.[13]

The costs were well beyond the reach of Chinese officials, whose policy priorities rested on resisting the Japanese advance and reclaiming Japanese-occupied lands more than they did on systematically reorienting wayward peripheries of the Republic. Thus, they focused their efforts on those Soviet mineral production sites that had already been extensively surveyed by Soviet geologists, constructed by Soviet engineers, and integrated into Soviet infrastructure and markets. For GMD officials, who prioritized the need to rapidly and inexpensively increase the production of critical wartime minerals, following the Soviet extraction blueprints, building atop the earlier layers, and concentrating on proven fields appeared to be the best strategy.

The presence of the large-scale Soviet mining and oil drilling operations appeared to be clear evidence of the potential that Xinjiang's resource wealth held for the Republic. Indeed, geologists made a beeline for the oilfield at Dushanzi and the tungsten mines at Bortala in western Xinjiang as soon as the region was opened to them. In July 1942, China's Minister of Economic Affairs Weng Wenhao (himself a Western-trained geologist) was invited by Sheng Shicai to tour Xinjiang. After a short stay in the provincial capital, Weng traveled directly to Dushanzi, where he happily noted that the facilities could produce 1,000 gallons of oil daily for the war effort and, with greater investment, could be easily ramped up to produce around 7,000 gallons.[14] The site, with its thirty-three wells, modern drilling and refining equipment, and sizable contingent of Soviet engineers, quickly became a place of pilgrimage for Republican geologists, mining engineers, and planners dispatched to survey the province. The refining equipment in particular was a source of optimism for Chinese scientists like Weng and a few months later Huang, who detailed the operation's high capacity and the fact that the gauges and switches were all top-of-the-line and fully automated.[15]

The Chinese government was in desperate need of oil to help prosecute its war with Japan. The campaigns to develop new oilfields in unoccupied Free China and the effort to draw on new non–petroleum based fuel sources have been well documented.[16] But the unexpected acquisition of Xinjiang in 1942 appeared to resolve the oil shortage problem once and for all. Fernando Coronil argues that petroleum has a deeper power for developing states beyond simply providing a source of fuel for powering combustion engines. Oil, he writes, "created the illusion that instantaneous modernization lay at hand, that the flow of history could be redirected, that oil money could launch the country into the future and grant it control over its own destiny."[17] The prospect of tapping the proven oilfield that appeared to stretch across much of north-central Xinjiang pointed not only to a source of gas to power the trucks, tanks, and airplanes needed in the war effort, but also toward a bright postwar future for China. Gaping at the substantial Soviet-built oil apparatus in the foothills of the Tianshan range helped inspire petroleum dreams among state planners in Chongqing.

The tungsten mine, located a stone's throw from the border with the Soviet Union, attracted similar attention from geologists and state planners. In an October 1943 conversation in Chongqing, Sheng suggested that Chinese officials tap Xinjiang's tungsten wealth in order to repay Soviet aid given to Chiang Kaishek and the government in the years immediately following Japan's invasion in 1937. He noted that Bortala's short distance from the Soviet border would largely eliminate transport costs and allow the debt to be paid down more quickly.[18] The idea was not farfetched, as the Chinese government had already prioritized tungsten production at various fields in southwest China. They used the high-value mineral to repay not only Soviet support from the late 1930s but also, more recently, American Lend-Lease aid. By 1942, large quantities of tungsten ore that had been extracted from Chinaproper were already being shipped by truck convoy across Xinjiang into the Soviet Union as well as being loaded onto planes at airfields in southwest China and shipped to Allied bases in India.

Bortala's proximity to Xinjiang's transport network and the high demand for tungsten ore prompted state planners to prioritize it over the fields at Koktokay in the far north.[19] At Bortala, the presence of the joint Soviet-Xinjiang operations, which channeled raw ore to the processing plant at Khorgos (see chapter 5), was clear evidence for Chinese officials of the economic potential that Xinjiang held for the Republic. Not long after the reassertion of Chinese control, a surveying team from Chongqing was dispatched to survey these lucrative ore fields. The annual 1944 work plan for the group, later named the Xinjiang Tungsten Engineering Office (Xinjiang wukuang gongcheng chu), was ambitious. The plan included a 29 million yuan outlay for the team to begin combing the three ore sites in Bortala in July and August. After establishing the site at Bortala, the team was to turn its attentions to Koktokay.[20]

Chinese planners also noted that Xinjiang's highway network, which had been constructed with Soviet loans and completed with the help of Soviet engineers, served to bind the province's resource wealth to Soviet markets and industry. The paved Dihua-Ili highway, which Huang noted was the most traveled and best maintained route in the province, bisected the province north of the Tianshan Mountains and had a paved nine-kilometer spur that connected it to the Dushanzi drilling operation as well as another connecting it to the Bortala tungsten fields. The region's transportation infrastructure had the added benefit of connecting these fields to the Soviet long-distance transport networks via the Turk-Sib rail line just across the border. By relying on these connections, Chinese officials could more cheaply import equipment and supplies and also transport finished ores to mineral markets in the Soviet Union and potentially other international markets via ports in British India and Persia.[21] As one report from the Ministry of Economic Affairs argued, it would allow China to "avoid large transport costs in [mineral] shipments through the northwest."[22]

The willingness of geologists like Huang Jiqing and state planners like Weng Wenhao to embrace Soviet blueprints in Xinjiang speaks to the power of the layers laid over Dushanzi and Bortala. The heavy investments in extraction, processing, and transport by Soviet planners helped steer future Chinese state investment and interest toward these exact same sites. While Huang and others recognized that Xinjiang sat atop large quantities of potentially lucrative resources spread throughout the province, the logistics of exploration and the high cost of building new facilities and infrastructure prompted them to concentrate their efforts on Dushanzi, Bortala, and to a lesser extent Koktokay. The layers of state interest in the form of surveys, facilities, and infrastructure initiated by Soviet planners in the 1930s and 1940s helped orient the efforts of their counterparts in the Republic of China.

The massive cost of extraction and processing equipment and the considerable difficulties of transporting raw and processed ores and petroleum prompted Chinese officials to do more than simply follow Soviet resource extraction blueprints. In order to avoid losing access to the massive Soviet capital investments in the province and quickly begin producing the oil and minerals desperately needed to maintain their war effort, they actively reached out to their Soviet counterparts to set up a joint resource extraction enterprise in Xinjiang. Their efforts centered around the development of joint oil operations. While they certainly could have benefited from Soviet aid in the tungsten fields in western Xinjiang, the relative ease of extracting ore with simple tools (as opposed to deep drills) and the ability to ship out unprocessed ore meant that they did not see Soviet aid as a necessity. Oil, however, which required a substantial refining operation was a different matter. Not long after exerting their political control over the province, Republican officials contacted their Soviet counterparts about establishing a joint operation at Dushanzi. Their willingness to reach out to the Soviet Union despite Chiang Kaishek's gnawing mistrust of the Soviet Union and its territorial intentions in Xinjiang, points to the desperation of the Chinese Republic to begin the process of incorporating the province's resources into central government plans.

## Competition v. Cooperation

The challenge for Chinese officials was how to walk the fine line between gaining Soviet cooperation in mineral and oil production while at the same time safeguarding their territorial sovereignty. The result was an often schizophrenic policy that swung wildly between requests for Soviet support and often aggressive attempts to minimize the Soviet presence in the region. Their task was made even more difficult by Sheng Shicai, whose priority was driving out Soviet influence and preserving his own power base within the province.

Seeking to sever fiscal connections with his previous patrons, Sheng sought to rapidly pay back Soviet loans. To do so, he purchased more than 50,000 horses in 1942 and 400,000 sheep in 1944 from pastoralists in Xinjiang at below-market prices and then drove them over the border. But the core of his larger effort was the campaign he waged against Soviet personnel in Xinjiang.[23] Sheng knew that the Soviet officials who had helped support him with loans, military aid, and technical support since the early 1930s would not take kindly to his decision to turn his back on them when they were at their most vulnerable. The fear of retribution from Soviet agents led to an aggressive policy by provincial officials that was intended not only to gain new allies in Chongqing but also to drive the Soviets out of Xinjiang once and for all. Throughout 1942 and 1943, as Chinese officials sought to draw on Soviet expertise, use Soviet infrastructure, and solicit Soviet investment in the oilfields around Dushanzi, Sheng actively sought to poison Sino-Soviet relations to ensure the elimination of internal Soviet threats to himself.[24]

In addition to accusing the Soviet consul and other high-ranking Soviet officials of colluding with Japan in early 1942, Sheng also undertook a vicious campaign of imprisoning Soviet experts and citizens—indeed, anyone affiliated with the Soviet administration of the province. In conversations with Chinese government leaders, the Soviet ambassador Aleksandr Panyushkin repeatedly complained about the atmosphere of suspicion surrounding Soviet citizens in Xinjiang. In a January 6, 1943, conversation with Sheng Shicai and his newly appointed GMD representative in Dihua, Panyushkin indignantly complained that policemen demanded to examine his passport despite the fact he had informed them multiple times that he was in fact the ambassador. The incident, he said, reflected a broad mistrust of Soviet citizens. Rejecting the accusation, Sheng denied the fact that there was any shift in attitude and instead reaffirmed Xinjiang's policy of "closeness with the Soviet Union."[25] The situation on the ground undermined Sheng's glib response. Various reports to Moscow pointed out the shabby treatment of Soviet citizens who were being regularly berated in the streets, not being sold food or other sundries by local merchants who were forbidden to do so on pain of immediate imprisonment, and were subjected to humiliating searches by overly eager policemen and border guards. As one 1943 report to the Soviet Union's Ministry of Foreign Affairs noted, "In April and May of this year the attitude at every level of government in the province toward Soviet citizens and organizations has taken a rapid turn for the worse."[26]

As far as Soviet officials were concerned, the tension on the ground was caused by Sheng himself and they did not hesitate to voice their displeasure with his administration at any and every opportunity. In a meeting with Deputy Foreign Minister Wu Guozhen, Panyushkin complained that "Xinjiang's local government had adopted every type of measure to block the movement and transport of Soviet citizens inside of Xinjiang."[27] In his memoir, Panyushkin blamed Sheng directly for the campaign of harassment. Sheng "justified and defended the illegal actions of the Chinese regarding Soviet citizens and government agencies in Xinjiang because he himself was their organizer," he wrote plainly.[28] Confronted with the ongoing concerns about the treatment of Soviet citizens and investment in the province, in a conversation that May with the Soviet ambassador, Wu Guozhen pointed the finger of blame at a "few Xinjiang officials." According to a Soviet Foreign Ministry report to Moscow, Wu seemed to squirm anxiously throughout the conversation, an attitude the ambassador thought reflected his discomfort with the situation he was being placed in by Sheng's aggressive policy.[29]

Things were no better in Dushanzi and other Soviet-sponsored enterprises in the province. Operating under vague instructions from above, in late 1942 provincial officials arrested several high-ranking Soviet engineers and technicians on questionable charges of sabotage.[30] According to Sheng, he was seeking to reexert control over an operation that had become dominated by the Soviet Union. In his account, Soviet engineers had ridden roughshod over any attempt to circumscribe their rampant hiring of new Soviet "experts," many of whom, he claimed, lacked any credentials at all. He also sought to curtail what he charged was a wanton theft of oil by Soviet technicians. In an investigation conducted over twenty days in September 1942, the local branch of the Xinjiang Public Security Bureau found that Soviet engineers had illegally taken nearly 30,000 kilograms of gasoline and more than 12,000 kilograms of kerosene directly out of the refining tanks and shipped them to the Soviet Union.[31] According to Sheng, it was insubordination, sabotage, and thievery that had led to the mass arrests of Soviet technicians on-site. "If someone destroys things they will not simply be removed from their position, instead they will be punished without mercy," Sheng warned in a conversation with Panyushkin in 1943.[32]

Whatever his rationale, Sheng's attempts to clean house at Dushanzi created an atmosphere of severe tension at the oil site. Strikes broke out among Chinese workers protesting unequal wages in November and later, in January 1943, in a show of force, the Soviet Union dispatched a group of soldiers from their garrison in Hami along with two tanks to Dushanzi, an action that only fueled tensions.[33] Later, after the withdrawal of the troops, a contingent of Chinese workers broke down the door of a locked Soviet office on-site, rifled through accounting papers and other documents, and made off with expensive equipment.[34] Soviet officials complained to China's Ministry of Foreign Affairs that Soviet workers were also frequently being violently harassed at the encouragement of plant higher-ups and government officials.

Despite any suspicions that they might have held about the Soviet Union's long-term intentions in Xinjiang, Chinese officials continued to believe that Soviet capital held the key to the exploitation of the province's petroleum wealth. As a result, in the midst of this tension, they opened talks with the Soviet Union about the possibility of establishing a joint oil extraction enterprise at Dushanzi. After a series of lower-level negotiations over the operation in late 1942 and an initial exchange of draft proposals, the official high-level negotiations over the establishment of a joint Sino-Soviet oil extraction operation at Dushanzi (among other issues) commenced in February 1943 in Chongqing. The Soviet negotiating team led by Panyushkin opened the meeting by asking for an equal 50-50 ownership split in any operation set up in Dushanzi. The proposal was countered by the Chinese side as being in violation of Chinese mining law; they made a counteroffer that would split the enterprise 51 percent to 49 in favor of China. Similar conflicts also arose over the makeup of the board of directors, as the Chinese felt that Chinese appointees should be in positions of authority, while the Soviet side insisted that management be equalized and offered to different sides on a rotating basis.

Soviet representatives felt that they were negotiating from a position of strength. As the Soviet ambassador noted in the first round of negotiations, "we would like to remind the Chinese side that one of the peculiarities of this enterprise is that no matter whether we are talking about now or in the past, all of the equipment has been provided by us." He went on to emphasize, "who best knows the production particulars and understands the production capabilities of the enterprise? There is not the slightest doubt that it is Soviet citizens."[35] Yet the Chinese side felt that they too were in a position to dictate terms. As a consequence, negotiations deadlocked over the two related issues of ownership and management. In a meeting a month later, the issues remained unresolved. After quickly locking horns over the same issues that had foiled negotiations in February, the Soviet ambassador concluded the March

1943 meeting by saying the "problem is quite complex and while we had hoped to reach a quick agreement, it is now clear that this is not possible."[36]

In the final moments of the last round of negotiations, as Soviet negotiators were preparing to leave, Weng Wenhao raised the prospect of purchasing Dushanzi's equipment.[37] Panyushkin promised to inquire with his superiors on the matter, but the sources addressing the Soviet position have not yet been uncovered. It is logical to assume, however, that the victory at Stalingrad less than a month before, a victory that helped protect Soviet oil production in the Caucasus, made the oil operation at Dushanzi less of a priority. This, paired with the campaign against Russian citizens, must have played a role in hardening Soviet negotiators against supporting any Chinese position. That April, receiving news about Soviet intentions to begin a full pull-out of both personnel and equipment from Dushanzi and other sites in Xinjiang, Wu Guozhen sought out the Soviet ambassador and expressed his "unparalleled surprise" about this new development.[38] Unmoved, Soviet representatives officially announced on May 17 that the oil operations would soon close, that technicians would be assembled, equipment would be broken down, and shortly thereafter the entire enterprise shipped back to Soviet territory.[39]

On May 24, Soviet leaders at Dushanzi informed the Chinese factory manager that the next day a fleet of sixty trucks would be arriving to begin the process of removing equipment and personnel. When Soviet technicians began to pull out of the area, they found their way impeded by a Chinese contingent who said they were operating under orders "from above" to block the transport of equipment and personnel out of the region. They even denied the convoy the use of the fuel depot to refuel their trucks.[40] More generally, Soviet officials reported that drivers working for various extractive industries at Dushanzi and other sites were being frequently stopped and harassed. In one case that month, Masim Turabaev, a Xinjiang resident who was involved in freight transport for the Soviet geological administration, was detained by provincial security agents and interrogated about the types of things he was transporting. He was let go with a stern warning that "if in the future he works for the [Soviet] geological administration then he will be immediately arrested." Turabaev then asked to be discharged from his driving duties.[41] In order to avoid harassment on the roads, Soviet agencies began sending trucks and vehicle convoys to and from the border at night.[42]

Despite the obstacles, over the next month, Soviet teamsters shipped out between 70 and 80 percent of the enterprise's equipment. By June 17, only the steel framing for drilling and piping for wells, along with pumps, a few boilers, and assorted buildings, remained on-site. Capping the tension and eliminating any shred of the cooperative spirit that had undergirded the operation,

an ironically apt fire of unknown cause burned the Joint Sino-Soviet Confer-
ence Room at Dushanzi to the ground that July.[43] As for the wells themselves,
which had held so much promise and seemed to be on the verge of a major
production breakthrough as late as 1942, Chinese officials in Xinjiang were relieved to find that they had not been sabotaged and had in fact been expertly
capped by Soviet engineers with cement and steel.[44]

In April 1944, the Ministry of Economic Affairs gave jurisdiction over Dushanzi to the Gansu province oil drilling office, and that September, China's
Ministry of Economic Affairs officially established state control over the site.[45]
Without the Soviet Union's deep pockets, however, production was slow. The
operation relied on one imported drill driven with a car engine powered by
a twenty-seven-kilowatt generator. The gleaming high-tech vacuum distillation refining system that Huang Jiqing had salivated over during his initial
trip to Dushanzi had been dismantled and in its place local technicians relied
on a rudimentary atmospheric distillation cauldron. All told, the Chinese operations in the region repaired seven former Soviet wells that together yielded
a relatively paltry ten tons or so of raw oil per day, an amount insufficient to
come close to even meeting provincial demand.[46]

Despite the small scale of the operations, Dushanzi continued to exert an
almost hypnotic allure for Republican officials who dreamed of someday being able to tap the oil ocean that seemed to sit tantalizingly just below the surface. The desire to rely on the petroleum richness of this distant border region
to transform not only Xinjiang but the Chinese Republic itself helped ensure
a continued focus on Dushanzi. The Soviet surveys and operation pointed the
way forward and helped concentrate efforts around this one oilfield in this oil-
rich province. While tungsten, beryllium, and lithium had less of the hypnotic
modernist allure of oil gushers, a similar desire by Chinese officials to quickly
and cheaply reap the region's mineral wealth in order to boost revenue and
power industry helped maintain the focus and interest around Bortala and
Koktokay at the expense of other, less heavily explored sites in Xinjiang.

### Occupying Ore Fields

The collapse of the negotiations in 1943 eliminated any hope of Sino-Soviet
cooperation in Xinjiang's oil and ore fields. In fact, the withdrawal of Soviet
personnel, equipment, and institutions in the province helped foster a simmering cross-border tension. That year, the Soviet Union imposed harsh new
trading rules that caused the volume of cross-border trade to drop by nearly
85 percent.[47] As a result, food, metal goods, tea, and sugar all grew increasingly expensive. According to an analysis by Owen Lattimore, the market

prices for these commodities increased by more than 8 times from 1940 to 1942 and escalated even more quickly in the subsequent years, increasing by 750 times by 1945.[48] Industrial-produced cloth in particular was scarce and according to witnesses, the cloth needed for Islamic burial shrouds became an extravagant luxury item for many in the province.[49] One provincial official wrote in a report to Governor Sheng following an investigation of the shortage in Dihua that "uniforms are all rotting away, you cannot even purchase cloth, it is truly an extremely difficult situation."[50]

If anything, things were worse for local producers. In a series of new trade regulations issued in 1943 by the Soviet Foreign Trade Committee, trade with Xinjiang in all goods with the exception of lamb skins and wool was expressly forbidden.[51] With an undeveloped transport network connecting the province to markets in China-proper, the closing of the Soviet-Xinjiang border ensured that local products piled up in markets around the province. In response, the prices for these goods dropped sharply, in a few cases as much as 90 percent.[52] The drying up of trade with the Soviet Union and the inability to access potential markets in China meant that local producers had no incentive to invest capital in herds or in agricultural production. A report from the Soviet consular officer in Dihua noted that in northern Xinjiang many local villages "did not produce any crops this year. According to some reports, only 20 to 30 percent of the total amount of land sown last year has been sown this year." In many cases, the report went on, former agriculturalists turned to hard labor in the region's coal mines to make ends meet.[53] Production in various industries declined significantly. In Turfan, once-vibrant cotton production dropped by half, the amount of wool produced in the province dropped significantly, and silk production, which had once been a mainstay of sideline production in rural southern Xinjiang, basically disappeared.[54]

The economic burdens helped create an atmosphere of tension within the province that Soviet officials actively sought to exploit. Throughout 1942, drawing upon the simmering unrest, the leaders of what came to be known by Chinese Communist Party historians as the "Three Districts Rebellion" (Sanqu Geming) embraced an anticolonial rhetoric that had been nurtured in the Soviet republics.[55] Leaders of the movement railed against Han ethnocultural domination of the province and pushed for a Turkic Muslim government that would rule a unified Xinjiang. "Our provincial government has stated the equality of the fourteen nationalities of the four million people of Xinjiang, and that the government would protect interests of religion, affirming it as one of the six great political principles," thundered one leader in a speech. Pointing to the star on the GMD flag that was said to represent the unity of China's peoples, he exclaimed, "this six-pointed star is a lie!"[56] A brochure written in Kazakh and seized in Tacheng in the north bitterly complains, "Our leaders have been eliminated and now the Han and their armies control the entire province." The pamphlet went on, "We cannot take this anymore. Let us initiate a glorious battle for freedom and equality."[57]

The growing unrest in the province prompted Chiang Kaishek to cashier Sheng Shicai in 1944. Republican officials hoped that removing Sheng, who was tapped to head the Republic's Ministry of Agriculture and Forestry in Chongqing, would reduce tensions and perhaps create a better relationship with the Soviet Union. Not long after his removal from office, however, a massive rebellion swept out of Xinjiang's western border regions. Recent scholarship and newly discovered archival materials reveal the centrality of the Soviet role not only in fomenting the unrest but also in materially supporting the uprising with weapons and training for disgruntled communities across northern Xinjiang.[58] As a consequence, when the uprising first began in the town of Gongha in the western stretches of Xinjiang province close to the Soviet border in November 1944, the rebels taking up arms against the local garrison were not merely an angry rabble armed with agricultural tools, but well-equipped soldiers with modern weapons, flags, and uniforms. After the occupation of nearby Ili in January 1945 by the Ili National Army, as the rebel forces were known, Soviet support became even more direct.[59]

Fearing an attack on the fabled oilfields of Dushanzi, two months after the beginning of the rebellion a contingent of Chinese oilfield workers were sent home. Not long after, in early 1945, the Ili National Army began its spring offensive in northern Xinjiang by launching an attack on Dushanzi. On April 19, General Zhu Shaoliang informed Chiang Kaishek that a rebellious military unit from Dushanzi made up of Uyghurs and Kazakhs attacked a Chinese cavalry unit on the road southeast of the oilfields. When the Chinese unit counterattacked, the Uyghurs and Kazakhs fled into the surrounding hills. Even more ominous for Zhu, however, was a smaller band of twenty "Soviet bandits" including two Soviet officers who were spreading rumors and threatening to attack the two companies of Chinese infantry stationed at Dushanzi. A several-month standoff was broken when the rebels, backed by Soviet soldiers and airplanes, closed in on the nearby town of Wusu. On September 6, little more than a week before the city fell, the remaining three hundred Chinese oilfield workers and technicians capped Dushanzi's oil wells and fled.[60] A few days later, the oilfields were "liberated" by the Ili National Army.

Chinese geologists and technicians laboring in the Bortala tungsten fields were caught completely off-guard by the uprising and, like their counterparts in Dushanzi, were quickly swept up in the violence. According to a message smuggled out in the winter of 1944, the team was trapped west of the Jinghe

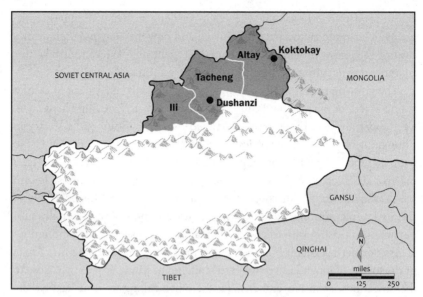

MAP 6.1 The three districts making up the East Turkestan Republic. Source: David Wang, "Nationalism or Power Struggle," in *Clouds over Tianshan: Essays on Social Disturbance in Xinjiang in the 1940s* (Copenhagen: NIAS, 1999), 36. Map by Debbie Newell.

River, cut off from government forces and largely on their own quickly after the initial uprising. The two units charged with defending the group were attacked on the road and the team was "blocked by ferocious bandits." With Ili and, by spring, much of northern Xinjiang in the hands of the rebel groups, the team found itself without food or supplies. While some in the group were successfully evacuated, others were less lucky. Of the fourteen engineers sent to the ore fields, nine were unaccounted for by the spring of 1945. With gaps in the archival record, the ultimate fate of the team is lost. In the end, the Xinjiang Tungsten Mine Engineering Office, which had been charged with uncovering the mineral wealth of this province, found itself not in the ore fields of northern Xinjiang, but stuck in the city of Lanzhou, the capital of Gansu province. As one member of the team wrote, "We fear that in the near future we will not be able to resume operations."[61]

In a series of victorious campaigns, the rebels extended direct control over the resource-rich border districts of Ili, Tacheng, and Altay. Finally, in September 1945, the Soviet Union ordered the Ili National Army to halt.[62] Rather than conquer the seven additional districts of Xinjiang, leaders of the movement consolidated control over this region and established the second East Turkestan Republic (ETR) (map 6.1). The separate administration of the three districts continued to exist in one form or another until 1949. There is not one simple reason for the Soviet Union's eagerness to underwrite armed rebellion in Xinjiang. Feelings of animosity toward Sheng Shicai for his betrayal and a desire for vengeance surely played some part in Stalin's calculation. A fear that the shift in orientation toward China would lead to the troubling prospect of American troops being stationed in Xinjiang, only a short march from Soviet territory, also unquestionably played a role in Stalin's reasoning. Yet the desire to gain access to the resource wealth at Bortala, Dushanzi, and Koktokay, which were not coincidentally located in the three districts of Xinjiang that made up the East Turkestan Republic, was surely an important element of the calculus.

Officials in the Chinese Republic firmly embraced this latter reason in their own assessments of the uprising. A GMD report argued that the impetus behind the Soviet patronage of the Ili National Army and later the East Turkestan Republic was a desire to gain access to the rich mineral wealth of the Altay in particular, noting that "the Soviet Union has coveted these resources for a long time." Another report argued that "for more than a year, desiring mining, the Soviets were upset that they could not do whatever they wanted and so they encouraged an attack on Altay."[63] For their part, American officials in the Central Intelligence Agency were later convinced (mistakenly) that the Soviet effort was centered around a desire to gain access to uranium ore in the resource-rich Altay range.[64]

It should not come as too much of a surprise that Chinese officials preferred to blame Soviet perfidy for the uprising rather than their own mismanagement of the province. But it seems fairly clear that the Soviet Union's ability to access lucrative tungsten, beryllium, petroleum, and tantalum along with other rare and lucrative minerals was indeed an important factor driving Soviet support for the movement. Indeed, well before the dust had settled in the province, Soviet planners reached out to officials in the ETR about signing a new agreement that would exchange loans for access to raw materials. Working with officials in the new regime, Soviet planners quickly dusted off old plans and mobilized mining labor and geologists to once again incorporate the province's rich ores into Soviet economic planning. For Soviet officials, the establishment of the ETR was an opportunity to ensure that the blueprints drawn up in the 1930s and early 1940s, as well as their substantial investment in resource extraction in the region, had not been wasted.

The newly established ETR, which like both Sheng Shicai and Chiang Kaishek before them intended to rely on resource production to pay off Soviet debts, quickly restarted operations. Shortly after the liberation of the oilfield, the government quickly issued a request for the former laborers at the site to return and aid the new government's efforts to produce oil. According to the memories of one man who answered the call, more than fifty workers returned, and the officials were able to recruit an additional hundred or so workers from the town of Ili. Headed by an Uzbek who was a former officer in the Ili National Army as well as a Russian assistant manager, the Dushanzi Oil Company quickly came back online and by 1947 had around three hundred workers on site.[65] The workers at the oilfield sought to refurbish the eleven capped wells with wooden and in some cases steel scaffolding, but in the end the operations were successful in restarting only four of the wells. These wells produced only around 4 or 5 tons of raw oil daily. For the four years between 1946 and 1949, the site produced a relatively meager 5,600 tons of raw oil. The petroleum was processed on site in a crude atmospheric distillation cauldron.[66]

Soviet technicians continued to aid local oil workers at Dushanzi. But the end of the threat to the Soviet Union's oil hub in the Caucasus helped reduce the importance of Xinjiang's petroleum for Soviet planners. Instead, their main focus in the late 1940s was on the tungsten wealth located in Bortala in western Xinjiang, as well high-value beryllium, lithium, and tantalum ores, located in the Altay Mountains in the northern stretches of the province. The result was a sustained Soviet investment in production, processing, and supporting infrastructure in these regions. Seeking to pinpoint important ore sites and build upon knowledge accumulated over the previous four decades, Soviet officials shipped the reports written by earlier Russian and Soviet expeditions to the teams charged with leading the extraction operations. Relying directly on these earlier reports, Soviet technicians, with the support of officials in the ETR, picked up right where they left off.[67]

According to Chinese reports, shortly after the uprising, Soviets reopened the ore fields at Bortala and the region's alluvial tungsten deposits were quickly being worked by more than 3,000 Kazakhs and Uyghurs. Less than a year later, the reports note that there were 10,000 workers on site and by 1947, 20,000. Soviet archives affirm the presence of a large production facility in the years following the founding of the ETR. These sources suggest, however, that the operation was not quite as large as Chinese intelligence reports implied. A Soviet report from 1946 notes that mineral mining operations in all of Xinjiang intended to hire a total number of slightly less than a thousand workers, though in fact by August of that year only 686 were actually employed on site. Of this number, 166 were Soviet citizens.[68] The population was significant enough that an official in the Soviet Ministry of Non-ferrous Metals called on the Ministry of Education to establish a seven-grade school in Xinjiang to educate the children of Soviet workers.[69]

Early Soviet geological expeditions had found that the ore fields around Koktokay in the Altay had large amounts of lithium, beryllium, and tantalum. In addition to their high value on global mineral markets, these rare minerals had important nuclear technology, rocketry, and other military applications. As a result, Soviet planners prioritized the development of Koktokay in the mid to late 1940s. At the beginning, these operations, which were led by the same Soviet work team leader who headed the group in the early 1940s, were said to employ around 600 workers.[70] Chinese reports, which were based on interrogations of former workers and intelligence reports, noted that production increased sharply in the late 1940s. The operations in the Altay Mountains were said to extract 825 *shijin* (around 400 kilograms) daily or 150 metric tons annually of beryllium, tungsten, and lithium ore; but with the import of advanced equipment from the Soviet Union, production spiked to 450 tons annually in 1946. By 1947, the operation was said to be producing 1,000 tons annually. Soviet sources on the operations are spotty, but they suggest that the operation, while not as large as Chinese claims, was a significant presence in the region. A planning report for extraction operations in the Altay for 1946 targets a total production of 200 tons of high-value lithium ore. There is little to suggest that the operations grew so significantly over the next year. But the enterprise, which exported all or nearly all of the ores to the Soviet Union via the Irtysh River, was a substantial presence in the Altay and played a critical role in Soviet planning.[71]

According to a report from former miners in the Altay who later fled into territory controlled by the Chinese government, the operation also boasted dormitories and offices, a repair shop, a power plant, a wireless station, and guards armed with machine guns.[72] An attack by Kazakh fighters supporting the Republic of China in 1946 drove off a large portion of their labor force and ended in the shuttering of two of the ore fields. But the production of ores, most notably beryllium, which fetched prices more than 35 times higher than tungsten on global metal markets, continued unabated.[73] Chinese reports published in the 1950s point out that at just one of three sites around Koktokay, the Soviet Union extracted nearly 39 tons of beryl ore in 1946. That number grew to nearly 170 in 1947 and 250 by 1949.[74] The finished ore was prepared for transport by Soviet technicians, who packaged it on barges on the Irtysh River at Burqin and shipped it directly into Soviet territory.[75]

Chinese officials were confident that the scope of Soviet illegal mining in the province was far greater than the reports they received from defectors and refugees from the ore-rich regions in the north suggested. As the author of one report, which was based on the interrogation of two miners who had fled the operation in the Altay, wrote bitterly, "This does not reflect the complete picture of Soviet unauthorized mining."[76] Even after a Soviet-mediated cease-fire and the official founding of a new coalition government in the province in June 1946 (the first governor of which was a Han Chinese official tapped by the Republic of China), the separation of the three districts along the Soviet border from the Republic of China was largely maintained. The ETR remained an ore-rich satellite of its Soviet neighbor, and, like Sheng Shicai and Jin Shuren, the regime chose to pay its debts through the granting of mining rights. Chinese leaders continually filed formal protests to Soviet diplomatic personnel about the unauthorized extraction and transport of mineral wealth that, they claimed, rightfully belonged to the Chinese state. Their protests, however, were met with silence, and Soviet-financed teams continued to extract, process, and transport these lucrative minerals back to the Soviet Union.

In the end, the rebellion and the founding of the ETR allowed for the consolidation of Soviet plans and the underscoring of a comprehensive infrastructural network in the region that facilitated the Soviet Union's unfettered extraction of Xinjiang's mineral wealth. For their part, Chinese officials sought to make the best of a bad situation. From 1944 to 1949, torn away from the richest and best-documented resources in the province, officials in China's Ministry of Economic Affairs and the National Resources Commission surveyed the minerals of arid eastern and southern Xinjiang, discovering several potential oilfields in the Tarim Basin region of southern Xinjiang.[77] Additional surveys conducted by geological teams from the Academia Sinica and the Xinjiang Geological Survey sought to uncover other potential ore sites. But the lack of sufficient transportation infrastructure, the high cost of transport, and new fiscal priorities in the postwar period ensured that these discoveries were not prioritized for investment.

### Back to the Negotiating Table

The loss of Xinjiang's most ore-rich regions forced Chinese officials to recalculate the cost of playing the hard line in the 1943 negotiations with the Soviet Union. Faced with the complete loss of Xinjiang's three districts and powerless to militarily resist, they felt they had no choice but to reopen negotiations in order to stake some semblance of a claim to the region's mineral wealth. An agreement with the Soviet Union would grant the Republic, which was already planning for a glorious postwar future, access to the raw materials it so desperately needed to transform itself into a powerful modern state. As early as January 19, 1945, high-ranking Chinese government officials submitted an outline plan to the Soviet ambassador laying out the framework for a future trade and economic cooperation agreement between China and the Soviet Union that was focused on Xinjiang province. The eight-part plan facilitated cross-border trade through loosened restrictions and also proposed the establishment of a joint Sino-Soviet oil, tin, and tungsten operation in the province.[78] The 1945 proposal offered substantial concessions, and in nearly every case accepted the Soviet negotiating position from the failed 1943 talks over joint oil operations. Nevertheless, Soviet officials rejected the agreement out of hand, explaining that the ongoing unrest in Xinjiang made negotiations impossible.

In June 1946, the Soviet Union mediated the establishment of a new "coalition government" in Xinjiang that included not only the seven China-controlled districts, but also the three border districts of the ETR. The new coalition government was headed by Zhang Zhizhong, a Han Chinese GMD official who also served as the special representative of China's Ministry of Foreign Affairs in Xinjiang. Despite the supposed unity of the province, the new government exerted little to no control over the territory controlled by the ETR or its resource wealth. Rather, ETR officials maintained their close relationship with the Soviet Union. Hoping to gain clearer access to Xinjiang's most productive regions, Zhang spearheaded the effort to reach an agreement with the Soviet Union. His main challenge was in convincing not only Soviet officials, but also anticommunist leaders in the central government, who were ideologically opposed to the idea of negotiating with the Soviet Union, to come to the table. In an August 1946 telegram to Chiang Kaishek, Zhang laid out an argument for an agreement with the Soviet Union that seems to have been tailor-made to tug at the patriotism of reluctant officials. He wrote that Xinjiang's "oil and metal mines are all in the three districts of Ili, Tacheng, and the Altay, regions that are outside of our government's control. I deeply fear that those illegally holding the regions will sign agreements with foreigners." Zhang went on to say, "In order to protect our nation's sovereignty, the central government must begin to negotiate with the Soviets straightaway."[79]

Zhang proposed expanding the scope of the agreement beyond simply focusing on tungsten, tin, and oil to all subterranean resources in order to gain far greater support in extractive operations. His suggestions were angrily rejected by anticommunist figures, including the Minister of Economic Affairs Weng Wenhao and the Minister of Foreign Affairs Wang Shijie. The latter fulminated, "If this is officially ratified then it will allow the Soviets to form even closer links at the local level, which will make control even more difficult."[80] Chiang Kaishek agreed with Wang and strongly critiqued Zhang's proposal, writing that "all of Xinjiang's mineral resources cannot be included so haphazardly into an agreement like this."[81]

Yet Zhang's larger arguments about mineral sovereignty proved convincing. As Wang conceded in a 1946 memo, "I think that the only resolution of this problem [of Soviet agents mining in the territory of the ETR] is to quickly negotiate an agreement over economic cooperation and reach an agreement at the earliest date possible."[82] After more than three months of hammering out the details of a proposed agreement, in November 1946, the Chinese negotiators forwarded a new proposal to the Soviet consul in Dihua. The proposal called for the establishment of oil, tungsten, and tin mining operations that were to be jointly owned at 50 percent each. Management would be split, though Chinese would be in the highest positions, and shared purchases of equipment and material would be mutually decided upon.[83]

Zhang's success in convincing anticommunist Chinese officials to come to the table was not matched by a success in negotiations with the Soviet Union. While Xinjiang was largely peaceful, geopolitical tensions resulting from the outbreak of China's civil war between the GMD and Mao Zedong's Chinese Communist Party (CCP) gave Soviet officials little incentive to open negotiations. Indeed, it was only the crumbling of GMD armies in central China beginning in the latter half of 1948 that prompted the Soviets to open negotiations over the establishment of a joint extraction enterprise. For their part, Soviet officials hoped that signing an agreement with the GMD government would help them institutionalize their role in Xinjiang and create an advantageous starting point for future negotiations with the CCP. In a December 1948 memo to Stalin, one high-ranking Soviet official argued that "renewing trade and economic cooperation will help advance and strengthen our position in Xinjiang." It will not only promote cross-border trade, he said, but it will also "legalize the Soviet Ministries of Metallurgy and Industry metal mining operations in the Altay and Ili border regions."[84]

Pressed by an unenthusiastic government that was increasingly distracted by its waning fortunes in its war against the CCP on one side and a Soviet side eager to extract concessions on the other, GMD negotiators were squeezed into a difficult spot throughout the summer of 1949. As the negotiating team sweated over an agreement that would establish equally held joint oil extraction and nonferrous mineral mining enterprises as well as a management structure that rotated among Chinese and Soviet leaders, the GMD government largely cut off communications with the negotiating team. Finally reaching an agreement with their Soviet counterparts in August, the Chinese negotiating team desperately sought authorization from their superiors. Officials in the doomed government who were already preparing their flight to Taiwan instead sent a tersely worded cable condemning Soviet perfidy in aiding the CCP and insisted that they would refuse to sign off on any agreement.[85] With that, the negotiating team left Xinjiang, and any hope that a China-based regime would be able to profit from the region's resource wealth would wait until after the victory of the CCP later that year.

A highly suspicious plane crash killed five leaders of the ETR in August 1949. This, combined with Stalin's willingness to trade Soviet control of Outer Mongolia for Chinese control of Xinjiang, meant that when Mao Zedong stepped atop the rostrum at Tiananmen Square to declare the formation of the People's Republic of China on October 1, 1949, the new regime was able to exert its claim to all of Xinjiang's mineral-rich regions. While 1949 ended the autonomy of the three districts of Ili, Tacheng, and Altay, officials in the newly established People's Republic of China understood that, like their predecessors in the former Republic, if they wanted to reap the resource wealth of northern Xinjiang that had been laid bare by nearly five decades of surveys and investments, they first needed to reach an agreement with the Soviet Union. Their powerful rhetoric about self-sufficiency and Mao's rhetorically powerful assertion that China had now "stood up" notwithstanding, the CCP simply lacked the capital, the technical expertise, and the access to distant transport networks to be able to go it alone in border regions like Xinjiang.

CCP officials grappled with many of the same financial problems and investment priorities that had precluded the Republic of China from heavily investing in the development of peripheral regions. The presence of the Soviet Union's strong, integrated Central Asian transport network, the large numbers of skilled Soviet technicians, and the high-tech machinery already in operation at Xinjiang's most lucrative ore fields served as an institutional and infrastructural foundation for resource extraction that CCP leaders were eager to build atop. As a consequence, these leaders, like their predecessors in the Republic, carefully followed Soviet-created developmental blueprints and actively solicited Soviet investment in mineral extraction enterprises in Xinjiang.[86]

Shortly after coming to power, the new regime obtained a copy of the unratified August 1949 draft agreement that been painfully hammered out by the GMD negotiating team in Xinjiang but which was never ratified by the central government. CCP officials sought to use the draft as a template for their own agreement over the cooperative extraction of minerals. In a January 1950 telegram to Mao Zedong, the vice chairman of the central government Liu Shaoqi argued that the government should "conclude an agreement with the Soviet government that is in large part exactly the same as this draft, in order to facilitate the use of Soviet capital to exploit Xinjiang's natural resources and develop Xinjiang's production."[87] Mao concurred, and the agreement, which laid out the foundation for the establishment of two joint-stock companies, one charged with drilling and refining oil (the Sino-Soviet Oil

Company) and the other with extracting tungsten, beryllium, and other rare minerals (the Sino-Soviet Non-ferrous and Rare Metals Company), was officially ratified by both sides on March 27, 1950. Operations officially got under way the next year.

Fears of Soviet intentions in Xinjiang that had helped shape the schizophrenic policy of the Republic of China toward Soviet investments in the early 1940s continued into the early People's Republic. Despite the CCP leadership's ideological kinship with the Soviet Union, the news of the signing of the joint agreement unleashed a wave of protests, as many people feared that the move signified a new form of colonial enterprise in western China.[88] As far as CCP officials were concerned, however, the rationale for soliciting help from the Soviet Union was clear: the new government was not capable of investing the amounts of funds needed to extract Xinjiang's minerals for the good of the new nation. As one 1950 geological report titled "Xinjiang Is China's Oil Depot" declared, the establishment of the two Soviet enterprises "is glad tidings for the people of Xinjiang and also is glad tidings for the people of China," as they would be critical in the task of "establishing the modernization of industry."[89] Similarly, the party's mouthpiece the People's Daily declared in an April 21, 1950, report justifying and explaining the establishment of the two enterprises that "Xinjiang has ample natural resources that urgently need to be developed but because the region is far and the transport difficult, we have difficulty opening this province."[90]

Under the terms of the Sino-Soviet agreement, China's capital investment in this distant province was minimal, as the Chinese side was charged only with providing the land upon which the extraction enterprise and refineries were situated as well as constructing the buildings needed for work and housing. The Soviets, on the other hand, were responsible for providing drilling machinery and refining equipment, as well as the liquid capital for the enterprise.[91] In the end, backed by substantial amount of Soviet capital and supported by legions of Soviet geologists, technicians, and economic planners, it should come as no surprise that the two enterprises closely followed Soviet mineral extraction blueprints. Going beyond blueprints, they also continued to draw upon Soviet equipment, the labor of Soviet technicians, and Soviet infrastructure. In addition, they also continued to draw on Soviet markets, as the vast majority of nonferrous minerals were shipped directly to the Soviet Union.

Geological operations for the nonferrous metals company hewed close to the framework outlined by earlier generations of Soviet geologists. The desires by the Chinese side to concentrate on resources that could be easily extracted and transported to the Soviet Union to pay back the Soviet loans taken on shortly after the founding of the People's Republic helped ensure a focus on the high-value beryllium, lithium, and tantalum-niobium ores demanded by Soviet industries. Production at the tungsten fields in Bortala had largely collapsed by the time of the founding of the People's Republic. The combination of an aggressive mining campaign in the first half of the 1940s that tapped out the region's veins, along with a boom in Soviet domestic tungsten production in the late 1940s and early 1950s, prompted a shift in priorities. This shift was reflected in the fact that regional work teams consistently drilled far fewer meters of holes and dug fewer meters of pits annually than any other teams throughout the early 1950s.[92] Efforts in the region collapsed completely in the middle years of the decade, and by the late 1950s the tungsten field at Bortala, which had been battled over by various parties in the mid-1940s, was largely abandoned.[93] Instead, the majority of the nonferrous metals company's activities were centered in the far north, as 60 percent of test drilling was done in the Altay in 1952, and 57 percent in 1954, the last year of the company.[94] Operations at Koktokay in particular expanded drastically after 1953 and the suppression of a series of Kazakh "bandit" uprisings that threatened CCP hold over the border region.[95]

Chinese industries lacked the technical capacity and demand for the non-ferrous metal ores produced in Xinjiang in the early 1950s. As a result, the company's activities were focused almost exclusively on extraction rather than processing. Most of the ores produced were raw and unprocessed: after ore-laden rock was chipped out of the ground at places like Koktokay, they were simply sorted on large sorting tables by workers armed with little more than hammers and a careful eye. From here, most were driven by truck to the port of Burqin on the Irtysh River and then shipped directly to the Soviet Union. Even if they had the technical capacity to use the finished ores, Chinese officials lacked the infrastructural network binding northern Xinjiang to industrial centers in China-proper. By contrast, Soviet industries demanded large amounts of lithium, beryllium, tantalum, and other ores and had a powerful transportation infrastructure that ensured their smooth transport. To facilitate the outflow and supplement the riverine shipments on the Irtysh, which could operate only for the half of the year when the water was high, economic planners undertook improvements to the highway link connecting the nonferrous metal mines at Koktokay to the Soviet border crossing at Jeminay in 1953.[96] From 1950 to 1954, the nonferrous metal operation shipped everything it produced to the Soviet Union: 11,368 tons of beryllium, 4,242 tons of lithium, and 15 tons of niobium and tantalum. The ores were shipped to Soviet factories at Ust-Kamenogorsk (modern-day Osekemen in Kazakhstan), Novosibirsk, and even as far as Leningrad (St. Petersburg).[97]

In the Sino-Soviet oil enterprise, the eighty-two Soviet geologists and oil engineers recruited to help their Chinese counterparts focused their efforts on known oilfields pinpointed by their predecessors. Both leaders of the Sino-Soviet Oil Company's geological department were Soviet citizens, as were six of the eight geological team leaders connected to the operation. In a report drawn up in 1950 by the Soviet Ministry of Oil expressly for the company, twenty-five potential oil sites were targeted for greater exploration. Of these, fourteen were in northern Xinjiang in the Zungharian basin, a region extensively surveyed by Soviet geologists in the previous decade, eight were near Kucha, just south of the Tianshan mountains in central Xinjiang, and only three were near Kashgar in the far south.[98] After some initial small-scale test drilling, all of the operations south of the Tianshan were shuttered in 1953, when orders from Beijing declared that before the establishment of a railroad connecting Dihua to China's rail network, "the focus of [geological] exploration should be on northern Xinjiang." The report went on to emphatically state that in order to hold down the cost of transporting raw petroleum, "production should be restricted to areas with existing [refining] equipment."[99] Test drilling was thus refocused on established ore sites like Dushanzi, where the company drilled seventy-one test wells in the 110–square kilometer area for a total depth of 75,000 meters. By contrast, in the far south, a relatively paltry eleven wells were dug between 1951 and 1954.[100]

The Soviet oil extraction and production infrastructure laid in Xinjiang in the 1930s and 1940s served to shape CCP policy in the region. The refining operation in particular, which was overseen by two Soviet managers, served as the point around which Xinjiang's oil industry rotated. The Dushanzi refinery was one of only a handful of modern, highly mechanized refineries in all of China. In addition to the roads and rails binding the province to the Soviet Union, the modern refining equipment, much of which had been originally sited and placed by Soviet engineers and technicians in the pre-1949 period, continued to shape the outlines of extraction operations and served to lock in a pattern of production centered around Dushanzi. In 1952, new refinery equipment increased the refining capacity of the operation by six times and the addition of two new refinery tanks increased the total capacity still further.

By the early 1950s, Soviet planners no longer sought access to Xinjiang's oil wealth. The region's oil, which played a critical role in Soviet wartime planning, was not prioritized in the postwar period. Instead, the petroleum produced at Dushanzi in the 1950s was primarily distributed in Xinjiang itself in order to reduce petroleum imports into the region. It might seem curious that the Soviet Union was willing to invest its resources in oil exploitation in Dushanzi when it appeared to be gaining little from the operation. On the one hand, Soviet support for the operation was part of its larger effort to provide critical technical assistance to the People's Republic through the provision of "experts" to Chinese work units. On the other, it seems reasonable that the ongoing Soviet assistance in the oilfields at Dushanzi was deemed necessary by Soviet officials to ensure a continued flow of critical nonferrous metals that were not available in large quantities in Soviet territory. The fiscal commitment to nonferrous ore extraction grew from 6.8 million rubles in 1951 to 17 million in 1952 and exploded to 31.6 million in 1953 and 40.8 million in 1954. The demand for these essential minerals made the retention of the two extraction operations worthwhile for Soviet planners.

Big plans to drastically expand test drilling operations and continue capital investments were already on the table in 1953. Yet for reasons that remain unclear, despite having a thirty-year time frame on the initial agreement, in 1954 Chinese and Soviet leaders announced the imminent closure of the two joint operations. On January 1, 1955, two new, wholly Chinese owned enterprises opened in their place. The decision to close the Sino-Soviet Oil Company and the Sino-Soviet Non-ferrous and Rare Metals Company was said to be mutual. Despite growing tensions between Mao and Stalin's successor Nikita Khrushchev as well as Chinese suspicions about Soviet intentions in Xinjiang, officials held a series of meetings in December 1954 that praised Sino-Soviet cooperation and thanked Soviet technicians for their selfless sacrifice. Publicly, CCP officials explained that the enterprise had served its purpose in preparing geologists, engineers, and planners to take over mineral extraction at Xinjiang's ore fields.[101] As the People's Daily put it, Chinese officials had now "gained sufficient experience to administer [operations] on their own."[102]

Despite the bootstrapping rhetoric, the People's Republic continued to draw heavily on Soviet assistance even after the closing of the two Sino-Soviet companies. On December 24, 1954, mere days before the shuttering of the enterprise, Premier Zhou Enlai sent a memo to various central government ministries desperately seeking a way to keep paying the salaries of those Soviet geologists employed by the oil company whether or not an official agreement to do so was reached with the Soviet Union.[103] In addition, even after the reestablishment of the Sino-Soviet Rare and Non-ferrous Metals Company as a wholly Chinese-owned company in 1955, 156 Soviets continued to serve as advisors and technicians.[104] Work units throughout the province continued to employ Soviet experts during this period, but the desire to institutionalize ongoing Sino-Soviet cooperation prompted the signing of an agreement formalizing Soviet assistance in the exploration of Xinjiang. Indeed, on June 30, 1955, Chinese and Soviet officials signed the number 6004 agreement, which created the framework for ongoing Sino-Soviet cooperation. According to a Chinese Ministry of Geology report, the agreement "allocated experts from the Soviet Geology and Mineral Protection Offices who will employ techniques and skills used by Soviet geological teams."[105]

In addition to technical assistance, the Soviet Union continued to serve as the central transport link for both companies. Nearly all of the equipment for both was purchased in the Soviet Union and shipped by Soviet trucks to Dushanzi and to the nonferrous ore fields in Koktokay by barge. In 1955, officials in the nonferrous metals company stationed in the Altay mountains took in over seventeen million yuan worth of equipment from the Soviet Union.[106] This steady stream of equipment only began to decline in 1957 with the uptick in Sino-Soviet tensions. In addition, in 1955 nearly 100 percent of the minerals produced in the Altay were packed onto barges and shipped into the Soviet Union as repayment for Soviet loans to China issued in 1950.[107] The Soviet Union's centrality as a destination for raw materials and as the source of critical equipment was reflected in the signing of a Sino-Soviet agreement in 1954 that laid the institutional foundation for a new rail line that would extend to the Soviet border at Alashankou, just north of Bortala in central Xinjiang. The line, beginning in Xinjiang's capital, would continue onto Aktogay in Soviet Kazakhstan, a transport hub on the Turk-Sib rail line. Planners sought to time the construction of the so-called friendship railroad with the completion of the Lanzhou-Xinjiang line, for which construction began in 1952.

∗

In 1954, a reporter touring the Dushanzi oil operation found himself awed by the massive enterprise tucked away in the northern foothills of the Tianshan Mountains. During the day, sunlight dazzled off the refinery and drilling equipment while at night, "the surrounding hillsides were awash in electric light, gleaming like stars in the sky."[108] Envisioning the integrated site from above, the reporter compared its shape to a massive poplar tree, as a long straight trunk road connected its various branches: office buildings, workshops, refining operations, and dormitories. Even if we take the visitor's effusive reporting for the sunny boosterism that it was, for those making the bumpy ride up from the provincial capital, Dushanzi must have been a sight to behold in the early 1950s. By 1954, it boasted cutting-edge refinery equipment imported from the Soviet Union, an army of drill rigs capable of reaching thousands of meters below the earth, and a massive labor force of more than 5,500 spilling out across the steppe. Workers there had access to hospitals, schools, libraries, and even a movie theater. While Dushanzi was larger than the province's other extraction enterprises, it was not unique.

Dushanzi and the other resource extraction operations were the manifestation of patterns of economic development and state investment that had been created by Soviet economic planners and assiduously followed by their GMD and later CCP successors. Each regime, eager to reap Xinjiang's minerals without investing heavily in new surveys and new extractive and processing operations, lay its own layers of investment and interest atop the layers laid by their predecessors. The growing attention by state planners in the 1950s to resource production in Xinjiang served to further institutionalize and set patterns of state investment and interest in plaster if not in stone. The continuities speak to the power of the layers of state investment and the strength of a path dependency created and institutionalized through infrastructural development. It also speaks to the weakness of the Chinese state in Xinjiang that existed not only in the Republican period, but also in the early People's Republic. In the end, both regimes were unwilling to invest their precious resources into the integration of this peripheral region. Content in having simply staked a territorial claim, CCP officials in Beijing were unwilling to shoulder the high cost of a surveying and infrastructural development campaign in Xinjiang that would fundamentally reshape the economic development blueprints drawn up by Soviet planners in the 1930s and 1940s.

The layering of decades' worth of sustained Soviet investment in transportation infrastructure, extraction enterprises, and centralized government planning helped create and reinforce enduring institutions established to channel lucrative minerals back toward Soviet markets and industry. But not only did the growing mineral extraction sites in northern Xinjiang represent Soviet blueprints come to life. They also were the seeds of CCP institutional control in the region. While the party apparatus was centered in the provincial population centers, most notably Dihua, or Urumqi as it was renamed in 1954, these resource sites came to serve as nodes of state power in an institutional network placed over the province. As government campaigns to increase industrial production grew in the late 1950s, state investment and attention at places like Dushanzi or the ore fields in the Altay grew substantially. This growth, which will be the focus of the next chapter, helped formalize the Soviet-inspired blueprints as new company towns popped up at these sites around the province and helped funnel state power down to largely unpopulated but resource-rich regions in northern Xinjiang that had been previously prioritized for development by Soviet planners.

# Petroleum, Lithium, and the Foundations
# of Chinese State Power

Echoing the thoughts of provincial officials stretching back into the late Qing period, in 1954 the Xinjiang party secretary Wang Enmao noted that "there is very little of anything above ground in Xinjiang—many areas are simply barren land—but buried below ground is a limitless supply of treasures."[1] The capital expenditures made by the Chinese government in the mid-1950s to exploit, process, and transport these so-called treasures—in this case oil and nonferrous minerals—served to shape the contours of modern Xinjiang. These expenditures, concentrated at isolated sites in northern Xinjiang prioritized and developed first by Soviet planners, helped draw in large populations of Han settlers, supporting industries, transportation infrastructure, and new institutions of state power that served to bind the region to China.

Chinese Communist Party planners in the 1950s were focused on the development of China's heavy industry sector. As Zhou Enlai explained in 1953, "First, we must concentrate [our energies] on developing heavy industry in order to establish a foundation for national industrialization and national defense modernization."[2] Relying on a "big push" development strategy, CCP planners allocated substantial amounts of capital to industrial enterprises.[3] The problem, however, was that in many cases, due to insufficient domestic resources and an ongoing international trade embargo, heavy industry was inhibited by a lack of key raw materials. In a report presented at a June 1955 meeting of the party's Central Committee, the vice chairman of the National Planning Commission, Bo Yibo, expressed his frustration with the slow pace of raw material production: "The coal, electricity, and oil supply is strained; production amounts in the steel, nonferrous metal, basic chemistry, and construction material industries are insufficient, the variety is limited, and the quality is not high."[4]

Seeking to alleviate the shortages, central government planners sought to increase production at domestic ore and oil fields. In the early 1950s they focused their efforts primarily on sites in Manchuria. After the 1931 Mukden incident and the founding of the puppet state of Manchukuo, Japanese planners lavished substantial amounts of investment in infrastructural development, surveys, and extraction operations in the region. They uncovered several areas that remained productive into the postwar period, including, most notably, the shale oil field at Fushun, which itself attracted a substantial amount of interest from CCP state planners.[5] But Fushun and other sites in Manchuria were not as productive as CCP officials were hoping for and shale oil was a less efficient fuel source and more expensive to produce than crude. As a result, geologists and surveyors blanketed China in the mid-1950s in an effort to resolve the ongoing resource bottlenecks that were inhibiting industrialization.[6] In Xinjiang, economic planners looked to the oilfields and nonferrous ore sites that had been uncovered by Russian and Soviet geologists, worked by jointly owned Soviet-Xinjiang enterprises, and finally exploited by the Sino-Soviet joint operations in the first half of the 1950s. Two sites in particular were the focus of Chinese state planners in Xinjiang in the mid-1950s: the oilfield centered around Dushanzi in the northern foothills of the Tianshan Mountain range and the nonferrous mineral site at Koktokay, located deep in Xinjiang's far northern Altay Mountains. Both sites had been extensively surveyed and developed by Russian, Soviet, and provincial leaders throughout the twentieth century, and in turn soaked up the bulk of Chinese state capital and attention in Xinjiang in the 1950s. Even Mao's Great Leap Forward (1958–1961), which appeared poised to expand Xinjiang's resource map, proved unable to shake the centrality of these two sites in the larger economic development plans for the region.

On some level, this investment in resource extraction was a reversal of the tight-fisted hands-off border policy embraced by China-based regimes stretching back to the late nineteenth century. In the 1950s, the desire to gain access to Xinjiang's resources was backed up with real money, as planners aggressively pursued resources at Koktokay and Dushanzi. The concentration of capital and interest into the discrete resource-rich pockets of Dushanzi and Koktokay helped shape long-term patterns of investment, settlement, and institutionalization. In the end, the institutions of Chinese state power in Xinjiang (which was renamed the Xinjiang Uyghur Autonomous Region in 1955) were laid in the 1950s atop the foundation of the resource extraction industry.

In Xinjiang, the multilayered apparatus needed to extract, refine, and transport petroleum as well as the network of connections needed to protect, support, and develop nonferrous ore fields shaped patterns of state spending, institutional development, and demographic change in Xinjiang. The desire to extract resources, bind these resources to markets in China-proper, import populations of Han Chinese laborers, and exert greater control over populations and resource-rich territory through the development of institutions of state power helped reinforce state power and authority in the region. The role of capital investments and industrial priorities in shaping border policy in the early PRC has been largely overlooked in favor of a narrative focused on state-sponsored agricultural reclamation and the efforts of the Xinjiang Production and Construction Corps (Xinjiang Shengchan Jianshe Bingtuan, or XPCC). In fact, with their largely Han populations, coercive apparatus, and substantial material presence, the resource production sites at Dushanzi and Koktokay, rather than the XPCC farms, served as the main nodes of Chinese power and institutional authority, from which leaders in Beijing extended their control over the resource-rich north. Sitting at the center of institutional and infrastructural networks, these sites should be viewed as outposts of the party state that have shaped the long-term economic, political, and social topography of this border province.

### Setting the Patterns of State Investment in Northern Xinjiang

Heavily influenced by the Soviet Union, the development models of CCP party planners in the early and mid-1950s focused on capital investments in heavy industry and raw material production. As a result, the period was witness to substantial increases in state capital spending, with spikes in 1953 and 1956 that drove capital investments as a percentage of GDP above 25 percent.[7] Yet the financial situation in the early PRC remained unstable and the list of spending priorities was long. As a result, government planners were forced to make specific choices about where exactly their resources should be invested. In Xinjiang, the weight of the layers of surveys, investment, and transportation infrastructure laid over the oilfield at Dushanzi and the nonferrous metal mine at Koktokay ensured that the planners, who were eager to quickly and inexpensively ramp up production, continued to follow the Soviet-derived planning blueprints for the region.

Cut off from global oil markets, CCP planners in the 1950s were particularly focused on recovering new domestic sources of petroleum. Frustrated with a long-standing trope among geologists about China's supposed "oil poverty," state planners made the discovery of new productive oilfields a top priority.[8] In Xinjiang, geologists pored back over old surveys and planning reports and identified a handful of potential new oilfields in relatively close proximity to the refining operation. There was a considerable amount of de-

FIGURE 7.1 The Number One Well at Karamay. Today the well is commemorated in a public park beneath a work of public art, titled "Large Oil Bubble" (Dayoupao). Photo by author.

bate among various geologists and surveyors about where to tap the oilfield that sprawled beneath north-central Xinjiang—whether it was in the foothills of the Tianshan or farther north in the Zungharian Basin. Earlier surveys pointed them toward a site 150 miles north of Dushanzi at Coal Tar Mountain (Heiyoushan). That Coal Tar Mountain had substantial amounts of oil was no secret. The field was one of twenty-five prioritized for development in the 1950 planning document produced by the Soviet Ministry of Oil for the Sino-Soviet Oil Company (see chapter 6) and, over the life of the company, a series of test wells revealed the presence of oil, including gushers at the relatively shallow depth of around five hundred meters at three different wells in 1951 alone.[9] Despite this evidence that the region was a promising oilfield, the complexity of the site's underlying geology had long given geologists and oil engineers pause. But new surveys and new optimism following the establishment of the new wholly China-owned Xinjiang Oil Company in 1955 prompted a return to Coal Tar Mountain.[10]

In early January 1955, geologists in the company wrote a report for the upcoming meeting of the Ministry of Geology's Oil Surveying Work Committee that called for a greater focus on the field. At the first annual meeting of the national Oil Surveying Work Committee, which met on January 20, 1955, in Beijing, high-ranking officials heavily touted Xinjiang's oilfields and Coal Tar Mountain in particular.[11] Convinced of the field's potential, government officials authorized the expansion of drilling at the field's Number One Well (figure 7.1). Drilling began in July, and on October 30, a sizable geyser bloomed over the arid landscape, producing seven tons of raw oil the first day and eight tons the next.[12] Reveling in their discovery, one Chinese member of the drilling team described the gusher as having turned the sky an auspicious shade of red that reminded him of "the rising sun emerging in all of its splendor."[13]

In a report published the next year, the former geologist of the Republic of China (who had surveyed Dushanzi in 1942; see chapter 6) and current member of the PRC's Ministry of Geology Surveying Committee, Huang Jiqing, insisted that the field on the northern side of the Zungharian basin was the most oil-rich spot in the northwest. He argued, "We should strengthen oil surveying work in the region of Coal Tar Mountain–Wu'erhe (the latter is around one hundred kilometers northeast of Coal Tar Mountain)."[14] A growing consensus among the geological community and economic planners prompted an orientation of extraction activities toward Coal Tar Mountain and away from Dushanzi. A report from Li Jukui, the head of the Oil Industry Office in Beijing, which was based on a tour he took of the site shortly after the gusher and which was submitted to high-ranking party members Chen Yun, Li Fuchun, and Bo Yibo, trumpeted the new discovery: "This proves that the large area from Dushanzi to Coal Tar Mountain is a desirable area where oil accumulates."[15]

Hoping to maximize production to meet the demands for oil, state economic planners chose to concentrate their efforts on uncovering highly productive new oil wells in the vicinity of Coal Tar Mountain. The strategy, which was coined "cast a larger net and catch bigger fish" by Kang Shi'en, vice chair of China's Oil Industry Office, called for the laying of a thick net of prospecting wells across the region to pinpoint the most productive potential wells. By May 1956, teams in the area (which was officially renamed Karamay, or Kelamayi in Chinese, that same month, the name being Uyghur for "coal tar"), had already drilled nineteen new test wells, nine of which were producing oil. By the end of the year, drilling teams had completed an impressive twenty-nine that produced more than 16,000 tons of raw oil, an amount making up one-third of the province's total production (see table 7.1). The next year, production at Karamay increased to over 70,000 tons.[16] As one account noted in the summer of 1956, oil derricks were "popping up like spring bamboo shoots after the rain."[17] State planners focused on the Zungharian basin oil corridor stretching from the Dushanzi refinery north to Karamay and northeast to the perceived edge of the oilfield at Wu'erhe.

Rather than undertaking the expensive and difficult task of relocating refinery equipment at Dushanzi 150 miles north to the new wells, officials chose to simply retain the equipment and built highway and pipeline connections binding the Karamay extraction site to the refinery. The result was the strengthening

TABLE 7.1. Oil production at Karamay

| | Production of crude (in thousands of tons) | Percentage of Xinjiang's total crude oil production |
|------|------|------|
| 1956 | 16.4 | 4 |
| 1957 | 70.2 | 74 |
| 1958 | 333.8 | 93 |
| 1959 | 961.1 | 98 |
| 1960 | 1,636.7 | 96 |

Source: Xinjiang Weiwu'er zizhiqu difangzhi bianzuan weiyuanhui, ed., *Xinjiang tongzhi: shiyou gongye* (vol. 40) (Urumqi: Xinjiang Renmin Chubanshe, 1999), 234.

of the integrated oil hub (Mitchell's so-called oil apparatus) centered around the refinery at Dushanzi.[18] By 1956, Dushanzi boasted a thermal cracker to produce high-octane fuels, a petroleum coking oven, and a bitumen-oxidizing operation for producing asphalt. As raw oil produced in Karamay increased, so did the operations at Dushanzi. In 1956, the refining operation had a total capacity of 70,000 tons, an amount that was expanded to 200,000 tons in 1957 and a second expansion the following year further expanded capacity to 500,000 tons.[19] At Karamay, officials developed a new paved highway that connected the oilfield to refinery operations, as well as to Xinjiang's main east-west trunk road. The highway received an ongoing series of upgrades throughout the 1950s. Making a nod to the role of roads and infrastructure in pacifying and integrating this border region, the highway was described in an October 1955 article in the *People's Daily* as a "sharp sword stabbing straight into the Zungharian basin."[20]

After the gusher later that month, total traffic on the road escalated to more than two hundred trucks per day, a number that quickly increased to well over five hundred, as machinery, food, piping, fresh water, and equipment were hurriedly shipped north to keep pace with the discovery of new oil wells around Karamay.[21] In 1958, hoping to further strengthen state control over oil and eliminate potential bottlenecks in the provision of raw crude to Dushanzi, technicians imported seamless steel piping from the Soviet Union and used it to connect the refinery to the oilfields at Karamay. Engineers completed the pipeline in May, and by December, five pumping stations arranged along its length enabled the flow of 530,000 tons of oil annually.[22]

Desperate to uncover oilfields capable of meeting domestic needs, state plans for Xinjiang in the mid-1950s remained focused on petroleum production. But the vast quantities of beryllium, lithium, and tantalum-niobium ores uncovered in the previous four decades also attracted substantial amounts

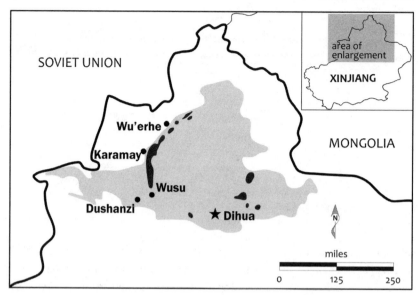

MAP 7.1 Northern Xinjiang's oil fields. Source: Xinjiang Weiwu'er zizhiqu difangzhi bianzuan weiyuanhui, ed. *Xinjiang tongzhi: shiyou gongye* (vol. 40) (Urumqi: Xinjiang renmin chubanshe, 1999), 81. Map
by Debbie Newell.

of state attention. Chinese industries in the early to mid 1950s had little demand for these raw materials with critical high-tech and nuclear applications. Instead, central government officials relied on these valuable minerals
to repay Soviet loans taken in the early 1950s and also to pay for arms, Soviet
technical assistance, and equipment. At first, Chinese economic planners
relied on agricultural products, light industry, and a smattering of strategic
materials such as raw rubber and tungsten ore to repay their debts. Beginning in 1956 and escalating in the late 1950s as Sino-Soviet tensions mounted,
planners began to rely on the far more valuable nonferrous metals to take
the burden off of agricultural producers and rapidly repay loans and other
debts. The majority of these minerals were extracted from the Altay Mountains, which, in addition to their rich mineral veins, were close to the Soviet
transport network.

Koktokay's massive Number 3 Ore Vein had been the primary locus of
mineral extraction operations for the Sino-Soviet Non-ferrous and Rare Metals Company until the closing of the company in 1954 (see chapter 6). After the
opening of the wholly China-owned company in 1955, it continued to focus
on that vein. Indeed, while the earlier Sino-Soviet operations had been active
at a number of ore sites scattered across the Altay Mountains, the proven success of the Koktokay ore fields and a desire to concentrate investment only at

productive sites in order to save money prompted Chinese officials to concentrate their efforts there. Officials downsized and in some cases shuttered secondary ore fields in the wider region.[23] New plans unveiled later in 1955 sought to further increase production at Koktokay by calling for the conversion of all of the field's underground tunnel mines into one massive open pit mine. Completed in 1956, the change facilitated the greater use of mechanized equipment, including excavators and heavy drills, and vastly expanded the amounts of ore extracted and processed.

Production expanded significantly at Koktokay in the mid to late 1950s, as officials in the Xinjiang Non-ferrous Metals Company sought to meet growing central government demands. In 1956 alone, the company sold more than 16,600 tons of lithium ore worth 24.5 million rubles to the Soviet Union, an amount nearly double that of 1955.[24] According to central government sources, between 1950 and 1962, over 100,000 tons of lithium, 34,000 tons of beryllium, and 39 tons of tantalum-niobium were shipped to the Soviet Union. As the only lithium-producing site in China and one of only a handful of beryllium and tantalum-niobium producers worldwide in the late 1950s, the Altay Mountains and Koktokay in particular played a central role in loan repayment.[25]

The nature of nonferrous metals differs substantially from that of oil. As a consequence, the industrial complex built up to support the production of beryllium, lithium, and tantalum-niobium at Koktokay looked quite different from that of Karamay-Dushanzi. Nonferrous metal mining, like coal mining in Timothy Mitchell's formulation, tends to be a far more decentralized operation and is easily disruptable at various links in the supply chain, whether it was workers chipping ore out of a vein, hand-sorting ores, or transporting ores from the extraction site to warehouses and ultimately to shipping destinations.[26] The growing desire to increase production in 1958 and 1959, as central government leaders sought to rely on strategic materials to pay for desperately needed defense imports from the Soviet Union, prompted the leadership of the Xinjiang Non-ferrous Metals Company to centralize control over production.[27]

In a series of renovations, the mine established specialized sorting rooms for beryllium and lithium ores and in 1957 created a separate on-site sorting factory, which by 1958 had over eight hundred workers hunched over long ore-sorting tables under specialty lamps. The desire to exert greater control over the process of ore sorting led to the installation of a mechanized wet spiral separator for separating tantalum-niobium ores in 1957 and the limited installation of a froth flotation sorter to increase the concentrations of beryllium ores the next year. With their eyes on the long-term formation of an integrated ore production network in Xinjiang, CCP officials in 1958 opened the 115 Factory in the capital city of Urumqi, which at the time was the only lithium engineering facility in China and specialized in synthesizing raw lithium ore into the lithium oxide and lithium salts critical in high-technology enterprises and in the production of nuclear weapons.

The desire to improve control over ores and facilitate state oversight over their export led to a greater investment in transport institutions. Complimenting a series of central government–funded improvements to northern Xinjiang's highway network made in the mid-1950s, beginning in 1958 several large warehouses were constructed in Urumqi as well as in ore production sites in the Altay and in the riverine transport hub at Burqin on the Irtysh.[28] The total square footage of these fully staffed warehouses that were managed by the Xinjiang Non-ferrous Metals Company doubled in size in the late 1950s. In the mid-1950s, officials expanded the port at Burqin, which was the prime conduit for mineral exports to the Soviet Union. The port, which was capable of accommodating barges weighted down with four hundred tons of raw ore in the high-water summer months, was expanded and improved upon in the mid-1950s.[29] At the same time, economic planners discussed the possibility of extending the planned rail line from the Soviet border to Urumqi (see chapter 6) up north from Kuitun through Karamay and ultimately ending at the town of Altay, 330 miles north of Xinjiang's main east-west trunk line and a comparatively short 150 miles from Koktokay.[30]

The interest and attention to petroleum production as well as lucrative nonferrous metals helped ensure that the twin poles of resource extraction in Xinjiang—Karamay-Dushanzi and Koktokay—played an increasingly prominent role in the PRC's economic planning in the mid to late 1950s. From 1955 to 1958, the PRC shipped more than 136,000 tons of nonferrous metals directly to Soviet factories, averaging more than 34,000 tons annually.[31] Likewise, the efforts invested at Karamay-Dushanzi helped ensure that this site played an increasingly prominent role in state economic planning. Indeed, it produced 74 percent of all of Xinjiang's petroleum in 1957, a number that grew to 93 percent the next year. And by 1958, oil extracted at Karamay represented 22 percent of China's total petroleum production (although nearly all of this was being consumed within Xinjiang).[32] These early successes helped prompt a greater attention to production in Xinjiang and a clearer connection in the minds of Chinese state planners between this border region and the production of resources prioritized by the state.

## The Foundations of Chinese Power in Xinjiang

The desire to exploit the region's resource wealth led the central government to invest substantial amounts of capital in Karamay-Dushanzi and Koktokay.

TABLE 7.2. Capital construction investment in the oil industry

| Year | Investment in million yuan (not including geological activities) |
| --- | --- |
| 1954 | 27.65 |
| 1955 | 78.60 |
| 1956 | 159.55 |
| 1957 | 159.49 |
| 1958 | 195.63 |
| 1959 | 139.70 |
| 1960 | 154.31 |
| 1961 | 37.87 |

Source: Xinjiang Weiwu'er zizhiqu defang zhi bianzuan weiyuanhui, ed., *Xinjiang tongzhi: caizheng* (vol. 57) (Urumqi: Xinjiang Renmin Chubanshe, 1999), 273.

Investments in Xinjiang's petroleum industry grew rapidly in the years after 1955. While the industry absorbed 27.65 million yuan in 1954, that number exploded two years later to 159.55 million yuan (see table 7.2). Drawing on funds not only from Xinjiang's department of finance (*caizhengting*), but also various ministries in Beijing, by 1957 the investment in the oil industry was double that of total provincial spending. The investments in oil made up more than 37 percent of the total investment in capital construction in the region and indeed outstripped total spending for various other large-scale spending categories, including small enterprises, agricultural aid, reclamation, and herding.[33] Spending on nonferrous metal mining was significantly less than investments in oil, but for the period of the First Five Year Plan it exceeded 67 million yuan, an amount that made up more than 21 percent of total provincial-level spending.[34]

Capital investments represent a tangible, material transformation of the physical world. These investments lead to the construction of new buildings, roads, refineries, pipeline networks, and drilling rigs that inscribed state priorities onto the landscape. But the concentration of capital in out-of-the-way, underpopulated stretches of northern Xinjiang in the mid-1950s also helped transform the economic, political, and social topography of the region, as new populations, infrastructure, and institutions chased the capital investments. In his work on the connection between urban spaces and frontier hinterlands in the American West, William Cronon notes that "western cities came into being when eastern capital created remote colonies in landscapes that as yet contained few people."[35] The largely immigrant, Han-majority cities at

Karamay-Dushanzi and at Koktokay should be viewed similarly, as colonies funded by capital from eastern China in this remote, underpopulated border region. These cities were a product of the capital investments made to extract certain resources. Drawing in large populations of Han Chinese settlers and facilitating the development of infrastructure and institutions that bound the sites directly to China-proper, Karamay-Dushanzi and Koktokay served as critical nodes of state power and authority in northern Xinjiang.

Focusing on the role that large-scale extractive operations played in a broader process of Chinese state formation in this border region helps reveal a new perspective on the driving force behind the integration of Xinjiang in the years following the founding of the People's Republic. For Chinese and Western scholars alike, the post-1949 transformation of Xinjiang from a largely unintegrated border region into a component part of the Chinese nation-state has been attributed primarily to the efforts of the XPCC.[36] The organization was founded in 1954 and charged with both shoring up border defenses as well as aiding in production. While the XPCC corpsmen were involved in a wide range of production activities, they are primarily known for their role in spearheading the large-scale reclamation campaign in the region. The organization's success in producing grain, transforming landscapes, and settling large numbers of migrants from China-proper on industrial farms in the mid-1960s should not be discounted. But when compared to the massive capital investments and substantial communities of workers at Karamay-Dushanzi, XPCC settlements were relatively small and underfunded throughout most of the 1950s and early 1960s. Indeed, throughout this period, total fixed capital investments in Xinjiang's oil industry, which were concentrated at Dushanzi, were comparable with fixed capital investments for the entire XPCC and, in at least one year, investments in oil production even outstripped investments in the organization.[37]

Further, the XPCC was centered largely in the south and along the Tianshan North Road, and was a minor presence in the Zungharian basin and farther north.[38] The well-funded extraction enterprises, along with the communities and supporting industries that emerged at new boom towns like Karamay and to a lesser extent Koktokay, powerfully shaped the distribution of state power, authority, and capital in the 1950s. For their part, during this period, XPCC units frequently played the role of supporting extractive industries, as they helped put down so-called bandit uprisings that threatened extraction operations (most notably the defeat of Osman Batur's group of nomadic Kazakhs), mined coal needed at the sites, built roads and highways connecting resource fields to transport networks, and shipped excess grain to the operations as needed. In the 1950s, resource extraction enterprises, more

so than the XPCC, shaped Xinjiang's relationship to China. The state capital that flowed directly to these resource production sites helped transform
them into nodes of Chinese state power, institutional control, and capital
investment.

By the end of May 1956, there were 1,000 laborers working in various oil-
related capacities at Karamay, but the wheels were already in motion to increase
this number to more than 4,000 by the end of the summer. A state-sponsored
campaign conducted through the state-run media continually called on loyal
citizens to drop everything and "aid Karamay." By early September, Karamay's
population of workers had ballooned to 6,000 and plans were already in place
to increase the population by several thousand by the end of the year. On January 1, 1957, workers and their families numbered 13,806, and officials expected
that number to grow to more than 30,000 by the end of the year.[39] The population increase was made up primarily by new Han Chinese migrants arriving in
Xinjiang from eastern and central China. As one contemporary account notes,
of the 6,000 workers in 1956, only 1,600 were from ethnic minorities. Later in
1959, official records point out that throughout all of Xinjiang's oil industry,
fewer than 20 percent of laborers were from non-Han ethnic groups.[40]

For laborers arriving in Karamay, at first accommodations were spartan.
Workers lived in the three hundred tents and twenty or so dugouts scattered
around the oilfields. Typically, each "well team," which consisted of thirty or
so laborers, shared one space. Yet a construction campaign undertaken with
military labor drawn from the XPCC in the summer of 1956 helped transform
the site. By August, sixty residential dormitory buildings were under construction, covering an area of more than fifty thousand square meters. In
addition to the living quarters, laborers also built new administrative and industry offices, as well as parks and various green spaces, a trading post where
workers could buy goods imported from China-proper and the Soviet Union,
a Xinhua bookstore, a network of farms to grow food for residents, a branch
of the People's Bank, a post office, and on August 23, after the import of a film
projector, a movie theater.[41]

The more secretive nonferrous metals industry did not lend itself to
sweeping pronouncements in the state-run media, and the nature of mineral extraction and processing did not require a massive campaign to recruit
workers from China-proper. Nevertheless, the integrated ore field at Koktokay expanded substantially in the late 1950s, as increased government investment and attention helped transform the site from an isolated ore field into a
node of state investment and development. Company officials eagerly sought
to fulfill central government demands for raw materials. The total number
of laborers working on site grew from 4,868 in 1957 to 5,979 in 1959, the vast

majority of whom were Han Chinese migrants from China-proper. That year, across the Xinjiang Non-ferrous Metals Company as a whole, total labor jumped to 35,454, up from 22,861 in 1958.[42]

To accommodate the growing size of the operation at Koktokay and the handful of sites stretched across the Altay Mountains, company officials undertook the creation of a vast array of supporting industries, including four eighty-three kilowatt power plants, a vehicle repair shop, a machine shop, an electrical shop, and a dynamite plant. Additionally, to support workers, administrators, and their families, land was reclaimed for new farms, and extensive housing built for workers and offices for staff. The impact of China's production priorities and the sustained state interest in Karamay and Koktokay were not confined to bricks and mortar. During his trip to the Altay in 1955 to visit a nonferrous open pit mine, the journalist Chu Anping marveled at the radio broadcasts, the biweekly movies, and the weekend dance parties that seemed so reminiscent of home in this desolate corner of the People's Republic. The presence of this Chinese outpost in this distant borderland seemed to Chu and others to represent the success of the Chinese state and the leadership of the party. "If there were no party then there would be no party support and leadership, and [as a result] the people would not have been able to produce these glorious results in this cold desolate region," he wrote.[43]

The ability of the state to create the cultural events and institutions that so pleased Chu in 1955 paralleled the extension and expansion of institutions of the party state deep into China's long-isolated far western border regions. In his work on oil production in the Niger Delta, Michael Watts argues that large-scale sites of resource extraction, processing, and transport are "the setting, at once institutionally dense and politically cogent, within which new governable spaces are manufactured."[44] The same can be said for Karamay-Dushanzi and Koktokay, as the desire to control production and maintain the stability of labor in these regions located so far from state political infrastructure led to the importation and development of institutional networks that bound the sites to centers of power in Urumqi and Beijing. These new "governable spaces" built upon the foundation of the earlier layers of surveys, state investments, and institutions, served as nodes of state power and authority, and stood out against the background of northern Xinjiang with their heavy state investment, sizable Han population, and depth of political organization and central government control.

The desperate drive to enforce state claims to resources, control workers and production, and oversee the unimpeded flow of products in directions benefiting the state helped transform these two mineral fields not only into production centers, but also into CCP political outposts by the early 1960s.

After 1955 and the establishment of the wholly Chinese-owned Xinjiang Oil and Nonferrous Metals Companies, the Ministry of Fuel Industry (and after July, the Ministry of Oil Industry) oversaw the operations at Karamay-Dushanzi, and the Ministry of Heavy Industry Office of Non-ferrous Metals oversaw nonferrous metals production in the Altay. With approval from the Ministry of Oil Industry in Beijing, managers installed new leadership in the Xinjiang Oil Company, bringing in Zhang Wenbin to head up the company in 1955. Having joined the party in 1936, and served as a political instructor and party secretary in a cadre school in Yan'an, party officials in Beijing were confident in Zhang's loyalty.[45] The Xinjiang Non-ferrous Metals Company was already in the hands of Bai Chengming, a long-time party member. But in order to strengthen on-the-ground control, after 1955 company leadership brought in new managers and party representatives who shared similar loyalist backgrounds and credentials.[46]

As extraction and processing operations grew, and as the population of laborers, workers in affiliated industries, and family members increased exponentially in these areas prioritized for increased production, it became clear to local and provincial officials that they needed to create a new political infrastructure at the sites. Karamay-Dushanzi in particular was witness to a massive and potentially destabilizing growth in population in the mid to late 1950s. "A new oil industry city is right now taking shape," wrote the authors of a report calling for a greater party presence in Karamay.[47] In January 1957, Xinjiang's party committee in Urumqi petitioned the State Council in Beijing to establish a new Karamay City with its own party committee institutionally separate from that of surrounding Wusu county. Noting the sizable population increase in the region, the request called for greater state oversight. "Social order is largely chaos; drunkenness, beatings, thievery, rapes, and arson are happening continuously and have severely impacted production," the report read.[48] With such a dire warning, the State Council quickly approved the establishment of a preparatory committee that would begin the process of political consolidation and incorporation in the oilfield.

The problem, as the preparatory committee saw it, was not only a growing population of ungoverned oil workers and their families, but also a lack of political unity across the oilfield. In a May 1957 report, they noted that the lack of unified political leadership across Karamay and Dushanzi threatened production, as "the provision of goods are sporadic and the provision of services is not sufficient to meet the life requirements for workers."[49] The report justified calls to create a Karamay City that was far broader than the oilfield alone and instead sought to create one large administrative area that folded the refining operation at Dushanzi, the oilfield at Karamay, a handful

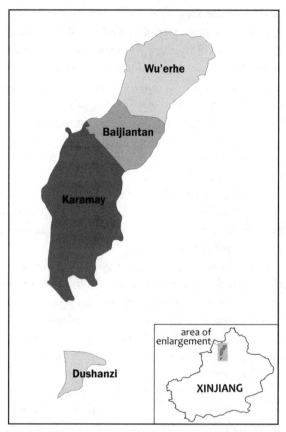

MAP 7.2 Karamay Municipal Region. Map by Debbie Newell.

of subsidiary oilfields, and several potentially oil-rich sites, as well as adjacent agricultural and pastoral lands into one centrally administered region. As the preparatory committee insisted, "The city's political power will be established and emanate from the current production site, but [we] must also consider suitable future development, and in order to facilitate management we must strengthen unified leadership."[50] In May 1958, the State Council in Beijing approved the creation of the Karamay Municipal Region. The borders of the new administrative area stretched more than sixty-five miles north of the city center of Karamay and, though not contiguously connected to the administrative area, it also included Dushanzi (map 7.2).

The campaigns to integrate these resource sites more clearly into the political infrastructure of the People's Republic were paralleled by an effort to extend institutions of the party state down to the local level. As these resource production sites grew, a network of institutions that sought to increase state control over workers and production grew alongside them. In order to extend China's coercive apparatus, the establishment of new public security offices closely tracked the opening of oil and ore fields in the province. Similarly, seeking to exert control over production and integrate workers in this isolated region into national political and production campaigns, leaders prioritized the recruiting of new party members, work floor–level party cadres, and propaganda personnel who were called upon to inform workers of new campaigns, production targets, and new slogans.[51]

At the center of the efforts to more clearly integrate these resource sites into the institutional infrastructure of the People's Republic was the priority placed on the development of the Lanzhou-Xinjiang rail line. A 1952 report of a conversation between Zhou Enlai and Stalin finds that CCP officials were focused on the construction of a rail line spanning Outer Mongolia that would connect Soviet production sites and markets to China. Stalin urged that they instead focus their efforts on a line through China's northwest, saying, "We think that you cannot abandon the Xinjiang [line], because it is an important route passing through rich oilfields."[52] Chinese planners certainly did not abandon the line dreamed about by multiple generations of their predecessors stretching back to the late Qing period. Indeed, the inching of the railroad west from Lanzhou toward Xinjiang throughout the mid to late 1950s pointed toward a future in which Karamay's oil and Koktokay's minerals could play a central role in China's economic planning.

Plans for an extension of the rail line from Urumqi to the Soviet border first hammered out in 1954 (See chapter 6) included a stop at Kuitun, just ten kilometers from the refineries at Dushanzi, and eventually a line that would connect Kuitun to Karamay and ultimately, to Altay in the far north.[53] The line seemed destined to rapidly increase the exploitation of Xinjiang's mineral wealth and facilitate its integration into China's increasingly ambitious industrial planning. An article in the People's Daily noted in July 1956 that "if you say that oil is the lifeblood of industry, then the Lanzhou-Xinjiang railroad line is the main oil artery."[54]

The institutional and infrastructural networks that orbited around Karamay-Dushanzi and Koktokay helped ensure that future state investment continued to follow the layers of surveys, extractive efforts, and capital investments laid over the past half century. The concentration of capital into these specific sites helped shape long-term political, economic, and demographic patterns in Xinjiang. Dushanzi and the Altay had long been only rhetorically connected into China-based industrial planning and political campaigns. The new infrastructure served to channel in new capital, new Han communities that served as critical supporters of Chinese state power in this sparsely populated border region, and new institutions that helped reinforce state monopolies over resources and also assert control over production. The evolution of these sites and their transformation into nodes of CCP state power in the mid-1950s allowed the government in Beijing to begin exerting more direct control over them at a moment when a series of aggressive production drives and campaigns were looming on the political horizon.

### The Great Leap and the Spatial Contours of Mineral Extraction

The push to increase production in the mid-1950s exploded in the waning years of the decade with the inauguration of Mao's Great Leap Forward (1958–1962). The Great Leap set sky-high targets for steel and grain production, but also prioritized the production of a wide assortment of raw materials including petroleum. The campaign sought to alleviate the reliance on large capital investments and high-tech Soviet imported equipment and at the same time unfetter China's productive potential by relying on the power of the masses. To do this, Mao sidelined central party planners seen to be too beholden to Soviet planning models. In order to unleash the power of the masses, the party emphasized a new strategy termed "walking on two legs" (*yong liang-tiaotui zoulu*), which placed equal emphasis on the development of highly capitalized large production centers as well as small-scale operations relying not on concentration of capital but on so-called "native methods" (*tufa*). To achieve the skyrocketing production goals, state capital investment, which was used to fund heavy industry, spiked from around 25 percent of total GDP in 1957 to well over 30 in 1959 and over 40 in 1960.[55]

The result in Xinjiang was a continued focus on Karamay-Dushanzi and Koktokay alongside simultaneous efforts to uncover new sites of production scattered throughout the vast region including the long-neglected south. The period 1958–1961 was one of massive expansion in surveying, extraction, and production. The head of the Karamay Party Committee opened a May 5, 1958, committee meeting by proudly noting the committee's participation in the 1957 Anti-Rightist Movement and pointed out that they were currently in the process of "unveiling the new forms of the Great Leap Forward."[56] In both the Zungharian basin and the Altay Mountains, the substantial increases in drilling in the mid-1950s paled in comparison to the increases undertaken in the late 1950s and early 1960s. Mao's call for the launching of satellites (*weixing*), which referred to the achievement of astronomical production targets, helped transform Xinjiang's geological maps, as planning committees set sky-high production goals. Relying on an institutional infrastructure set in the mid-1950s and

FIGURE 7.2 An image of the Number 3 vein at Koktokay, with the slogan "Long live the Great Leap Forward" written in white ore-bearing rock from the mine on the hillside. Photo by author.

centered around Karamay-Dushanzi and the Altay Mountains, the Great Leap Forward drove a massive increase in the meters drilled by geological teams, the amounts of earth processed by extraction operations, and a sharp, even if temporary, growth in production. The result was the discovery of a series of new oil and ore fields scattered in the vicinity of Karamay and Koktokay but also at a wide variety of fields located throughout Xinjiang province.

In February 1958, Deng Xiaoping criticized planners putting together the Second Five-Year Plan (SFYP) for their lack of ambition when it came to the Karamay oilfields. He noted that the plans for 1959 called for the oil enterprise to produce 400,000 tons of oil, a reasonable amount considering the fact that the production in 1958 topped out at little more than 333,000 tons. This, he suggested, however, was "too little." Deng estimated that all of Xinjiang was capable of producing a massive 3,000,000 tons annually and should be producing at least 2,000,000 tons annually by the end of the SFYP.[57] Later, Deng's enthusiasm was embraced by officials in Xinjiang, who at an April 30 meeting of the party committee of the Xinjiang Oil Oversight Office, called for a "leap forward in planning to serve as the foundation for an even greater leap forward." They called for teams in the province to drill more than 450,000 meters of wells in 1958, a more than three-fold increase over 1957, and by 1962 to be producing 5,000,000 tons of oil annually.[58]

These marching orders were extended to work units toiling in oilfields throughout Xinjiang. In October 1958, at an on-site meeting of the Oil Oversight Office held at Karamay, which was attended by 1,000 high-ranking officials, workers, and cadres, the leadership issued new drilling targets calling on drilling teams to "exceed 1,000 [meters] monthly and 10,000 annually."[59] In 1958, seventy-eight teams were able to exceed the 1,000 meters monthly mark with one team drilling a total of 4,525 meters in one month. For the year, nineteen teams exceeded the 10,000 meters mark, with one team drilling a total of 18,975 meters.[60] The results of teams competing to exceed drilling targets were widely publicized in front-page articles in the industry publication, *Xinjiang Oil Worker*, throughout the Great Leap. At a February 1959 meeting unveiling the annual report for the Dushanzi Mining Affairs Office, the head of the office, Wang Youtian, gave the opening convocation and praised workers and cadres for their efforts. He noted that they "were full of enthusiasm, and were so absorbed in their work that they forget to eat and sleep, that they did not notice blowing snow and severe cold." Wang went on, you have "made our production results leap and leap again" and concluded by pointing out that drilling and oil extraction had exceeded annual plans.[61]

Officials focused their efforts on established oil sites like Karamay, blanketing the region with new wells as they sought to squeeze out every last drop. A November 1959 meeting of the leadership of the Xinjiang Oil Oversight Office called for strengthening surveying and test drilling in established oilfields in order to "ferret out second-tier tectonic structures" capable of yielding oil. In Karamay, officials sought to find "the second Karamay" and in their annual planning for 1960, they called for drilling sixty-two new wells in the region reaching a total depth of 161,300 meters. In order to find this new Karamay, they staked out an ambitious and, some suggest, risky drilling plan in which twenty-two of the test wells would be dug within a mere two kilometers of one another and thirty within four kilometers of one another.[62] Officials hoped that the plan would lay bare 100 million tons of new oil reserves. Plans for 1961 called for an additional sixty-six wells closely packed in this stretch of the Zungharian basin reaching a total depth of 200,000 meters.[63] Altogether, the total number of oil wells drilled in Xinjiang increased by nearly seven times from 1957 to 1958, growing from 148 wells to 997.[64]

A similar dynamic helped shape the ore fields scattered throughout the Altay Mountains in the late 1950s and early 1960s. In 1959, the 701 Geological Team, which was charged with exploring the mineral wealth of the region, called for an even greater expansion of surveying and extraction operations. They argued that the surrounding ore fields "contain many smaller veins, but in recent years, work in these smaller veins has been insufficient."[65] In addition to the political imperatives of producing for the Great Leap, the growing tensions with the Soviet Union, which culminated in the 1960 Sino-Soviet split, helped unleash an aggressive push to produce the nonferrous metals

TABLE 7.3. Oil wells and meters drilled in Xinjiang

| Year | Wells drilled | Meters drilled |
|------|---------------|----------------|
| 1954 | 38 | 36,612 |
| 1955 | 42 | 61,230 |
| 1956 | 116 | 116,293 |
| 1957 | 148 | 164,468 |
| 1958 | 997 | 627,524 |
| 1959 | 814 | 438,474 |
| 1960 | 513 | 498,377 |
| 1961 | 133 | 111,454 |
| 1962 | 69 | 45,147 |

Source: Xinjiang Weiwuer zizhiqu difang zhi bianmu weiyuanhui, ed. Xinjiang tongzhi: shiyou gongye (vol. 40) (Urumqi:
Xinjiang Renmin Chubanshe, 1999), 122.

needed to rapidly pay back Soviet loans in the late 1950s and early 1960s. China's state-run media would later brag that despite the devastation of the Great Leap Forward–driven famine, the loans along with interest were repaid on time. "Those years that were the most difficult for our nation were those in which we repaid the most on our loan," read an editorial in the People's Daily.[66] Without discounting the sacrifices made by Chinese peasants during the Great Leap, it is worth noting that the success in paying back the loans was due in large part to the large shipments of valuable nonferrous minerals that were arduously chipped out of the Altay Mountain ore fields by a grow-ing legion of laborers.[67]

The drastic calls to increase production and meet the sky-high rhetoric of the Great Leap led to the opening of ore sites scattered throughout the Altay Mountains. The ore fields that had been abandoned by the Xinjiang Non-ferrous Metals Company to cut costs and concentrate production in the mid-1950s were reopened in the late 1950s, along with a number of nonfer-rous metal fields that had been first discovered by Soviet geologists in the 1930s and 1940s. Additionally, the general increase in surveying and test drill-ing allowed company geologists stationed in the Altay Mountains to discover several new veins, particularly those located in the area northwest of Kokto-kay and north of the town of Altay. In the ore fields west of Koktokay, from 1957 to 1962, the number of workers nearly quadrupled to 3,640. While those in Koktokay did not increase quite so dramatically, they still grew by nearly 2,000 workers to nearly 7,000 by 1960.[68] The drive to produce nonferrous minerals in combination with Great Leap Forward rhetoric also led to massive increases in the effort expended by these laborers. The Great Leap years were witness to substantial increases in the amounts of earth processed at this network of sites radiating across the Altay Mountains. The volume of earth processed at Koktokay increased by more than five and a half times from 1955 to 1959.[69] Official statistics record similar increases in processing at ore fields scattered all across the mountain range.

The demands of the Great Leap led to a tidal wave of geological and extraction teams breaking over the vast province. These teams, pushed by the ever-increasing calls to discover new ore veins and oilfields and to put up production and drilling satellites, explored regions that were well off of Xinjiang's production priority lists. Expanding their focus beyond the layers laid over the previous six decades, they discovered several important new resource sites in the region. Geological teams concentrated their efforts on the exploration of potential oil sites in eastern Xinjiang in the Toksun Basin near Turfan, as well as several sites in the southern foothills of the Tianshan Mountains. But the bulk of their efforts were focused on the exploration of the vast Tarim Basin south of the Tianshan Mountains. Five years after the central government report calling for the focus of geological activities on northern Xinjiang and the closing of test wells in the Tarim (see chapter 6), in 1958, the Xinjiang Oil Oversight Office triumphantly opened the Tarim Mining Affairs Office, which focused exclusively on the lands south of the Tianshan. As the garish headline in the July 23, 1958, edition of the *Xinjiang Oil Worker* newspaper screamed, "Raise the red flag high above the Tianshan, raise a ruckus in the Tarim!"[70]

The strength of the Zungharian basin oil complex, however, served as a major obstacle to the geographical expansion of operations. Xinjiang's poor transportation infrastructure, particularly in the south, ensured that broad swaths of potentially oil rich lands had no access to the high-tech refinery located at Dushanzi, and planners were unwilling to build another large capital-intensive refinery in this distant region that still had not been aggressively surveyed. Embracing the potential of mass-based solutions to technological bottlenecks (a faith characteristic of the Great Leap), oil officials in Xinjiang began to experiment with small-scale, low-technology equipment. "Although the processes from looking for oil to refining oil are scientific, that does not mean that they cannot be simplified," explained an official at a meeting in May 1958. He went on, "When you produce big things you waste money and energy, when you produce small things you save money and energy."[71]

In addition to the use of shorter drills, officials also turned to native method refining equipment, which was cheaper and less technologically intensive. Experiments conducted by engineers working at Dushanzi, who were charged with developing native method technologies for oil production, found that with an investment of fifty yuan and seven or eight hours of time, one could make one's own low-tech atmospheric distillation cauldrons. They claimed that these cauldrons were capable of producing refined oil 58.9 percent as pure as that coming out of the high-tech Dushanzi refinery. The technological innovation, which was merely an embrace of native method technologies and was intended to decentralize oil production in Xinjiang by breaking the reliance on Dushanzi, was unveiled at a May 1958 meeting with representatives of Xinjiang's twelve prefectures. As an article in the *Xinjiang Oil Worker* explained, "Villages and towns with oil veins (*youmai*) will be able to refine their own raw oil."[72] At the May meeting, oil engineers at Dushanzi distributed oil distillation cauldrons to delegates as "gifts," intending that participants bring the technology back to their home districts.[73] With the decentralization of production and the spatial expansion of operations, officials placed new, sky-high targets on production, calling on Xinjiang to produce more than twenty million tons of petroleum annually by 1962. One-quarter of this amount was to be produced in as yet undiscovered fields south of the Tianshan Mountain range.[74]

Having freed themselves from the shackles of Dushanzi, geological teams fanned out throughout southern Xinjiang. To uncover the oil wealth of this region, which remained largely a blank spot on China's geological maps, these teams focused on old geological reports from the Sino-Soviet oil operation, reports from local officials, and rumors about places in the broad Tarim basin where oil bubbled out of the ground. In the end, however, they focused their efforts on only a handful of promising sites, including Kashgar in the far south, and Kucha and Luntai in the southern foothills of Tianshan.[75] One oilfield in particular, at an isolated spot 120 kilometers northwest of Kucha, was the primary object of interest. After less than two months of intensive drilling, in October 1958 the Yiqikelike well began to spew a significant amount of oil.[76] "This is only the first blast in opening all of the oilfields of the Tarim," wrote one confident journalist.[77] The oil from this site, located on the opposite side of the towering Tianshan Mountain range and a long and dusty 500 kilometers from the large-scale refineries at Dushanzi, was processed onsite with two small atmospheric distillation cauldrons capable of producing twenty tons of oil daily at full capacity.

The contours of nonferrous metal exploration likewise grew in the Great Leap period. Expanding outward from the Altay Mountains, geological teams focused careful attention on the western Altay district on the border with the Soviet Union, eastern Xinjiang in the Toksun basin, the area around Kucha in the northern stretches of the Tarim basin, and the northern foothills of the Kunlun Mountain range in the far south. All of these sites experienced significant increases in geological activities during the Great Leap period. To accommodate the increase, over the course of the Great Leap the number of workers in the Xinjiang Non-ferrous Metals Company increased substantially, growing by more than six times from 1955 to its high-water point of more than 24,000 workers in 1960.[78] The growth in both the oil and nonferrous metal operations resulted in substantial increases in production. Total oil production grew from 95,000 tons in 1957 to 357,000 tons in 1958 and jumped again in 1960 to 1.66 million tons.[79] At nonferrous metal mines across Xinjiang, production likewise increased, as laborers worked punishing hours to meet production demands. In the ore fields north of the city of Altay, production of lithium ore doubled from 1957 to 1958 and from 1957 to 1960 the total value of ores extracted and processed nearly doubled, increasing from 5.5 million yuan to more than 10 million.

A number of the sites uncovered by geologists and drilling teams during the Great Leap were later opened to large-scale extraction and exploitation, to meet growing domestic and international demands. Of Xinjiang's fifteen known oilfields today, six were discovered during the first two years of the Great Leap. Yet, the intensive focus on increasing production during the Great Leap also ensured a greater focus on the proven ore and oilfields at Karamay-Dushanzi and Koktokay. Indeed, the production push ensured that contiguous regions with even the hint of potential were aggressively drilled and surveyed by teams who were eager to meet their targets. As a result, these areas came to stand out on geological maps with even greater clarity than other regions scattered throughout the vast province. The fact that infrastructure and processing plants were located nearby helped further ensure that as funding dwindled, production declined, and the call for satellites fell silent in the years after the Great Leap, planners would return to these well-surveyed, well-integrated initial sites.

## The End of the Great Leap

Many of the gains recorded in the Great Leap Forward were illusory. Indeed, when it came to nonferrous metals, it is clear that most of the growth in ore production was simply a product of the massive and unsustainable amounts of earth being processed.[80] In addition, recent analyses note that in their efforts to reach the sky-high targets, many teams simply drilled and dug randomly. Further, the inefficiencies of the native method distillation cauldrons meant that the oil produced was largely unusable as gasoline. The distances of many of the newly discovered sites from Dushanzi and the provincial road network ensured that raw oil could not be easily shipped to the refinery or elsewhere.

The result was a painful contraction of Xinjiang's resource and economic development map in the early to mid-1960s, as the Great Leap fizzled and as the People's Republic completed the repayments on its loans to the Soviet Union. During this period, state planners sought to cut waste and consolidate investment and manpower, a shift embodied in the post–Great Leap slogan, "calibrate, consolidate, replenish, and grow." Throughout China, the small, highly localized operations relying on the native methods technology that made up one of the "two legs" of Great Leap planning were shuttered by the thousands, as state planners sought to reconcentrate their investments on large, capital-intensive enterprises previously emphasized by state planners in the early to mid-1950s. With the shift, capital investments in Xinjiang's oil industry plummeted from 1960 to 1961 by nearly 75 percent, while investments in nonferrous metal mining dropped by nearly half.[81] The result was a shrinking of Xinjiang's planning map, the concentration of efforts at well-established sites already integrated into provincial infrastructure, and a reversion to the spatial contours of extraction prioritized by geologists and economic planners in the mid-1950s. With only a few exceptions, the traces of the ambitious oil extraction and nonferrous metal mining operations in far-flung corners of the province established during the Great Leap were wiped from the landscape, their memories retained only as fading spots on China's geological maps.

As the size of the Soviet loans began to dwindle in the early 1960s and the export of minerals to the Soviet Union began to drop off, China's pursuit of a homegrown nuclear weapon and its investment in the development of a missile program helped maintain central government interest in nonferrous metal production. The ores emphasized shifted, however, to meet the new demands, as production of beryllium, which was primarily being packaged for export to the Soviet Union, was officially deprioritized in 1963 in favor of tantalum-niobium and lithium ores, which played critical roles in China's rocketry and nuclear engineering programs.[82] This decision led to a scaling back of the nonferrous mineral operations across the Altay and a refocusing of operations around the proven resources of the already integrated and developed Number 3 vein at Koktokay. The earlier demand for the large amounts of nonferrous metals was simply no longer there by the mid-1960s. Expecting to pay off the remaining Soviet loans within the next two years, in 1963 officials shuttered several of the most promising ore sites in the Altay, particularly those centered around the town of Altay itself, west of Koktokay. While the number of workers at Koktokay declined substantially from around 6,500 workers in the early 1960s to less than 2,000 in the mid-1960s, the declines were even more abrupt elsewhere in the Altay, where workers dropped by about 87 percent to around 500 in 1965.[83] The massive expansion of the Great Leap was decidedly temporary and the contours of state investment in nonferrous metals reverted back to its focus around Koktokay.

Several factors pushed the focus of state planners away from the oilfields in southern Xinjiang and back toward the wells in Karamay-Dushanzi. First and foremost was the failure of the so-called native method of refining to produce usable fuels. In this period of scaling back production and capital investment, the power of the large-scale, high-tech refining operation, its supporting infrastructure, and the large number of geological surveys that had long focused on the area meant that the cost of extracting and processing petroleum was lower. Furthermore, the completion of the Lanzhou-Xinjiang rail line in 1962 and the development of supporting internal highway networks served to concentrate attention on the Karamay-Dushanzi oil complex. The rail line ended at the Urumqi West railway station, which was specially engineered to accommodate oil tankers and oil loading equipment. In the first year of the rail line's operation, over 400,000 tons of petroleum products were shipped out of the province. Strengthening the connection between the oilfield and China-proper, a highway-based transport network and teams of trucks and drivers organized under Xinjiang's Oil Industry Transport Company served as the institutional connection between the refineries at Dushanzi and the rail line binding them to China-proper. The improvements to the network of pipelines that connected raw oil extracted at Karamay to refining equipment at Dushanzi, as well as the highway that bound the refinery to the transport hub at Urumqi, not only facilitated oil production but also helped lock in patterns of investment and extraction that centered around the refinery at Dushanzi.

The reversion back to Karamay-Dushanzi in the 1960s was also the product of a shift in the spatial imaginations of party leaders. Beginning in the early 1960s, they increasingly looked away from the northwest and back toward the northeast to fulfill China's demand for oil, as new discoveries seemed more promising and accessible than Xinjiang's wells. The discovery of oil at Daqing in Manchuria in 1959 was greeted with great excitement by Mao and other officials, who celebrated its large reserves and its proximity to transportation networks and industry. After an aggressive campaign of exploration and exploitation of the field, by 1963 Chinese leaders officially declared the end of China's reliance on foreign oil. While leaders continued to emphasize production at proven oil sites like Karamay, the concentrated investment and attention on Xinjiang, once billed as "China's oil depot," dropped off in the 1960s. The massive influx of capital into the region that began in the mid-1950s eased in the post–Great Leap period, as planners embraced more realistic production targets and as officials in Beijing looked elsewhere for the raw materials to fuel their industrial development.

   The reduction in state investment prompted officials in Xinjiang to refocus interest and investment on resource sites that had already been extensively mapped, surveyed, drilled, and integrated into extant production, processing, and transport networks. As the Great Leap fervor died in the mid-1960s, state planners almost reflexively returned to those sites prioritized by the planners and officials who came before them. Standing out in sharp relief against a province that had not been subject to the blanketing campaign of surveying, capital investment, and infrastructural development, the small handful of sites aggressively pursued by a wide assortment of state and nonstate actors, both Chinese and non-Chinese, once again drew their attention. Eager to increase production but lacking the means to invest in an ambitious, large-scale production campaign, they followed the layers of state interest, investment, and institutions back to a small handful of sites in northern Xinjiang prioritized for development over the previous five decades.

*

Economic policy oscillated wildly throughout the 1950s, 1960s, and 1970s, as a political struggle raged between Soviet-influenced state planners and those empowered by Mao Zedong's efforts to decentralize planning and unfetter development from concentrated capital investments. While the post–Great Leap period was witness to a sharp drop-off in state investment in resource production in Xinjiang, a new commitment to developing a large-scale industrial base in China's vast interior (a campaign known as the Third Front) in the face of multiple military threats prompted renewed capital investments in major production sites in the region in the mid-1960s. A pullback in the late 1960s with the Cultural Revolution was again reversed in the mid-1970s following the normalization of relations with the United States and a new hope to generate revenue through international oil exports. But in the end, the head-spinning political and economic changes did little to shift the overall contours of state planning and investment, which to greater and lesser degrees continued to conform to the patterns developed over the course of the first half of the twentieth century. The layers of surveys, capital investments, and infrastructural development laid over Karamay-Dushanzi and Koktokay helped ensure that when the periodic campaigns ended, the state funds slowed to a trickle, and the priority placed on developing Xinjiang more generally declined, patterns of investment returned to earlier blueprints and to the layers lain over the previous three decades.

These two resource production sites served as political outposts of Chinese state power in northern Xinjiang. The reputation of both sites as safe, politically integrated cultural outposts, complete with plenty of high-paying jobs both in mineral extraction and the wide network of supporting industries, ensured that the population of Han Chinese migrants only increased in the 1950s and 1960s. For those looking to escape famine in the late 1950s and early 1960s or for those "sent-down" students, intellectuals, and cadres called upon to serve the nation by opening the borderlands in the 1960s and 1970s, Karamay and Koktokay were primed for state-sponsored immigration and settlement. The foundation laid in the 1950s, as leaders in the central government eagerly sought to increase the production of the minerals needed to fuel their lofty industrialization goals, served to populate and arguably "pacify" the province in ways that the XPCC never did in the early years of the PRC.

The resource outposts in modern Xinjiang were eventually supplemented with a far more aggressive military presence in the region, as Chinese government leaders increasingly feared the possibility of a Soviet invasion of China's far west. The 1960 Sino-Soviet split and, even more, the 1962 Yi-Ta (Ili-Tacheng) incident, during which 60,000 mostly Kazakh nomads flooded out of Xinjiang and into the Soviet Union, prompted a tightening of security in the province and an expansion of the activities of the quasi-military XPCC. In contrast to their relatively minor presence in the 1950s, as of 2017 there were seventeen total XPCC agricultural farms located north of the foothills of the Tianshan and of these, more than two-thirds were established in the period immediately following the Yi-Ta incident. Growing Sino-Soviet tensions in the years after 1962 further increased the state support for the XPCC in northern Xinjiang. Throughout the late 1960s the amount of cultivated hectares and the populations on the XPCC's network of state farms increased substantially.

While the importance of resource extraction in a larger CCP border policy dipped in the late 1960s, the state's emphasis on the production of oil and nonferrous metals beginning in the mid-1950s had already helped lay the contours of modern Xinjiang. The institutional and infrastructural networks that bound Koktokay and Karamay to markets, industry, and political capitals in China-proper continue to shape patterns of capital investment, settlement, and state power in Xinjiang. As the markets for petroleum and nonferrous metals have grown significantly in recent years, the layers of maps, surveys, and economic plans designed to aid in the large-scale extraction of the region's petroleum and nonferrous metals that were laid thick across northern Xinjiang set the framework within which and upon which expansion has taken place. In the end, central government demand for minerals in the 1950s and early 1960s helped shape the contours of economic development and political control in Xinjiang. The import of institutions and the creation of infrastructure helped reinforce the layers of state investment and state power that have shaped modern Xinjiang.

# 8

# The Enduring Power of Layers

## The Resonance of Layers

Mao Zedong's death in 1976, and the rise of Deng Xiaoping in 1978, marked a watershed in the history of twentieth-century China. The unveiling of Deng's new "reform and opening" (*gaige kaifang*) policy heralded a shift from a self-sufficient command economy toward a more globally integrated market economy. But the view for much of China's vast interior changed little in the late 1970s and 1980s. In Xinjiang, the shift in economic orientation did little to even out the layers that had developed at select resource sites in the north. As a result, state investment continued to conform to the patterns dug into the soil of the province over the course of the twentieth century.

Deng's economic strategy in the early 1980s depended on focusing state efforts on coastal regions, intending to use them as an economic engine for driving growth elsewhere in China.[1] From 1980 to 1981, the CCP established new "special economic zones" in the coastal cities of Shenzhen, Zhuhai, Shantou, Guangdong, and Xiamen, and state investment was channeled into these regions in larger and larger amounts.[2] The result was what many in the West have termed the "China miracle," as the country's annual GDP reached double-digit rates frequently in the 1980s. Not surprisingly, this rapid rise was not evenly distributed, as the productive capacity of the eastern seaboard began to vastly outpace that of interior provinces.[3] While per-capita GDP in Xinjiang climbed steadily in the 1980s, it was not witness to the increases witnessed farther east.[4] The spikes in per capita GDP, the skyrocketing standards of living, and the conspicuous consumption that began to characterize life in the east coast boomtowns of Shenzhen and other special economic zones were alien to residents of Xinjiang.

By the 1990s, there was a well-justified fear among many intellectuals as well as high-ranking party officials that China's economic reform strategy was creating a vast chasm between the wealthy east and a poor interior.[5] As a consequence, officials began funneling greater amounts of state investment into central and western China. In Xinjiang, state investments more than doubled in the first half of the decade. The shift was completed in the spring and summer of 1999, as the general secretary of the CCP, Jiang Zemin, who officially took over from Deng in 1989, expressly called for greater attention to the development of the interior. "From now on, the Party and the government must regard the great opening of the west as a major strategic mission and give the issue priority over everything else," Jiang explained in a June speech. Party leaders proudly trumpeted the new "Great Open the West" (Xibu Dakaifa) campaign, which was intended to clear the way for massive state investment.[6] In Xinjiang, the campaign prompted planners to funnel more resources into infrastructural development, namely the construction of new rail links that connected the capital of Urumqi to the southern city of Kashgar as well as greater investment in the extractive industries in the province. According to official data, from 2000 to 2010 the Open the West campaign succeeded in directing around US $3 trillion into western regions, including $60 billion for Xinjiang.[7]

The growing domestic demand for petroleum and China's increasing participation in global resource markets in the 1990s all helped create a renewed emphasis in Xinjiang on the production of raw materials.[8] As a consequence, despite the substantial sums spent in the development of the region's growing rail, highway, and airport networks as part of the campaign, the desire to rapidly increase the production of oil and nonferrous metals meant that state capital investments continued to flow disproportionately toward sites prioritized for investment during the first six decades of the twentieth century. This was made possible by the fact that the mushy goals of the Open the West campaign allowed provincial leaders significant leeway over how the large quantities of state funds flowing into Xinjiang were to be spent.[9] Following the blueprints laid out by their predecessors, planners channeled 70 percent of government fixed investments in the region to the north. The so-called Tianshan Mountain economic belt alone, which includes Urumqi and Karamay-Dushanzi, absorbed over 50 percent of that investment.[10]

While planners did invest in oilfields discovered in the south, the state continued to prioritize Karamay for production. By 1999, the site was producing nearly 30,000 tons of crude oil daily. The expansion in global markets for minerals such as lithium, an element critical in new battery technologies among other uses, led to a resurgence in production at the Soviet-discovered ore fields in Xinjiang's far north, which had been shuttered in 1999 because of declining production. The high price that lithium was fetching on

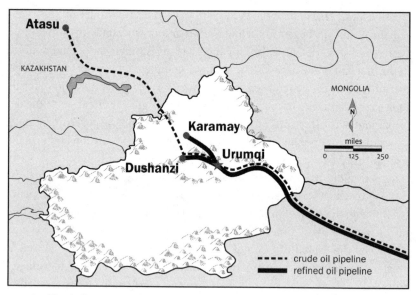

MAP 8.1 The pipelines connecting Xinjiang to China-proper and Eurasia. Source: PetroChina. Map by Debbie Newell.

international markets led government officials to reopen the Koktokay ore field.[11] Several new oilfields prioritized for production also came on line in the 1990s to meet growing demands, and a new oil boomtown began to emerge at Korla, south of the Tianshan Mountain range. But despite this, the power of the layers of investment and state interest laid during the twentieth century continue to point the way north, and still channel state investments in directions prioritized by an earlier generations of Russian, Soviet, Chinese, and provincial-level planners.

The more recent efforts to strengthen the economic connections between China and South and Central Asia have been constructed atop these earlier layers laid in Xinjiang. The so-called One Belt One Road (*yidai yilu*, or OBOR) project unveiled in 2013 and promoted heavily by General Secretary Xi Jinping seeks to strengthen overland and maritime connections binding China to Eurasia. The project showered substantial amounts of capital into the northwest, as it sought to improve the infrastructural ties connecting Xinjiang to Central Asia and beyond. Spending largely followed the patterns developed by earlier generations of surveyors, and in many respects has served to reinforce the layers laid over the region in the twentieth century. The centerpiece of the plan was a new high-speed rail network binding Xinjiang to the old Soviet border crossing at Khorgos. The reinforcement of the region's transport network as part of the OBOR project parallels the development

of a transnational pipeline network concentrated around the refinery at Dushanzi. In a stark reversal of the cash for raw materials exchange that shaped
Xinjiang for much of the twentieth century, China and Kazakhstan signed
a series of agreements in the early 2000s to trade raw petroleum pumped
out of oilfields in northwestern Kazakhstan for Chinese yuan.[12] Eager to
quickly begin processing the raw petroleum, Chinese and Kazakh planners
looked to Dushanzi and the refinery developed first by Soviet planners and
technicians. The completion of a new pipeline connecting the refinery at
Dushanzi to oilfields in northern Kazakhstan's oilfields and beyond in 2006
led to substantial new investments in capacity and technology—new layers
that sat comfortably atop the layers laid over this site since the early twentieth
century (map 8.1).

### Inequality, Ethnicity, and the Legacy of Xinjiang's Layers

In his work on the power of the transport systems developed to deliver new
forms of energy in the United States, Christopher Jones reveals how pipelines
and electrical grids shape and reinforce regional disparities. He notes the
ways in which these technologies channel resources to certain regions at
the expense of others and how the presence of this infrastructure promoted
the unequal distribution of environmental degradation, as new delivery technologies allowed sites of production to be located far from sites of consumption.[13] My work highlights a different spatial impact of these technologies, as
the infrastructure developed to produce, process, and transport resources in
the twentieth century in Xinjiang has played a critical role in promoting and
exacerbating inequalities.

The industrialization campaigns of the 1940s helped create a division between a largely rural Uyghur-dominated south and the immigrant Han majority north. While these divisions had long promoted inequalities, the relatively small amounts of capital invested in Xinjiang in the 1960s, 1970s, and
1980s helped ensure that they remained manageable and the income gap between south and north was relatively narrow. But from 1990 to 2000, the
number of counties in the region afflicted by major income disparities more
than doubled. In 1990, only four counties were in the impoverished "high-
income gap" category identified by one scholar, and all four of these were in
the southern half of the province. By 2000, however, more than twenty-seven
counties found themselves included in this category, all but one of which
were located in the south.[14] In fact, according to 2000 data, Xinjiang has the
fourth-highest level of rural-urban income inequality of any Chinese provincial level unit. In 2003, the average per capita GDP for southern Xinjiang was

5,207 yuan, a number only 60 percent of the provincial average of 8,382 and less than half of the average of 12,723 for prefectures north of the Tianshan.[15]

The problem of growing inequality in the post-Mao era is an issue that CCP leaders have been grappling with throughout China since the 1980s. Indeed, the tensions between northern and southern Xinjiang reflect the greater class divide that separates the coastal haves from the interior have-nots. The trouble for party officials, however, is that in Xinjiang, the geography of economic inequality has been increasingly grafted onto the geography of ethnicity. Scholars have revealed a distinct correlation between income and ethnicity in the province, finding that those prefectures with the highest percentages of Uyghurs and other non-Han minorities are the poorest prefectures. Indeed, the three prefectures with the highest concentrations of non-Han minorities are also the three poorest prefectures in Xinjiang, a pattern that holds true to one degree or another throughout the province.[16] The stark differences between the wealthy Han-dominated (78 percent) prefecture of Karamay with its per capita GDP of 45,033 yuan as opposed to poor, rural Uyghur-majority Khotan (96.8 percent) in the south, with its per capita GDP of only 1,977 yuan illuminates a troubling reality for Chinese leaders. The problem of inequality between south and north, Uyghur and Han in the province appears to only be getting worse, as the layers laid in northern Xinjiang in the first half of the twentieth century channel an on-going stream of state investment toward the north at the expense of the south.

The challenge for Chinese Communist Party officials is that the connection between economic inequality and ethnicity in Xinjiang seems to have fueled a growing resentment among Uyghurs in particular. Ernst Gellner and others have pointed to a correlation between unequal development and increases in nationalism, a phenomenon that is highly applicable to the Xinjiang case, as a growing Uyghur ethnonationalism, the embrace of stricter forms of Islam, and simmering anti-Han sentiments appear to have increased in parallel with the growing inequalities in the region.[17] There has been a long-standing dissatisfaction among many Uyghurs with the People's Republic's ethnicity policy and frustration with inequalities stretching back to the 1950s.[18] But before the 1990s, violent incidents remained rare.[19] As standards of living for Han migrant communities in resource-rich counties in the north climbed toward levels experienced in the boomtowns of coastal China while those in south have remained largely stagnant, the incidents have grown in their frequency and violence. While at first these incidents were primarily occurring in urban areas in the north, where Uyghur communities perhaps best understood the increasingly stark gaps, today they have spread throughout the province. While by no means the only factor in driving interethnic tensions in Xinjiang, the development of the infrastructures of the Chinese state in the twentieth century, indeed the very layers that have formed the region, have played a critical but largely unexamined role in shaping the socioeconomic geography of the region.[20]

Taking this analysis a step further, there is evidence that the chasm between the majority-Han north and the majority-Uyghur south has contributed to the creation of a wider Uyghur underclass in China and has shaped profoundly negative Han impressions of Uyghurs as a social group. The loosening of the enforcement of the PRC's residency regulations in the 1990s and the wealth of job opportunities in coastal China meant that during this period of growing inequalities, many of China's largest cities were witness to an inflow of large numbers of migrants from the interior. Large Uyghur communities from the poor southern oases, a region largely left off of state investment priority lists throughout much of the twentieth century, emerged in cities like Beijing, Shanghai, and Xi'an. Lacking the residency permits that would facilitate housing and employment, these poor, often illegal migrants frequently had no choice but to be involved in semilegal enterprises. For local Han who had few if any other interactions with Uyghurs, these migrants aided in the formation of a perception of Uyghur ethnic identity not tied to the sterilized cultural ethnic markings promoted by the state, but rather one linked to poverty, dirt, and crime.[21] With the rise in the cycles of violence in the region and a perception that Uyghurs are becoming increasingly radicalized, for many Han Chinese, Uyghur identity is becoming inextricably linked to terrorism and violence.

Seeking to resolve the so-called ethnic problem in Xinjiang, economic planners in Beijing appear themselves to be convinced that there is indeed a connection between spatial patterns of investment, growing inequality, and escalating ethnocultural unrest in Xinjiang.[22] There is clearly a belief among many that the growth in state investment since the mid-1990s, but which skyrocketed after 2000 has done little to rectify the tension in the province and in fact appears to have exacerbated it. The fears of rapidly increasing inequality and the yawning gaps between Uyghurs and Han in this border province have prompted planners in Beijing to introduce even more aggressive policies of state intervention. Recent plans have increased investment in the region but have also sought to find ways of channeling that investment directly toward counties with the largest percentages of minorities and with the highest rates of poverty.[23] These efforts seek to level the distribution of state investment and build new layers in the south capable of competing with those constructed in the north over the course of the twentieth century. Scholars have argued that these larger strategies will do little to rectify the fundamental inequalities, as the vast majority of the gains are filtering toward Han migrants with governmental connections rather than a Uyghur underclass in southern Xinjiang that is mired in stifling, ever-accumulating debt.[24] Even if, against all odds, CCP planners were able to fundamentally break Xinjiang's socioeconomic moorings in the north, what is not clear is whether this effort is too late. The question remains whether the layers of state investment and the subsequent strengthening of inequalities in the region have fundamentally scarred the relationship between Uyghurs and Han in ways that larger and larger amounts of state investment will be unable to rectify.

The power of resources in shaping ethnic relations is not unique to Xinjiang. Indeed, these lessons can be applied well beyond this particular distant, resource-rich corner of the Chinese nation-state. The recent intensification of Chinese efforts to gain access to Tibet's rich copper, chromite, lithium, uranium, and gold reserves has played an important role in spearheading greater surveying, the laying of new highway and rail networks, and an outflow of new institutions and larger numbers of Han migrants into Tibet. Chinese surveying teams, engineers, and economic planners have been involved in the process of layering investment in the region in ways that will continue to shape patterns of investment, economic development, political institutions, and immigrant settlement in the future. The wave of Han settlers and greater state control that have paralleled these efforts has been met with protests in Tibet as well as in Tibetan regions like southwestern Gansu, Qinghai, and western Sichuan. This outcome points to a connection between ethnic tensions and resource extraction that has much in common with the Xinjiang case. To what extent future flows of capital investment, the strengthening of state institutions, and the arrival of new migrants that accompany Chinese extractive operations will further exacerbate extant ethnic tensions in the region remains a major source of worry for party leaders in Beijing.[25] In the end, Tibetan ethnic identity, growing resistance to the state, and interethnic violence are critical elements in understanding contemporary Tibet and other Tibetan regions of China. But as in Xinjiang, there is a need to balance this analysis with a broader inquiry into the spatial contours of state power, investment, and economic development and the role that they have played in contributing to ongoing tensions in the region.

The decisions made by various state and nonstate actors over the course of the twentieth century to channel investments into a handful of resource sites centered in northern Xinjiang had real consequences for both the Chinese state and residents of this border region. These decisions had the advantage of facilitating production at a relatively low financial cost; there was, however, a high sociopolitical price. This choice set in stone a pattern of state investment and institutionalization that helped foster internal inequalities among Uyghurs and Han that today runs counter to the broader interests of the Chinese state. The consequences of this decision continue to ripple through Xinjiang in cycles of unrest and state oppression. And yet, despite the best efforts of Beijing to reorient state investment, the layers lain thick over the northern half of Xinjiang continue to shape the contours of state investment and institutional development.

## The Layers Beneath Our Feet

The siren song of Xinjiang's lucrative natural resources and local products entranced a wide assortment of imperial agents, provincial officials, and Chinese state planners in the twentieth century. As the previous seven chapters have shown, their efforts to stake claims to gold, wool, petroleum, tungsten, and lithium among others things at a handful of sites in the northern stretches of the region has shaped long-term patterns of state spending, immigrant settlement, and institutional development. In excavating the transnational layers of state interest and investment, this book reveals the infrastructure that has shaped the contours of the Chinese state in the region and offers a new material perspective on the long-term resonance of Western imperialism and informal empire in Xinjiang. But the connection between natural resources, global markets, and patterns of state investment is not one unique to this singular border region. Rather, this connection has powerfully shaped patterns of economic development and institutionalization as well as influenced state-society relations all along China's borders and beyond.

Beginning in the late nineteenth century, the Qing court's unwillingness to fund costly integrationist efforts in Taiwan along the southeast coast, Manchuria, and Inner Mongolia in the north and Yunnan in the southwest effectively opened the door to a wide assortment of competitors all eager to stake claims to lucrative resources. Taking advantage of the hands-off border policy, powerful empires actively worked to stake claims to the resource wealth in the Qing empire's border regions (map 8.2). The interest of these imperial powers in identifying, extracting, and transporting these essential natural resources prompted them to send out surveying teams, invest in extraction and processing enterprises, and construct transport and other infrastructural networks. The layers of investment and interest helped inscribe their priorities into the landscape. Subsequent Chinese regimes, eager to quickly and cheaply exploit these same resources in these distant, often-rugged border regions, adopted these priorities as their own.

In the nineteenth century, the British and other European empires were intensely focused on the discovery of coalfields along the China coast that

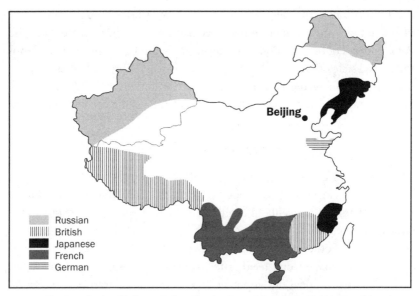

M A P 8.2 Foreign spheres of influence in late Qing border regions. Map by Debbie Newell based on a widely distributed online map. Oswego City School District Regents Exam Prep Center (1999), http://regentsprep.org/Regents/global/themes/imperialism/china.cfm/.

could be exploited to help power their trading vessels and warships. This interest prompted a growing focus on the potential of the Qing empire's resource wealth. The discovery of rich coal seams in the Qing empire's province of Taiwan prompted an interest in the island by a number of imperial powers that culminated in its annexation by Japan in 1895, following the Sino-Japanese War.[26] In Taiwan, Japanese imperial planners undertook extensive geological surveys, created a new rail line that connected the province north to south, and developed several harbors, all of which served as a blueprint for Chinese planners when they took the island over from Japan in 1945. In south China, reports about rich caches of copper, tin, and gold prompted the outflow of French surveyors from Indochina into southern Yunnan province in the late nineteenth century. Operating out of a newly established consulate in the southern Yunnan town of Mengzi, French surveyors, often backed up by wealthy French investors, fanned out into the region in the 1890s. Their efforts verified mineral wealth at several resource sites including the Gejiu tin ore fields. To support these efforts, French officials laid the tracks for a rail line that bound the provincial capital of Kunming to Hanoi and was intended to ferry ores and other local products into French Indochina. While the line would later be abandoned, the legacies of surveys and investments in the region lasted into the twentieth century. The French interest and investments in the region had a particular resonance following the Japanese invasion of China in 1937 and the retreat of the government of the Republic of China to the southwest, when planners relied heavily on ores discovered by the French surveyors to help pay off Lend-Lease aid from the United States.

The clearest parallel with the Xinjiang case is in Manchuria. In the so-called three eastern provinces (*dong sansheng*), Russia and, after 1905, Japan were heavily engaged in the task of developing rail lines, highways, and trade networks that would allow them access to the region's various products. Japanese surveyors were active in surveying Manchuria's minerals and fossil fuels, and the discovery of several important sites served to bolster the arguments for Japan's imperial expansion. After the 1931 Mukden incident, in which Japanese Kwantung Army officers engineered an incident that led to the establishment of the puppet state of Manchukuo, Japanese surveyors and planners were actively engaged in the task of identifying, extracting, processing, and transporting the various minerals and fossil fuels needed to support the war effort. The sizable investments at places like Fushun, which was called upon to produce massive amounts of coal and later shale oil, transformed the site. Planners in the Republic of China after 1945 and the People's Republic after 1949 built directly upon the layers developed by Russian and Japanese planners. The capital investments ensured that Manchuria was a centerpiece of state planning in the early People's Republic and continued to receive substantial quantities of state investment in the First Five Year Plan. This investment helped transform the region into China's industrial backbone for most of the Mao period.[27]

In many ways, Tibet is an outlier. While it existed as a protectorate of the British Empire for much of the first half of the twentieth century, its rugged, mountainous topography and geographic isolation helped limit the influx of external surveyors, capital, and infrastructure. The high price tag associated with extracting, processing, and transporting its resources ensured that neither British nor Chinese leaders were willing to invest substantial amounts of capital into the region.[28] But in other ways, Tibet also helps reveal the power of natural resources in shaping the larger process of state integration in the region. Indeed, the heavy Chinese investment in infrastructural development in Tibet in the 2000s has helped spur state efforts to identify and draw up plans for the extraction of the region's rich resource wealth. Chinese surveying teams, engineers, and economic planners have been involved in an accelerated process of layering investment that will continue to shape patterns of investment, economic development, political institutions, and immigrant settlement in Tibet.

With the notable exception of Tibet, all along China's vast borders the material legacy of formal and informal empires remains clearly visible. Indeed, beginning in the late Qing period and continuing well into the Republic, imperial powers played a substantial role in China's border regions in particular. Whether or not they sought outright territorial concessions, the imperial powers sought direct access to lucrative resources and other economic advantages. The investment and infrastructure prioritized by imperial agents to facilitate the extraction of natural resources continues to shape the priorities of China's economic planners. In these border regions, as in Xinjiang, the investment of capital by deep-pocketed foreign powers helped set future patterns of investment and institutional development, as GMD and later CCP officials proved unwilling or perhaps unable to muster the economic or political capital to change these patterns. The layers laid thick in border regions continue to shape the socioeconomic and political geography of China in ways that demand greater focus and attention. Excavating the transnational layers that have formed modern Xinjiang reveals the often hidden logics that first shaped and later undergirded patterns of state spending and the contours of political power and authority. These logics, driven by imperial interest and cash, have been hidden by a hegemonic, nation-centered narrative that has sought to paper over the transnational forces that have powerfully shaped Chinese border regions like Xinjiang.

The lessons learned in Xinjiang can be applied beyond China. Throughout the global south in particular, a region shaped by the power of formal and informal empires, foreign capital and international demands for certain raw materials have played a central role in shaping long-term patterns of state investment. Paul Baran first explored these legacies with his 1957 inquiry into what came to be termed "dependency theory." This theory, which was later built upon by scholars like Andre Gunder Frank and others, reveals the contours of an enduring global system that was built by imperialism and maintained by demand for raw materials and a flow of capital from former imperial metropoles.[29] Whether located in Asia, Latin America, or Africa, for many states in the global south sitting atop resources demanded by this global system has not resulted in peace and prosperity. Instead, in a wide-ranging debate surrounding what has been called the "resource curse," some scholars have noted that these resource-rich states, eager for revenue, have channeled investment into extraction at the expense of other economic sectors. In so doing, they have helped create imbalanced economies and reinforced authoritarian regimes. Evaluating the merits of this larger debate is beyond the scope of this book. But the case of Xinjiang suggests that perhaps we should view the emerging regional inequalities as a localized "curse" of its own.[30] Pulling back the layers that have shaped patterns of state investment and economic development in Xinjiang offers a new perspective on the long-term impact of imperialism and the socioeconomic consequences of empire.[31]

The case of Xinjiang points to how investment in surveying, extraction, processing, and infrastructure creates long-term spatial patterns of economic and institutional development. But Xinjiang is not unique. Throughout the global south, imperial powers have played central roles in finding, extracting, processing, and transporting natural resources. Whether it is American capital investment in copper mines and railroads in northern Mexico in the late nineteenth century, Soviet oil investments in northern Persia in the 1920s and 1930s, or Dutch and American investments in Venezuelan oilfields in the 1930s, foreign powers had a powerful role in shaping long-term patterns of economic and institutional development.[32] From a more contemporary perspective, it is still too early to understand the long-term power of predominately American surveys, technological investments, and infrastructural development in places like Afghanistan or Iraq since 2001. It is also too early to understand how China's investments in mining operations and infrastructural development efforts at various sites in sub-Saharan Africa since the early 2000s will shape long-term patterns of economic development there. But considering the power of layers in poor states with little capacity for large-scale investments in extractive regimes, the efforts will surely play some role in shaping patterns of investment and development for the foreseeable future.

This effort to excavate the layers of modern Xinjiang is not merely an abstract academic exercise. Indeed, the layers undergirding its landscape not only have a tangible, material presence, they also have very real socioeconomic and political resonances. The geological surveys, drilling rigs, railroads, open pit mines, and processing plants scattered across northern Xinjiang have shaped spatial patterns of state investment, income disparities, and the distribution of state institutions and immigrant communities. Pulling back the layers that have shaped the contours of modern Xinjiang reveals a complex multinational stratigraphy that is layered beneath the landscape of many border regions. The layers continue to exert a powerful but often overlooked influence, shaping their connections to the state, to the wider region, and to the world.

# Abbreviations

AHA:    Academia Historica Archive (Guoshiguan), Taipei
APRF:   Archive of the President of the Russian Federation (Arkhiv Prezidenta
        Rossiiskoi Federatsii), Moscow
AVPRF:  Archive of Foreign Policy of the Russian Federation (Arkhiv vneshnei
        politiki Rossiiskoi Federatsii), Moscow
FHA:    First Historical Archives (Diyi lishi dang'anguan), Beijing
IMHA:   Institute for Modern History Archive (Jindaishisuo dang'anguan), Taipei
KWD:    Wang Xi and Li Enhan, eds., *Kuangwu dang* (Taipei: Zhongyang Yanji-
        uyuan Jindaishi Yanjiusuo, 1960)
NGAC:   National Geological Archive of China (Quanguo dizhi ziliaoguan),
        Beijing
QDXJMJ: *Qingdai Xinjiang mijian zoudu huibian* (Urumqi: Xinjiang Renmin
        Chubanshe, 1996)
RGAE:   Russian State Archive of the Economy (Rossiiskii gosudarstvennyi
        arkhiv ekonomiki), Moscow
RGASPI: Russian State Archive of Socio-Political History (Rossiiskii gosudarstven-
        nyi arkhiv sotsial'no-politicheskoi istorii), Moscow
XJA:    Xinjiang Uyghur Autonomous Region Archives (Xinjiang Weiwuer
        zizhiqu dang'anguan), Urumqi
XJTZ:   Yuan Dahua, ed., *Xinjiang tuzhi* (Taipei: Wenhai Chubanshe, 1906,
        1923, 1965)

# Notes

## Chapter One

1. Yuan Dahua, "Zouwei Xinjiang chouban xinzheng minli weijian ying weiyuan chaban kaifa huangfang bing pi ziyuan yi fucai yuan shi" (Xuantong 3 [1911], 6/6), Imperial Rescript Memorial Collection: 04-01-30-0111-002, FHA.

2. Laura Newby addresses this perspective in Qing dynasty sources, arguing that it was a product of a Qing "textual apartheid." See "The Chinese literary conquest of Xinjiang," *Modern China* 25, no. 4 (1999), 451–474.

3. For more on this system, see Joseph Fletcher, "Ch'ing inner Asia c. 1800," in John K. Fairbank, ed., *The Cambridge history of China, late Ch'ing 1800–1911*, vol. 10, part 1 (Cambridge: Cambridge University Press, 1978); and Joseph Fletcher, "The heyday of the Ch'ing order in Mongolia, Sinkiang, and Tibet," in *The Cambridge history of China, late Ch'ing 1800–1911*, vol. 10, part 1.

4. For more on the pluralistic vision of empire, see James Millward, *Beyond the pass: economy, ethnicity, and empire in Qing central Asia, 1759–1864* (Stanford: Stanford University Press, 1998), 197–203. See also Pamela Crossley, *A translucent mirror: history and identity in Qing imperial ideology* (Berkeley: University of California Press, 1999).

5. Millward, *Beyond the pass*, 58–75.

6. Ibid.; see the conclusion in particular.

7. Gong Zizhen, "Xiyu zhi xingsheng yi," in *Jindai Zhongguo shiliao congkan* (Taipei: Wenhai Chubanshe, 1965), 2888–2893.

8. See Joseph W. Esherick, "How the Qing became China," in Joseph W. Esherick, ed., *Empire to nation: historical perspectives on the making of the modern world* (Berkeley: University of California Press, 2006); Dahpon Ho, "The men who would not be amban and the one who would: four frontline officials and Qing Tibet policy, 1905–1911," *Modern China* 34, no. 2 (April 2008), 210–246; Mary Clabaugh Wright, ed., *China in revolution: the first phase, 1900–1913* (New Haven: Yale University Press, 1968), 5–7.

9. According to Jurgen Osterhammel, informal empires "are a means to the end of securing significant economic interest (trade, direct investments, loans, etc.) that often came about without political support." Jurgen Osterhammel, *Colonialism: A theoretical overview*, tr. Shelley Firsch (Princeton: Markus Wiener Publishers, 2002), 20. For the classic literature on informal empire, see John S. Galbraith, *Reluctant empire: British policy on the South Africa frontier, 1834–1854* (Berkeley: University of California Press, 1963); Ronald Robinson and John Gallagher with

Alice Denny, *Africa and the Victorians: The official mind of imperialism* (London: Macmillan and Co., 1961). See also Peter Duus, Ramon H. Meyers, and Mark Peattie, eds., *The Japanese informal empire in China, 1895–1937* (Princeton: Princeton University Press, 1989).

10. Lin Hsiao-ting, *Tibet and Nationalist China's frontier: intrigues and ethnopolitics, 1928–1949* (Vancouver: University of British Columbia Press, 2006), 13.

11. Richard White, *The middle ground: Indians, empires, and republics in the Great Lakes region, 1650–1815* (Cambridge, Cambridge University Press, 1991), xi.

12. Since the 1980s a number of scholars have begun to challenge this long-standing trope. In particular, see William Kirby, *Germany and Republican China* (Stanford: Stanford University Press, 1984); William Kirby, "Engineering China: birth of the development state, 1928–1937" in Wen-hsin Yeh, ed., *Becoming Chinese: passages to modernity and beyond* (Berkeley: University of California Press, 2000), 137–160. See also Jay Taylor, *The generalissimo: Chiang Kai-shek and the struggle for modern China* (Cambridge: Harvard University Press, 2011), chapter 3 in particular.

13. For more on this effort in China-proper, see Shellen Wu, *Empires of coal: fuelling China's entry into the modern world order, 1860–1920* (Stanford: Stanford University Press, 2015), chapters 3, 4. See also Grace Shen, *Unearthing the nation: modern geology and nationalism in Republican China* (Chicago: University of Chicago Press, 2014).

14. James C. Scott, *Seeing like a state: how certain schemes to improve the human condition have failed* (New Haven: Yale University Press, 1998).

15. See Prasenjit Duara, *Culture, power, and the state: rural north China, 1900–1942* (Stanford: Stanford University Press, 1988), 2. Relying on a definition distilled from Charles Tilly's work (Tilly, ed. *The Formation of National States in Western Europe* (Princeton: Princeton University Press, 1975)), Duara argues that state making includes an "impulse toward bureaucratization and rationalization, the drive to increase revenues for both military and civilian purposes, the often violent resistance of local communities to this process of intrusion and extraction, and the effort by the state to form alliances with new elites to consolidate its power."

16. Timothy Mitchell, *Carbon democracy: political power in the age of oil* (New York: Verso Books, 2011), 2.

17. Christopher Jones, *Routes of power: energy and modern America* (Cambridge: Harvard University Press, 2014), 9. For more on the power of infrastructure, see Thomas Parke Hughes, *Networks of power: electrification in Western society, 1880–1930* (Baltimore: Johns Hopkins University Press, 1993).

18. Chandra Mukerji argues that the material efforts of the state to control the natural world served as a critical element in legitimizing the political authority of the sovereign. Chandra Mukerji, *Impossible engineering: technology and territoriality on the Canal du Midi* (Princeton: Princeton University Press, 2009).

19. Michael Watts, "Resource curse? Governmentality, oil, and power in the Niger Delta, Nigeria," *Geopolitics* 9, no. 1 (2004), 50–80, 60.

20. David Bachman suggests that the desire for resources helped drive a stronger and more aggressive Chinese policy in the region and has helped facilitate the expansion of a coercive apparatus in the region. Bachman, "Making Xinjiang safe for the Han? Contradictions and ironies of Chinese governance in China's northwest," in Morris Rossabi, ed., *Governing China's multiethnic frontiers* (Seattle: University of Washington Press, 2004).

21. Karen Barad, "Posthumanist performativity: toward an understanding of how matter comes to matter," *Signs: journal of women in culture and society* 28, no. 3 (2003), 801–831.

22. The geographer Robert Sack defines this process as "the attempt to affect, influence, or control actions and interactions (of people, things, and relationships) by asserting and attempting to enforce control over a geographic area." Sack, "Human territoriality: a theory," *Annals of the Association of American Geographers* 73, no. 1 (March 1983), 55–74. See also Stuart Elden, *The birth of territory* (Chicago: University of Chicago Press, 2013). For more on mapping, see Matthew Edney, *Mapping an empire: the geographic construction of British India* (Chicago: University of Chicago Press, 1999); Laura Hostetler, *Qing colonial enterprise: ethnography and cartography in early modern China* (Chicago: University of Chicago Press, 2001). For more on mapping in Xinjiang, see Peter Perdue, "Boundaries, maps, and movement: Chinese, Russian, and Mongolian empires in early modern central Eurasia," *International history review* 20, no. 2 (1993), 263–286. For more on the performance of identities, see Peter Sahlins, *Boundaries: the making of France and Spain in the Pyrenees* (Berkeley: University of California Press, 1991).

23. Regarding the arterial nature of power in the colonial context, Cooper writes: "If Foucault saw power as 'capillary,' it was arguably arterial in most colonial contexts—strong near the nodal points of colonial authority, less able to impose its discursive grid elsewhere." *Colonialism in question: theory, knowledge, history* (Berkeley: University of California Press, 2005), 48–49.

24. "Zhonggong zhongyang guanyu Zhong-Su shiyou gongsi he Zhong-Su youse ji xiyou jinshu gongsi ruogan wenti de jueding" (May 6, 1953), in Zhonggong Kelamayishi, Xinjiang shiyou guanliju weiyuanhui shizhi bangongshi, ed., *Zhong-Su shiyou gufen gongsi* (Urumqi: Xinjiang Daxue Chubanshe, 1997), 55.

25. For more on the process of accretion, see Nikhil Anand, "Leaky states: water audits, ignorance, and the politics of infrastructure," *Public culture* 27, no. 2 (2015), 305–330. See also Nikhil Anand, "Accretion," in "The infrastructure toolbox," Hannah Appel, Nikhil Anand, and Akhil Gupta, eds., Theorizing the contemporary series, *Cultural anthropology* website (September 24, 2015), https://culanth.org/fieldsights/715-accretion.

26. Owen Lattimore, *Pivot of Asia: Sinkiang and the inner Asian frontiers of China and Russia* (New York: Little Brown, 1950). See also David Wang, *Under the Soviet shadow: the Yining incident, ethnic conflicts, and international rivalry in Xinjiang, 1944–1949* (Hong Kong: Chinese University Press, 1999); Allen Whiting and General Sheng Shih-ts'ai, *Sinkiang: pawn or pivot?* (East Lansing: Michigan State University Press, 1958); John W. Garver, *Chinese-Soviet relations, 1937–1945: the diplomacy of Chinese nationalism* (Oxford: Oxford University Press, 1988), particularly chapter 6.

27. Much of this scholarship is focused on Japan; see in particular, Prasenjit Duara, *Sovereignty and authenticity: Manchukuo and the east Asian modern* (Lanham: Rowman and Littlefield, 2004). See also various selections in Peter Duus, Ramon H. Meyers, and Mark Peattie, eds., *The Japanese wartime empire, 1931–1945* (Princeton: Princeton University Press, 1996); Daqing Yang, "Unclaimed prize: oil explorations in pre-1941 Manchuria," unpublished paper, 2013. For a more recent work that does seek to draw out more of the longer-term connections, see Victor Seow, *Carbon technocracy: east Asian energy regimes and the industrial modern, 1900–1957* (Ph.D. dissertation, Harvard University, 2014).

28. Susan Leigh Star, "The ethnography of infrastructure," *American behavioral scientist* 43, no. 3 (November/December 1999), 377–391, 379.

29. I. Beller-Hann, M. C. Cesaro; R. Harris, and J. Smith Finley, *Situating the Uyghurs between China and Central Asia* (Aldershot: Ashgate, 2007); Ondrej Klimes, *Struggle by the pen: the Uyghur discourse of nation and national interest, 1900–1949* (Boston: Brill, 2015); Rian Thum, *The sacred routes of Uyghur history* (Cambridge: Harvard University Press, 2014). See also Gardner

Bovingdon, "The history of the history of Xinjiang," *Twentieth century China* 26, no. 1 (2001), 95-139.

30. For examples, see Joanne Smith Finley, *The art of symbolic resistance: Uyghur identities and Uyghur-Han relations in contemporary Xinjiang* (Leiden: Brill, 2013); Gardner Bovingdon, *The Uyghurs: strangers in their own land* (New York: Columbia University Press, 2010); Gardner Bovingdon, "The not-so-silent majority: Uyghur resistance to Han rule in Xinjiang," *Modern China* 28, no. 1 (2002), 39-78; Gardner Bovingdon, *Autonomy in Xinjiang: Han nationalist imperatives and Uyghur discontent* (Washington: East West Center, 2004).

31. The Chinese Communist Party has sought to enforce a historical narrative of Xinjiang that highlights the enduring connection between China-based capitals and this border region. For examples of this narrative, see Li Sheng, *Xinjiang of China: its past and present* (Urumqi: Xinjiang People's Publishing House, 2005). See also Ma Dazheng, *Xinjiang shijian* (Urumqi: Xinjiang Renmin Chubanshe, 2006); Tian Weijiang, *Xinjiang lishi* (Beijing: Wuzhou Chuanbo Chubanshe, 2001).

32. David Brophy, *Uyghur nation: reform and revolution on the Russia-China frontier* (Cambridge: Harvard University Press, 2016); Justin Jacobs, *Xinjiang and the modern Chinese state* (Seattle: University of Washington Press, 2016). See also Eric T. Schluessel, *The Muslim emperor of China: everyday politics in colonial Xinjiang* (Ph.D. dissertation, Harvard University, 2016); for a work focused on the formation of earlier political systems, see Kim Kwangmin, *Borderland capitalism: Turkestan produce, Qing silver, and the birth of an eastern market* (Stanford: Stanford University Press, 2016).

33. Star, "The ethnography of infrastructure," 377.

34. Newby, "The Chinese literary conquest of Xinjiang," 464-465.

35. Millward, *Beyond the pass*, see chapter 6. Various uprisings in Xinjiang reaffirmed the wisdom of this policy for Qing officials in the nineteenth century.

36. This was true even under regimes largely controlled by indigenous ethnic groups. The clearest example of this is the second East Turkestan Republic (1944-49), which I address in chapter 6.

37. For more on the Zunghar Empire and Qing campaigns against it in the eighteenth century, see Peter Perdue, *China marches west: the Qing conquest of central Eurasia* (Cambridge: Belknap Press, 2010).

## Chapter Two

1. Hengfu, Yu Minzhong, and Liu Tongxun, eds., *Qinding huangyu xiyu tuzhi*, section 34 (Taipei: Shangwuju, 1983, 1762).

2. Peter Perdue reveals the reclamation strategy employed by the Yongzheng emperor in his northwestern campaigns in the mid-eighteenth century. Perdue, *China marches west*. The strategy was part of a broader effort, as David Bello notes that the Qing court embraced a larger campaign of borderland reclamation beginning in the early eighteenth century in response to the explosion of the empire's agrarian Han population. Bello, *Across forest, steppe, and mountain* (Cambridge: Cambridge University Press, 2016), 43-44.

3. In 1784, the Shaan-Gan governor-general Fukang'an noted that the farms centered around Urumqi, Suilai, and Jimusa, all of which are located along the northern road, produced enough grain in one year to support the troops stationed in the region for three. Xinjiang Weiwu'er zizhuqu difangzhi bianzuan weiyuanhui, ed., *Xinijang tongzhi di liushiliujuan liangshizhi* (Urumqi: Xin-

jiang Renmin Chubanshe, 2000), 50; for more on the Qing agricultural garrisons in the West, see Perdue, *China marches west*, chapters 9, 10.

4. Eric T. Schluessel convincingly argues that the reconquest of Xinjiang by Zuo and his New Hunan Army should be viewed not as an effort in Qing colonialism, but rather as what was in many respects a colonial project undertaken by Hunanese statecraft adherents. See Schluessel, "The Muslim emperor of China," especially chapter 1.

5. For more on Zuo's perspective on agriculture, see Peter Lavelle, "Cultivating empire: Zuo Zongtang's agriculture, environment, and reconstruction in the late Qing," in Sherman Cochran and Paul G. Pickowicz, eds., *China on the margins* (Ithaca: Cornell East Asia Series, 2010), 43-64.

6. Scott, *Seeing like a state*.                                              .

7. For more on this process, see Peter Lavelle, "Water and agricultural development in post-reconquest Xinjiang," unpublished paper.

8. After liberating Karashar in central Xinjiang, Zuo set up reconstruction bureaus and ordered them to distribute agricultural items: "give aid in the form of seeds and wait until the harvest and then tax them in terms of tilling and pasturing." Quoted in Hua Li, *Qingdai Xinjiang nongye kaifashi* (Harbin: Heilongjiang Jiaoyu Chubanshe, 1998), 229, 231.

9. In 1876, the Qing court called on local officials to reclaim land in areas around Urumqi in order to give these poor people "a way to earn a living and prevent them from wandering and becoming bandits." Quoted in ibid., 228.

10. XJTZ, 14.

11. Ibid., 16.

12. The report from Governor Liu Jintang is cited in Lavelle, "Water and agricultural development in post-reconquest Xinjiang," 26.

13. Zuo was particularly influenced by Gong Zizhen, who called for a large-scale agricultural reclamation campaign that would facilitate the integration of Xinjiang into the empire. For more on Gong, see Millward, *Beyond the pass*, 241.

14. Millward argues that a series of uprisings in the first half of the nineteenth century prompted the Qing court to adopt a new policy in which immigrant groups brought in from China-proper were to serve as a demographic counterweight to the large population of Turkic Muslims in the region. Ibid., 211–231.

15. Liu Jintang noted on several occasions that manual laborers in northern Xinjiang demanded daily wages of two to three copper cash daily, an amount far higher than anywhere in China-proper. See Liu Jintang, "Xinjiang yizhan jingfei qing canzhuobu yiliang wei bian tong zhe" (Guangxu 11 [1885], 2/26), in QDXJMJ, vol. 1, doc. 177, 268–269; Liu Jintang, "Xinjiang Cheng zhu ge gong gaojun qing jiang zhe" (Guangxu 13 [1887], 7/26), in QDXJMJ, vol. 1, doc. 301, 425–426.

16. Liu Jintang, "Xinjiang nanlu xi sicheng xingxiu ge gong wanjun bing chouban ying xiu ge gong zhe," in QDXJMJ, vol. 1, doc. 74, 68.

17. For more on interprovincial assistance, see Millward, *Beyond the pass*, 58–63. The vast majority of interprovincial assistance came from the treasury surpluses of four coastal provinces still known for their high agricultural production: Fujian, Guangdong, Zhejiang, and Hubei.

18. Liu, "Xinjiang yizhan jingfei qing canzhuobu yiliang wei bian tong zhe," 268.

19. Quoted in Nailene Chou, "Frontier studies and changing frontier administration in late Ch'ing China, 1759–1911" (Ph.D. dissertation, University of Washington, 1976), 199. These fears were not without foundation. In June 1871, the Russian Empire, taking advantage of the chaos

in the region during the Yakub Beg rebellion, occupied 1,220 square miles of the Ili River valley. The land was eventually handed back in 1881 following a military standoff with General Zuo Zongtang's army, but the event convinced many in the court of the need to establish clearer claims to borderlands like Xinjiang.

20. See Perdue, "Boundaries, maps, and movement." See also Esherick, "How the Qing became China."

21. XJTZ, section 29, 16.

22. For more on the cultural power of landscape transformation, see Ruth Meserve, "The inhospitable land of the barbarian," *Journal of Asian history* 16, no. 1 (1982); Almaz Khan, "Who are the Mongols? state, ethnicity, and the politics of representation in the PRC," in Melissa Brown, ed., *Negotiating ethnicities in China and Taiwan* (Berkeley: Institute of east Asian studies, 1996). Nicola Di Cosmo addresses the origins of the wasteland-field dichotomy in the Han dynasty in Di Cosmo, *Ancient China and its enemies: the rise of nomadic power in east Asian history* (Cambridge: Cambridge University Press, 2004).

23. See Di Cosmo, *Ancient China and its enemies*, chapter 8; Nicholas K. Menzies "Strategic space: exclusion and inclusion in wildland policies in late imperial China," *Modern Asian studies* 26, no. 4 (1992), 724. According to Kenneth Pomeranz, reclamation was part of a "liberal project" undertaken by Ming and Qing officials that was intended to lift the Confucian morality of "the people" by improving their material condition. Pomeranz, "The transformation of China's environment, 1500–2000," in Edmund Burke III and Kenneth Pomeranz, eds., *Environment in world history* (Berkeley: University of California Press, 2009), 121.

24. Liu Jintang, "Zunzhi nishe nanlu junxianzhe" (Guangxu 8 [1882], 7/3), in QDXJMJ, vol. 2, doc. 97, 103.

25. "Qingban Xinjiang tunken zhe" (Guangxu 9 [1883], 11/18), in QDXJMJ, vol. 2, doc. 426, 612.

26. Quoted in XJTZ, section 29, 1.

27. Quoted in Ibid. In 2013, production rates in the U.S. were at record highs of sixty-four bushels per acre. See Tom Doran, "Record tying U.S. average wheat yield projected" (July 26, 2013), in *Agrinews* (http://agrinewspubs.com/Content/News/Markets/Article/Record-tying-U -S--average-wheat-yield-projected-/8/26/7704). Assuming that a little less than two bushels of seed need to be planted per acre (according to Dan Folske, "How many seeds per acre?" in *North Dakota Extension Service, Burke County* [January 21, 2013] http://www.ag.ndsu.edu/burkecoun tyextension/crops/how-many-seeds-per-acre), this points to a yield-to-seed ratio of 32.5:1, less than 40:1–50:1.

28. Zuo's statement was made addressing the efficacy of the karez, which were spring-fed irrigation canals retained in underground tunnels. Quoted in Lavelle, "Water and agricultural development in post-reconquest Xinjiang," 21.

29. Officials cited the claims that Han dynasty soldiers transformed five thousand hectares of land in central Xinjiang from wasteland into a region with a "mild climate with beautiful fields fed by irrigation canals and sown with the five grains." Huang Shulin, *Ershisishi jiutong zhengdian leiyao hebian*, section 320 (Taipei: Hongqiao Shudian, 1968 reprint), 38, 6.

30. Liu Jintang, "Xinjiang zhuken renfan choukuan ancha qingxing" (Guangxu 12 [1886], 12/20), in QDXJMJ, vol. 1, docs. 268, 385–387.

31. Liu, "Xinjiang liunianfen zheng shou e'liang shuili shumu pian."

32. Liu, "Xingban tunken bing ancha hukou chabao yinliang zhe."

33. Liu Jintang, "Xingban tunken bing ancha hukou chabao yinliang zhe" (Guangxu 13 [1887], 2/12), in QDXJMJ, vol. 1, doc. 269, 387–388.

34. Wei Jianhua, "Qingdai xiexiang zhidu gailun," in Wu Fuhuai and Wei Changhong, eds., *Xinjiang jinxiandai jingji yanjiu wenji* (Urumqi: Xinjiang Daxue Chubanshe, 2002), 231.

35. Li Lei and Tian Hua, "Qingdai Xinjiang jianshenghou de fushui zhidu yanjiu," in *Xinjiang jinxiandai jingji yanjiu wenji*, 341–423, 394.

36. Liu Jintang, "Chaming Xinjiang yongkuan wuke shanjian cunzhu baobu zhe," in QDXJMJ, vol. 1, doc. 262, 376.

37. Liu, "Xinjiang nanlu xi sicheng xingxiu ge gong wanjun bing chouban ying xiu ge gong zhe."

38. For more information on local canals, see XJTZ, sections 73–78.

39. Hua, *Qingdai Xinjiang nongye kaifashi*, 243; for more on the larger process of reclamation, see Lavelle, "Water and agricultural development in post-reconquest Xinjiang."

40. See XJTZ, sections 73–78. See also Hua, *Qingdai Xinjiang nongye kaifashi.*

41. Ibid., section 30, 3.

42. Liu Jintang, "Ken enhuo mian guanwai Zhen-Di dao shu linian min qian gexiang yinliang zhe" (Guangxu 10 [1884], 10/16), in QDXJMJ, vol. 1, doc. 167, 254.

43. Hua, *Qingdai Xinjiang nongye kaifashi*, 262.

44. Tao Mo, "Fuzou kaohe qianliang zhengdun lijin ge jie zhe" (Guangxu 21 [1895], 9/28), in QDXJMJ, vol. 2, doc. 673, 1004–1005.

45. Wei, "Qingdai xiexiang zhidu gailun," 233.

46. Xinjiang Weiwu'er zizhiqu difangzhi bianzuan weiyuanhui, ed., *Xinjiang tongzhi, caizheng* (vol. 57) (Urumqi: Xinjiang Renmin Chubanshe, 1999), 34.

47. Ibid., 35.

48. "Shaan-Gan Zongdu shengxun zou yugu guanneiwai sanshisannian xiexiang zhe" (no date), Grand Council Memorial Collection, FHA, cited in Wei, "Qingdai xiexiang zhidu gailun," 231; "Shaan-Gan zongdu Chang Geng yuzhu Xuantong sannian guanneiwai xiexiang zhe" (Xuantong 2 [1910], 6/27), quoted in Wei, "Qingdai xiexiang zhidu gailun," 234.

49. Samuju, "Shitun bozhong wanjun zhe" (no date), in QDXJMJ, vol. 2, doc. 865, 1121–1123. Qing sources are clearly estimating these numbers, as they are exactly the same from year to year. This figure does not represent the production in Burultokay specifically, but rather all of the wider region.

50. Samuju, "Qing reng choubo tuntian jingfei pian," in QDXJMJ, vol. 2, doc. 935, 1166.

51. Ibid.

52. Samuju, "Buluntuohai qutun ge gong gao cheng qing jiang yongkuan kaidan baoxiao zhe" (1903), in QDXJMJ, vol. 2, doc. 962, 1183–1184.

53. Ma Liang, Guangfu, "Yili Tegusitaliu bingtun renzhen geng zuo zhe" (Guangxu 29 [1903], 12/27), in QDXJMJ, vol. 3, doc. 1074, 1324–1326.

54. Ma Liang, Guangfu, "Qingzhun Tegusitaliu difang jieban tunken pian" (no date), in QDXJMJ, vol. 3, doc. 1115, 1368–1369.

55. Ibid.

56. Yuan Dahua, "Kaipi liyuan yi shibian yu" (Xuantong 3 [1911], 6/1), in XJTZ, section 106, 12.

57. Ibid., 29, 3.

58. For more on these declines, see Kataoka Kazutada, *Shincho Shinkyo toji kenkyu* (Tokyo: Yusan Kaku, 1991). These declines in arable land were combined with increases in grain tax collection particularly in the north. This seeming inconsistency is due to the substantial increase in percentages taken on productive fields. XJTZ, section 30, 1.

59. See Millward, *Eurasian crossroads: a history of Xinjiang* (New York: Columbia University Press, 2007), 102–105. This stands in contrast to Manchuria, where the imperial household department organized foraging parties of Qing banner troops to acquire tributary furs, wild ginseng, and pearls. See Jonathan Schlesinger, *A world trimmed with fur: wild things, pristine places, and the natural fringes of Qing rule* (Stanford: Stanford University Press, 2016), chapter 2; see also Bello, *Across forest, steppe, and mountain*, chapter 2.

60. Millward, *Beyond the pass*, 80–112.

61. Quoted in Zhao Fengtian, *Wanqing qushi nian jingji sixiang shi* [English title: Economic thought during the last fifty years of the Ch'ing period] (M.A. thesis, Harvard Yanjing Center, 1968), 42. For more on the shift regarding mining, see Wu, *Empires of coal*.

62. Zhao, *Wanqing qushi nian jingji sixiang shi*, 42. His calls for the state's involvement in mining points to an essential argument for the expansion of mining operations: a recognition that in the age of avaricious empires, minerals and other lucrative resources were both an opportunity and a threat. Shellen Wu explores this tension that resources presented, as they offered both opportunity for wealth as well as risk by attracting the attention of outside powers. See Wu, *Empires of coal*.

63. Since the early modern period, Western statecraft thinkers had emphasized the obligation of rulers to fully manage and exploit resources present in sovereign territory. This approach served as the precursor to the modern statist approach of aggressively promoting mineral and other forms of production through the employment of science and technology. Chandra Mukerji argues that this perspective on territorial management was rooted in Christian humanism of the sixteenth century. She argues that these Christian humanists sought to restore biblical Eden through enlightened human action, a perspective that allowed for a greater human intervention in the natural world. See "Material practices of domination: Christian humanism, the built environment, and techniques of Western power," *Theory and society* 31, no. 1 (2002), 1–34. For more on the early modern connection between the state and the material world, see also Mukerji, *Impossible engineering*.

64. Shellen Wu, "The Search for coal in the age of empires: Ferdinand von Richthofen's odyssey in China, 1860–1920," *American historical review* 119, no. 2 (April 2014), 357.

65. Ibid., 360; for more on the nascent geological community, see Shen, *Unearthing the nation*.

66. Bruce Braun, "Producing vertical territory: geology and governmentality in late Victorian Canada," *Ecumene* 7, no. 1 (2000), 15–16.

67. Scott, *Seeing like a state*, 51. David Bello argues that the Qing did pursue some level of "legibility" in border regions in order to facilitate their ethnic policy, which was closely tied to the protection of certain forms of production. Bello, *Across forest, steppe, and mountain* 158. This legibility, however, was relatively limited and did not extend to state-sponsored production.

68. See Ma Dazheng and Huang Guozheng, eds., *Xinjiang xiangtuzhi gao* (Beijing: Quanguo Tushuguan Wenxian Suwei Fuzhi Zhongxin, 2010). This source was originally published in the late nineteenth and early twentieth centuries. See also Wu Tingxie, *Xinjiang daji bubian* (Beijing: Zhongyang Minzuxue Yuanshao Shu Minzu Guji Zhengli Chuban Guihua Lingdao Xiaozu, 1983).

69. Justin Jacobs discusses the Qing "imperial repertoire" in Xinjiang in *Xinjiang and the modern Chinese state* (Seattle: University of Washington Press, 2016), chapter 1. For a more general discussion of imperial repertoires, see Jane Burbank and Frederick Cooper, *Empires*

*in world history: power and the politics of difference* (Princeton: Princeton University Press, 2010), 3.

70. XJTZ, section 28, 3.

71. Ibid., section 29, 1.

72. For more on the role of gold mines in settling border regions, see Judd Kinzley, "Turning prospectors into settlers: gold, immigrant miners, and the settlement of the frontier in late Qing Xinjiang," in Sherman Cochran and Paul Pickowicz, eds., *China on the margins* (Ithaca: Cornell East Asia Series, 2010).

73. In practical terms, these critics were absolutely right, as the bulk of the funds from interprovincial assistance tended to be drawn from treasuries in the southeast. See Wei, "Qingdai xiexiang zhidu gailun," 224-225.

74. XJTZ, section 28, 1.

75. Yuan Dahua, "Zou wei Xinjiang chouban Xinzheng minli weijian ying weiyuan chaban kaifa huangfang bing pi ziyuan yi fucai yuanshi" (Xuantong 3 [1911], 6/6), Imperial Rescript Collection: 04-01-30-0111-002, FHA.

## Chapter Three

1. Su Beihai, *Xiyu lishi dili* (Urumqi: Xinjiang Daxue Chubanshe 1993), 316. See also Ma and Huang, eds., *Xinjiang xiangtuzhi gao*, 744. See also XJTZ, section 29.

2. E-tu Zen Sun, "Mining labor in the Ch'ing period," in Albert Feuerwerker, Rhoads Murphey, and Mary Clabaugh Wright, eds., *Approaches to Chinese history* (Berkeley: University of California Press, 1967), 48. See also E-tu Zen Sun, "Ch'ing government and the mineral industries before 1800," *Journal of Asian studies* 27, no. 4 (August 1968), 835-845. See also Kinzley, "Turning prospectors into settlers," 17-41.

3. Shellen Wu argues that late Qing officials embraced the "giddy promise of science as the key to the West's wealth and power." Wu, *Empires of coal*, 67.

4. It should be noted that Russian geologists uncovered resource sites with the help of indigenous guides, advice from locals, and published Chinese gazetteers and reports. Aside from brief mentions in reports, I have not been able to uncover the depth of their impact on the expeditions. But the decisions planners made after discovery, as they prioritized certain sites over others is more important in this narrative, as leaders tended to emphasize resources located in close proximity to the Russian border and Russian transport infrastructure. For a case of native informants shaping the patterns of surveys, see Erik Mueggler, *The paper road: archive and experience in the botanical exploration of western China and Tibet* (Berkeley: University of California Press, 2011).

5. For more on Richthofen's influence, see Wu, *Empires of coal*; "great underground race" appears on 131. French surveys are addressed in William Collins, *Mineral enterprise in China* (New York: MacMillan Company, 1918), 52-54. For the Chinese side, see KWD, vols. 2 (for Shandong), 6 (for Yunnan), 7 (for Heilongjiang and Jilin), and 8 (for Xinjiang and Mongolia [Kulun]).

6. Xu Jingcheng, "Jinchen yangren cetan Xinjiang Hetian yidai jinkuang qingxing zhe," in QDXJMJ, vol. 2, doc. 548, 856.

7. "All of Yudianzi [modern day Yutian, located just east of Hotan and north of the Kunlun Mountains] has large amounts of gold and jade," writes the author of the *Hanshu*. Quoted in Xinjiang Weiwu'er zizhiqu difangzhi bianzuan weiyuanhui, ed., *Xinjiang tongzhi: shiyou gongye* (vol. 40) (Urumqi: Xinjiang Renmin Chubanshe, 1999), 494.

8. For more on this role for miners see Kinzley, "Turning prospectors into settlers."

9. Xu, "Jinchen yangren cetan Xinjiang Hetian yidai jinkuang qingxing zhe."

10. "Zunyi Xinjiang nanlu jinkuang qingxing qingzhi chi Shaan du Xin fuxiang cha tuoyi" (March 26, 1893), in KWD doc. 2759, 4847.

11. Ibid., 4848.

12. *Qing shi lu*, section 330, 10.

13. "Zongshu shou junjichu jiaochu Heilongjiang jiangjun Hong Tang chaozhe" (January 20, 1888), in KWD, doc. 2553, 4360.

14. XJTZ 29, 34.

15. Tao Mo, "Fuzou Hetian jinkuang qingxing zhe" (Guangxu 21 [1895], 11/6), in QDXJMJ, vol. 2, doc. 676, 1010–1011.

16. Liu Jintang, "Qing bo bu kuan mibu Xinjiang suomian lijin bing jieji jinxiang zhe" (Guangxu 8 [1882], 9/22), in QDXJMJ, vol. 1, doc. 101, 112.

17. Chang Geng, "Zouwei Xinjiang siku shicun yinyuan shajin tiaojin qing liubei banli xinzheng zhe" (Guangxu 33 [1907], 12/18), Imperial Rescript Collection: 04-01-35-0852-004, FHA.

18. *Xinjiang tongzhi: caizheng* (vol. 57), 35.

19. See Liu Jinzao, *Qingchao duwenxian tongkao*, vol. 1 (Shanghai: Zhejiang guji chubanshe, 2000), *Guoyong* 6 section 68, 8235.

20. *Xinjiang quan sheng caizheng shuoming shu* (Nanjing: Jingji Xuehui, 1914), 528.

21. Tao Mo, "Fuzou kaohe qianliang zhengdun lijin gejie zhe," in QDXJMJ, vol. 2, doc. 673, 1004.

22. Chang Geng, "Zouchen tiankou liezhi gekuan jianping yinliangcun houbo yongshi" (Guangxu 34 [1908], 3/28), Imperial Rescript Memorial Collection: 04-01-35-0841-064, FHA.

23. Liankui, "Zouchen Xinjiang Wuke juanraomin shi" (Guangxu 34 [1908], 3/12), Imperial Rescript Memorial Collection: 04-01-35-0585-006, FHA.

24. The edict is quoted in "Zongshu shou junjichu jiaochu Xinjiang xunfu Rao Yingqi deng chazhe" (September 22, 1897), in KWD doc. 2768, 4859.

25. "Zongshu shou shu Gansu Xinjiang xunfu Rao Yingqi wen" (February 29, 1896), in KWD doc. 2761, 4849.

26. See XJTZ, section 29, 35.

27. Ibid.

28. Ibid.

29. "Zongshu shou junjichu jiaochu Xinjiang xunfu Rao Yingqi wen," in KWD doc. 2761, 4850.

30. See Kinzley, "Turning prospectors into settlers."

31. "Lukuang zongju shou Xinjiang xunfu Rao Yingqi wen" (March 3, 1901), in KWD doc. 2766, 4855.

32. Ibid.

33. Miners were said to collect only one or two *fen* per day of washed gold at the most. "Lukuang zongju Xinjiang xunfu Rao Yingqi wen fu zougao" (February 4, 1902), KWD doc. 2767, 4856.

34. See Yang Zuanxu, *Xinjiang chuyi* (Wuchang: Wuchang Tu'an Yinshua Gongsi, 1913, 1919), 7.

35. XJTZ, section 29, 40.

36. This figure comes from Japanese traveler Tachibana Zuicho, who investigated a gold mining site on the Tianshan South Road at Qiemo in 1908. Ju Ruichao, *Ju Ruichao xixingji*, trans. Liu Hongliang (Urumqi: Xinjiang Renmin Chubanshe, 1999), 85.

37. Ibid.

38. See Ma and Huang, *Xinjiang xiangtuzhi gao*.

39. Ju, *Ju Ruichao xixingji*, 85.

40. This list was drawn from Wu Tingxie, ed., *Xinjiang daji bubian*, section 8, 263–395.

41. As an added bonus, the revenue generated in these ore sites was often not reported to Beijing and thus would not undermine the annual provision of interprovincial assistance.

42. "Zongshu shou Heilongjiang jiangjun Yi-ke-tang-a wen fu Mo-Gan liangkuang Guangxu 10 nian 10 yuefen shouzhi jingshu qingzhe" (February 6, 1890), in KWD doc. 2592, 4462.

43. Wu, *Empires of coal*, 131.

44. Ibid., 134–145.

45. "Zongshu shou junjichu jiaochu Beiyhang dachen Li Hongzhang chaozhe" (January 20, 1888), in KWD doc. 2553, 4360.

46. Wang Shunan, "Taolu laoren sui nianlu," in Zhang Bofeng and Gu Ya, eds., *Jindai bihai* (Chengdu: Sichuan Renmin Chubanshe, 1988 reprint), 71.

47. Tao Mo, "Fuzou Hetian jinkuang qingxing zhe," 1008.

48. "Zongshu shou Xinjiang shou xunfu Rao Yingqi wen fu zougao ji Zhong-E keban jinkuang hetong" (August 5, 1899), in KWD doc. 2773, 4865.

49. Ibid.

50. V. A. Obruchev, *The minerals of Dzungaria* (Washington, D.C.: U.S. Joint Publications Research Service, 1961), 36. This work is a U.S. government translation of an earlier work published by Obruchev. To put the yield in perspective, gold veins at Cripple Creek in Colorado, one of the most significant gold strikes of the late nineteenth century, typically yielded an average of nineteen ounces per ton of ore.

51. "Lukuang zongju shou Xinjiang xunfu Rao Yingqi wen fuzou pian" (February 14, 1901), in KWD doc. 2775, 4873.

52. "Lukuang zongju shou Xinjiang xunfu Rao Yingqi wen fuzou gao" (February 14, 1901), in KWD doc. 2776, 4876.

53. In his report, Obruchev argued that overconfidence in the site's ore wealth led to poor decisions about how to allocate capital. *The minerals of Dzungaria*, 35–36.

54. Ibid., 74.

55. Obruchev lists the importance of these two geologists in his report on northern Xinjiang, Ibid.

56. Ibid., 75.

57. "Waiwubu shou Xinjiang xunfu zi fufu E lingshi zhaohui" (May 3, 1905), in KWD doc. 2785, 4891–4893.

58. Obruchev, *Minerals of Dzungaria*, 75.

59. "Waiwubu shou Xinjiang xunfu zi fufu E lingshi zhaohui," in KWD doc. 2786, 4894.

60. Wang Lianfang, "Jiu Zhongguo Xinjiang shiyou dashi nianbiao," in Habudoula, ed, *Xinjiang shiyou gongye shiliao xuanji*, vol. 1 (Urumqi: Zhengxie Xinjiang Weiwu'er zizhiqu weiyuanhui wenshiziliao he xuexi weiyuanhui chubanshe, 2005), 23.

61. Wang, "Taolu laoren sui nianlu," 73.

62. Overall, the mining and refining operations employed seventy-two people and cost investors 10,870 taels annually. *Xinjiang quan sheng caizheng shuoming shu*, 602–603.

63. Wang, "Taolu laoren sui nianlu," 73.

64. Wang, "Jiu Zhongguo Xinjiang shiyou dashi nianbiao," 24.

65. Yang Zengxin, "Diancheng ni jigu sheli kuangyou gongsi wen," in *Buguozhai wendu*, Li Yushu, ed. (Taipei: Wenhai Chubanshe, 1965).

66. Yang, "Diancheng wunianfen zhongyang chuankuan linan zeng chouwen" (November 8, 1915), in *Buguozhai wendu*, 2956.

67. Yang, "Diancheng choukuan shouhui Yili zhibi buyi di jie ezhai wen" (November 27, 1914), in *Buguozhai wendu*, 2817. According to the British consulate in Kashgar, the loan was made against grain tax collection as well as coal mines in the vicinity of Ili. "Kashgar Diaries, July 31, 1912," in *Kashgar Diaries: 1912–1920*, British India Office Collection: L/PS/10/825 (British Library, London), 276.

68. Yang Zengxin, "Zhiling kaqiang bang shenyuan Long Xilin chafu Yingren daowa jinkuang wen" (January 16, 1914), in *Buguozhai wendu*, vol. 5, 2448.

69. Yang Zengxin, "Zhi Zhou Daoyi lun Ashan yi zhuzhong kenhuang kaikuang han" (September 24, 1919), in *Buguozhai wendu*, vol. 2, 792.

70. Ibid.

71. Yang, "Ling she linshi qingli caizheng suowen" (August 1, 1912), in *Buguozhai wendu*, vol. 5, 2777.

72. For more on early Republican finances in Xinjiang, see Judd Creighton Kinzley, "Staking claims to China's borderland: oil, ores, and state-building in Xinjiang province, 1893–1964" (Ph.D. dissertation: University of California, San Diego, 2012), 86–93.

73. British sources point to the richness of the Altay's gold wealth. According to a report, gold of a purity of 985 per mlle was often panned at the rate of 10–15 grams per ton of ore. "Kashgar Diary for December 1923 and January 1924," in *Kashgar Diaries, 1921–1930*, British India Office Collection: L/PS/10/976 (British Library, London), 1.

74. "A'ertai Zhong-E kuangwu jiashe an" (Minguo 3 [1914], 11th month), Ministry of Foreign Affairs Collection, 03-03-012-02-022; 03-03-012-02-018; and 03-03-012-02-017, IMHA.

75. For more on the impact of the Russian Empire's collapse in Xinjiang, see Jacobs, *Xinjiang and the modern Chinese state*, 51–74.

76. See Daniel Yergin, *The prize: the epic quest for oil, money, and power* (New York: Free Press, 1992), 167–302.

77. "Wu-Su liang xian difang youkuang" (Minguo 4 [1915], 11/22), Ministry of Foreign Affairs Collection: 08-24-61-001-01, IMHA, 7.

78. Ibid.

79. 25,000 would be raised from merchants. The provincial government would only put up 5,000. "Wu-su liang xian difang youkuang" (Minguo 4 [1915], 11/23), Ministry of Foreign Affairs Collection: 08-24-61-001-01(Institute of Modern History Archive, Academia Sinica, Taipei), 13.

80. Ibid.

81. Even in Xinjiang's isolated market, the rapidly increasing price of oil was clearly visible. Yang noted in a 1919 report to Beijing that the cost of lamp oil had more than quadrupled over the course of the war: oil that had once sold for just over 1.5 copper cash per catty of oil (slightly over one pound) was now being sold for well more than 6 cash.

82. Lin Jing, *Xibei congbian* (Taipei: Wenhai Chubanshe, 1930), 265.

83. *National Geological Survey of China, 1916–1931* (Nanjing: National Geological Survey of China, 1931).

84. Wong Wen-hao [Weng Wenhao], *The mineral resources of China (metals and non-metals except coal)* [Chinese title: *Zhongguo kuangchan zhilue*] in *Memoirs of the Geological Survey of China*, series B, no. 1 (July 1919), 243–245.

85. Xie Jiarong, "Zhongguo kuangye jiyao," *Dizhi huibao* 2 (December 1926), 107. He relies heavily on a report from the *Far Eastern review* that itself relies on the published findings of a Russian explorer named Karamisheff (W. Karamisheff, *Mongolia and western China: social and economic study* (Tianjin: La librairie Francaise, 1925). The article concludes its description of Xinjiang's oil wealth by saying "our description of these resources has been taken from materials of Russian industrialists who have, naturally, only noted those fields which they have come across by pure chance." "Petroleum in far west China," *Far Eastern review* 9 (September 1925), 600–603.

86. "Wu-Su liang xian difang youkuang," 24.

87. Obruchev, *Minerals of Dzungaria*, 74. A 1925 English-language report based on second-hand knowledge sneers that at this site, "there exists a very primitive way of working these wells that cannot be called exploitation." The report goes on, "the local inhabitants gather the petroleum on the surface and sell it in crude form, as a lubricating substance for cart wheels." See "Petroleum in far west China."

88. "Zhong-Ying heban Xinjiang shiyoukang gongsi shi" (Minguo 9 [1920], 12/18), Ministry of Foreign Affairs Collection: 03-03-043-01-016, IMHA.

89. The negotiators' "actions will place Xinjiang in British hands and we cannot fathom what evil intentions they hold," the telegram warned darkly. Ibid.

90. This policy effectively relinquished the provincial government's claims to the 2,688 ounces of gold being mined annually in the province. Yang Zengxin, "Zicheng yuanbu miancai Yutian Qiemo dengxian guanjin bing mian weijin dike wen" (March 1927), in *Buguozhai wendu, sanbian* (Taipei: Wenhai Chubanshe, 1954, original print 1934), 430.

91. V. A. Obruchev, *Progranichnaia Dzhungariia: otchet o puteshestviiakh sovershennykh v 1905, 1906, i 1909 na sredstva Tomskago tekhnologicheskago insituta imperatora Nikolaia II* (Moscow: Akademiia nauk SSSR, 1912).

92. Obruchev, *Minerals of Dzungaria*, 29.

## Chapter Four

1. Hengfu, Yu, and Liu Tongxun, eds., *Qinding huangyu Xiyu tuzhi*, section 34. Wool would become an important commodity only in the nineteenth century, as previously cotton and silk were the primary materials used for the production of fabrics. See James A. Millward, "The Chinese border wool trade of 1880–1937," https://sites.google.com/a/georgetown.edu/james-a-millward/other-publications.

2. In the Qing period, the term *tuchan* included subterranean resources as well as commodity products. It is only in the Republican period that the two categories become more clearly differentiated. For the sake of clarity, I am using "local products" to refer to commodity products.

3. "As one British India official surveying the trading terrain grumbled, 'the Russian side is so naturally easy as to have needed little or no road construction.'" G. Macartney, *Notes on the Road from Kashgar to Aris (Tashkent Railway) via the Turgat Pass, Narin, Tokmak, Pishpek, and Chimkent* (Simla: Gov't Central Branch Press, 1909), in British India Office Collection: L/PS/20/A98. For additional materials that that address the question of transport in the British India Office Collection, see "Letter from the Ambassador to Moscow to the Undersecretary of State for India, translated articles in the Commercial and Industrial Gazette of St. Petersburg of March 27–April 9, 1909 by A. Levitoff" (December 12, 1910), British India Office Collection: L/PS/10/297, 259–271 (British Library, London).

4. XJTZ, section 29, 16.

5. Xinjiang Weiwu'er zizhiqu difangzhi bianzuan weiyuanhui, ed., *Xinjiang tongzhi: shangye* (vol. 61) (Urumqi: Xinjiang Renmin Chubanshe, 1992), 91.

6. Ibid., 101.

7. XJTZ, section 29, 15.

8. The term "commerce war" was frequently used in local gazetteers. For example, see XJTZ, section 29, 14. But the phrase was widely used outside of Xinjiang as well. See Susan Mann, *Local merchants and the Chinese bureaucracy, 1750–1950* (Stanford: Stanford University Press, 1987), 147.

9. Chang Geng, "Zou X Yili XX pimao youxian gongsi shanggu yi zhaozu XX ding X ming zhancheng shi" (November 27, 1909), Imperial Rescript Memorial Collection: 04-01-01-1100-032, FHA.

10. Yuan Dahua, "Qingjiekuan xiutong dongxi tielu yi baoxiyu er gu quanju zhe," in XJTZ, section 106, 568.

11. See "Zhen-Di dao Chi zhuan beige zunyi fu Xinjiang xunfu Yuan Dahua zouqing xiuzhu dongxi tielu yi zhe zhi zhawen" (Xuantong 3 [1911], 10/20), Qing Dynasty Collection: Q15-34-3055 (Xinjiang Uyghur Autonomous Region Archive, Urumqi); "Zhen-Di dao chizhuan Shangbu ju zou ge sheng chouzhu tielu jiying tongchou quanju yuding luxian yi zhi zha wen Tulufan tongzhi Shanshan xian ling xiang fu dao chi xiangkan di shi yuding lu xian yi an zhi shen wen bing Xinjiang xunfu zhi piwen" (Guangxu 32 [1906], 7/21), Qing Dynasty Collection: Q15-32-2367, XJA, 5–8.

12. Wang Shunan, "Taolu laoren sui nianlu," 397.

13. Yang Zengxin, "Chengfu Yilihe chuanye qingxing wen," in Li, ed., *Buguozhai wendu*, vol. 2, 70.

14. Sun Yatsen, *Shiye jihua* (English title: *The international development of China*) (Shanghai: Commercial Press, 1920).

15. Lin Jing, *Xibei congbian* (Taipei: Wenhai Chubanshe, 1930), 397–398.

16. According to Soviet sources, most of these furs were shipped out of Xinjiang and transported on to Leipzig, which was home to several prominent furriers who distributed their products internationally. "Dlya svedeniya Vypiska iz ekonomicheskopravovogo doklada konsul'stva v Kul'dzhe ot 25/1-1930 goda" (January 25, 1930), 7590-411 (RGAE), 144. See also A. Anokhin, "Pravleniya Vneshtorgbanke" (April 28, 1930), 7590-474, RGAE, 192.

17. Li Sheng, *Xinjiang dui Su (E) maoyishi, 1600–1900* (Urumqi: Xinjiang Renmin Chubanshe, 1992), 324; Zhang Dajun, *Xinjiang fengbao qishinian*, vol. 4 (Taipei: Lanxi Chubanshe, 1980), 2260–2265.

18. Their involvement in trade was strictly prohibited under the 1920 trade agreement.

19. "Shengzhang Yang Zengxin guanyu Akesu daoyin Zhu Ruichi suocheng Xin-Su maoyi ruogan bi qing yishi gei jiaoshezhu de xunling" (September 26, 1926), in Xinjiang Weiwu'er zizhiqu dang'anguan, ed., *Xinjiang yu Su'E shangye maoyi dang'an shiliao* (Urumqi : Xinjiang Renmin Chubanshe, 1994), 230.

20. "Yili daoyin Chang Yongqing guanyu Sucha daoguan yian gei jiaoshezhu zhuzhang Fan Yuenan de ziwen" (November 21, 1925), in ibid., 218–220.

21. "It is believed that they [the Soviet consulate] wish to corner the whole of the wool and silk trade. A great proportion of the latter now goes to India, but they are said to be prepared to outbid all Indian competitors, and the loss of still another branch of trade with India appears to be imminent" ("Kashgar Diary for March 1928," section 47 in *Kashgar Diaries, 1921–1930*, British India Office Collection: L/PS/10/976, 77 (British Library, London).

22. Li, *Xinjiang dui Su (E) maoyishi*, 335.

23. "Shengzhang Yang Zengxin guanyu Akesu daoyin Zhu Ruichi suocheng Xin-Su maoyi ruogan biqing yishi gei jiaoshezhu de xunling," 231.

24. Quoted in Li, *Xinjiang dui Su (E) maoyishi*, 346.

25. "Sheng zhuxi Jin Shuren guanyu Tacheng zhongshang qingqiu zishe zhuanyun gongsi yi shi gei jiaoshezhu de xunling" (November 26, 1928), in *Xinjiang yu Su'E shangye maoyi dang'an shiliao*, 244.

26. "Sheng zhuxi Jin Shuren guanyu dizhi Sulian shangwu shi gei jiaoshezhu de xunling" (November 26, 1928), in *Xinjiang yu Su'E shangye maoyi dang'an shiliao*, 246.

27. Li, *Xinjiang dui Su (E) maoyishi*, 367–368.

28. Ibid., 367.

29. "Tacheng shanghui huizhang Song Zhizhang guanyu Sumao gongsi zai Ta she pushouhuo shi gei sheng zhuxi Jin Shuren de daidian" (March 24, 1931), in *Xinjiang yu Su'E shangye maoyi dang'an shiliao*, 281.

30. Ibid. See also "Sheng zhuxi Jin Shuren guanyu qudi Su zai Tacheng she pushouhuo yian gei Tacheng xingzhengzhang de xunling" (April 8, 1931), in *Xinjiang yu Su'E shangye maoyi dang'an shiliao*, 282; "Sheng zhuxi Jin Shuren guanyu Ashan diqu Zhongshang ti Sushang dai mai huowu yian gei waijiao banshichu de xunling" (May 13, 1931), in *Xinjiang yu Su'E shangye maoyi dang'an shiliao*, 284.

31. Anokhin, "Banku dlya vneshney torgovli OKU" (August 3, 1930), file number 7590-474, RGAE, 38.

32. "Torgovlya SSSR s Sin'tszyanom" (no date), file number 7590-867, RGAE, 38–65.

33. The construction of the line was not without controversy in the Soviet Union. Indeed, while advocates suggested that the new line could help deliver Central Asian cotton needed by Soviet light industry, opponents complained about its high price tag. See Mathew J. Payne, *Stalin's railroad: Turksib and the building of socialism* (Pittsburgh: University of Pittsburgh Press, 2001), 15–23.

34. From a translated 1927 Soviet work report attached to a report from the Chinese consul at Irkutsk. "Su'E shixing jianzhushang xitielushi cheng song Sulian jiaotongbuzhang zhi baogao ji luxian tushi" (April 1927), Ministry of Foreign Affairs Collection: 03-17-059-02-001, IMHA.

35. Ibid.

36. Ibid.

37. Ibid.

38. "Fu Benbu Xianzi Diliujiuwuhao Han Guanyu Su'E Jianzhu Shixi Tielushi" (Minguo 16 [1927], April), Ministry of Foreign Affairs Collection: 03-05-059-02-004, IMHA.

39. "Dihua Jixiangtong shangxing jingli Hu Saiyin jiu yu Su maoyi ying yi xianjin jiaoyi weizhu yiji yu Dihua sheli yanghuo shuru zonggongsi dengshiyi gei waijiao banshichu de bingwen" (June 6, 1931), in *Xinjiang yu Su'E shangye maoyi dang'an shiliao*, 294.

40. In a 1929 report, Jin noted that "to resist the import of foreign products you must increase imports from the internal provinces [China-proper] into Xinjiang." In *Xinjiang sheng zhengfu gongbao* 9 (December 1930), 92.

41. Owen Lattimore, *The desert road to Turkestan* (New York: Kodansha Press, 1995, reprint), 332. Gucheng was a caravan hub that had long linked Xinjiang to China-proper through the town of Suiyuan in Inner Mongolia. At the time, Suiyuan was the western terminus of the Beijing-Suiyuan rail line.

42. Xinjiang Weiwu'er zizhiqu jiaotong zhizhi bianzuan weiyuanhui, ed., *Xinjiang gonglu jiaotongshi*, vol. 1 (Beijing: Renmin Jiaotong Chubanshe, 1992), 16.

43. Zhu Jin, "Qingmo minchu caoyuan shanglu yanjiu," in *Xinjiang jinxiandai jingji yanjiu wenji* (Urumqi: Xinjiang Daxue Chubanshe, 2002), 498.

44. You Yinzhao, *Sui-Xin kanlu baogao yijuan* (Nanjing: Jingji Yanjiushi Bianyi, 1936), 422, 424.

45. Quoted in *Xinjiang gonglu jiaotongshi*, 23.

46. See Jacobs, *Xinjiang and the modern Chinese state*, 78.

47. Ibid., 82–83. See also Mai Yuhua, "Jianlun Jin Shuren zhu Xin," *Journal of the Wuhan Engineering Institute* 16, no. 3 (September 2004), 62–64.

48. Andrew D. W. Forbes, *Warlords and Muslims in Chinese Central Asia: a political history of Republican Sinkiang, 1911–1949* (New York: Cambridge University Press, 1986), 70.

49. Baoerhan [Burhan Shahidi], *Xinjiang wushinian* (Beijing: Wenshi Ziliao Chubanshe, 1984), 126, 160.

50. "Lian'gong (bu) zhongyang zhengzhiju huiyi di 54 hao jilu: Xinjiang he Zhongdong tielu" (August 5, 1931), RGASPI, in Shen Zhihua, ed., *Eguo jiemi dang'an: Xinjiang wenti* (Urumqi: Xinjiang Renmin Chubanshe, 2012), 1–2. This volume is a reprinted collection of various materials related to Xinjiang that were uncovered in various former Soviet archives.

51. "Waijiao tepaiyuan Chen Jishan wei qing Sufang jiang junshi shiye zhizaopin maigei Xinsheng yishi zhi Su waijiao tepaiyuan Silawucike de han" (September 1931), in *Xinjiang yu Su'E shangye maoyi dang'an shiliao*, 302.

52. Brophy, *Uyghur nation*, 237.

53. Li, *Xinjiang dui Su (E) maoyishi*, 375.

54. V. A. Barmin, *SSSR i Sin'tszian, 1918–1941* (Moscow: Barnaul, 1999), 96.

55. Quoted in Li, *Xinjiang dui Su (E) maoyishi*, 381.

56. Ibid. See also "Sheng zhuxi Jin Shuren guanyu Sufang shanlan shangquan Zhongmin da shouqi hai dengqing gei waijiao banshichu de xunling" (May 16, 1932), in *Xinjiang yu Su'E shangye maoyi dang'an shiliao*, 339. Later, during the wartime period, these merchants who continually sought to stem the tide of Soviet economic power in the region were aggressively demonized as "Japanese spies" by the governor Sheng Shicai. See "Shidalin deng yu Sheng Shicai tanhua jilu: Zhong-Su guanxi" (September 2, 1938), from the APRF], in Shen, ed., *Eguo jiemi dangan*, 62.

57. Ibid.

58. "Lian'gong (bu) zhongyang zhengzhiju huiyi di 143 hao jilu: Xinjiang gongzuo" (August 15, 1933), RGASPI, in Shen, ed., *Eguo jiemi dangan: Xinjiang wenti*, 15–18.

59. Officials frequently sought to underbid local producers. In one case a leader of the Torghut Mongols complained that the lump sum payment used to purchase marmot pelts, camel hair, and wool was insufficient to cover the market value of the products. He warned officials in the provincial capital that the Mongols might deface the goods if officials choose to not cover the additional costs. See "Manchukezhabu wei qingling shengzhengfu gou pimao yukuan shizhi shengzhengfu de cheng" (January 4, 1933), Xinjiang Weiwu'er zizhiqu dang'an guan, ed., *Jindai Xinjiang Menggu lishi dang'an* (Urumqi: Xinjiang Renmin Chubanshe, 2006), 247.

60. Li, *Xinjiang dui Su (E) maoyishi*, 395–396.

61. "Xin-Su linshi tongshang xieding de youlai ji qi tiaowen jieze" (September 6, 1932), in *Xinjiang yu Su'E shangye maoyi dang'an shiliao*, 380.

62. "Duoerfu guanyu Xinjiang nongmin yundong qingkuang gei Maliyaer de baogao" (September 18, 1931), RGASPI, in Shen, ed., *Eguo jiemi dangan*, 1–2. See also Barmin, *SSSR i Sin'tszian*, 108.

63. Barmin, *SSSR i Sin'tszian*, 106–107.

64. "Lian'gong (bu) zhongyang zhengzhiju huiyi di 143 hao jilu: Xinjiang gongye."

65. No title (July 1, 1933), Republican Collection: 2-3-88, XJA, 77.

66. No title (November 24, 1933), Republican Collection: 2-3-828, XJA, 56.

67. No title (September 21, 1933), Republican Collection: 2-3-828, XJA, 60–61.

68. No title (July 18, 1934), Draft Manuscripts Collection: 002-060100-00084-003, AHA.

69. Quoted in Zhang Junzhao, ed., *Minguo shiqi Xinjiang dashiji* (Urumqi: Xinjiang Meishu Sheying Chubanshe 2003), 51.

70. Quoted in Cai Jinsong, *Sheng Shicai zai Xinjiang* (Zhengzhou: Henan Renmin Chubanshe, 1987), 196.

71. Ibid., 197.

72. Quoted in *Xinjiang gonglu jiaotongshi* 31.

73. You, *Sui-Xin kanlu baogao yijiuan*, 422, 424.

74. Quoted in *Xinjiang gonglu jiaotongshi*, 31.

75. Quoted in *Xinjiang tongzhi: caizheng* (vol. 57) (Urumqi: Xinjiang Renmin Chubanshe, 1999), 124.

76. Barmin, *SSSR i Sin'tszian*, 139.

77. For more on the company and its operations see Li, *Xinjiang dui Su (E) maoyishi*, 432–464.

78. Li, *Xinjiang dui Su (E) maoyishi*, 439.

79. "Guanyu junxu yang jianmao ji pi jiaoyu maosi huiqu huowu cong zhong jian li, qing cha jubao" (February 10, 1940), in *Mao Zemin yu Hami caizheng* (Urumqi: Xinjiang Renmin Chubanshe, 1993), 159–163.

80. Li, *Xinjiang dui Su (E) maoyishi*, 432–435. For more on the asset seizure campaigns, see Jacobs, *Xinjiang and the modern Chinese state*, 113–117.

81. For the whole agreement, see Li, *Xinjiang dui Su (E) maoyishi*, 458–460.

82. Li Sheng, *Xinjiang dui Su (E) maoyi shi, 1600–1990*, 433.

83. For more on the effort to pacify nomadic groups, see Jacobs, *Xinjiang and the modern Chinese state*, 120–121.

84. "Orientirovochnaya stoimost' namechaemogo promyshlennogo stroitel'stva po Sin'tszyanu ustanavlivaetsya v summe 742000 rubley zolotom" (no date), file number 7590-726, RGAE, 1–7.

85. "Lian'gong (bu) zhongyang zhengzhiju huiyi di 11 hao jilu : chongjian Xinjiang jingji" (August 5, 1934), RGASPI, in Shen, ed., *Eguo jiemi dang'an*, 62.

86. "Lian'gong (bu) zhongyang zhengzhiju huiyi di 8 hao jilu : Xinjiang wenti" (June 9, 1934), RGASPI, in *Eguo jiemi dang'an*, 63–64.

87. Kemal, "Dokladnaya zapiska" (September 16, 1934), file number 7590-727, RGAE, 54–60.

88. "Agreement" (no date), file number 7590-45, RGAE, 726.

89. "Lian'gong (bu) zhongyang zhengzhiju huiyi di 11 hao jilu: chongjian Xinjiang jingji."

90. Both of these groups often felt overburdened by their obligations. A provincial official in 1936 overheard a conversation as his group took shelter from a summer rain storm in a small village in which a peasant complained that "road construction is a huge obligation, it occupies our

fields and irrigation canals, and in the spring planting and fall harvesting season the Highway Office comes to grab peasants for laborers." No title (July 24, 1936), Republican Collection: file number 2-7-105, XJA, 47–53.

91. *Xinjiang gonglu jiaotongshi*, 32.

92. The Bountiful Xinjiang Company closed in 1946. A new company, named the Northwest Trading Company, was established in 1949 following the normalization of Sino-Soviet relations.

## Chapter Five

1. "Mao Zemin guanyu Xinjiang caizheng, jinrong qingkuang zhi Luobu, Zedong tongzhi dexin" (April 18, 1938), in Zhonggong Xinjiang Weiwuer zizhiqu weiyuanhui dangshi gongzuo weiyuanhui, ed., *Kangri zhanzheng shiqi zai Xinjiang caijing zhanxianshang de Zhongguo gongchangdang ren* (Urumqi: Xinjiang Renmin Chubanshe, 1993), 38.

2. "Lian'gong (bu) Zhongyang zhengzhiju huiyi di 11 hao jilu: chongjian Xinjiang jingji," 41.

3. "A conversation between cdes. Stalin, Molotov, and Voroshilov and the governor Shicai Sheng which occurred in the Kremlin on 2 September 1938" (September 2, 1938), RGASPI, f.558, op. 11, d. 323, l. 32-41, History and Public Policy Program Digital Archive, translated by Gary Goldberg, http://digitalarchive.wilsoncenter.org/document/121901

4. See Duara, *Sovereignty and authenticity*; Daqing Yang, "Unclaimed prize: oil exploration in pre-1941 Manchuria"; Seow, "Carbon technocracy."

5. Administrative costs made up more than 62 percent of Xinjiang's total expenditures during its second Three Year Plan (1938–1940). Zhang Dajun, *Xinjiang fengbao qishinian*, vol. 8 (Taipei: Wenhai Chubanshe, 1980), 4385.

6. Ibid., 3801–3802.

7. "Zonghui jiguan jieyue jingsai gongzuo jihua" (March 13, 1941), in Gongqingtuan Xinjiang Weiwuer zizhiqu weiyuanhui, ed., *Xinjiang mingzhong fandi lianhehui ziliao huibian* (Urumqi: Xinjiang Qingshaonian Chubanshe, 1986), 337.

8. Cai, *Sheng Shicai zai Xinjiang*, 192.

9. Ibid.

10. "Mao Zemin guanyu Xinjiang caizheng, jinrong qingkuang zhi Luobu, Zedong tongzhi de xin."

11. "Zonghui jiguan jieyue jingsai gongzuo jihua," 337. There is evidence that at least some of the funds donated for the war effort may have made their way back to the Soviet Union. Thanks to Natalie Belsky for pointing out evidence from the State Archive of the Russian Federation (Gosudarstvennyy Arkhiv Rossiyskoy Federatsii) on this.

12. Wu Aichen, *Xinjiang jiyou* (Shanghai: Shangwu Yinshuguan, 1935).

13. XJTZ, 1156.

14. "Ashan jinkuangju jianzhang" (Minguo 24 [1935], 3/27), Republican Collection: 2-7-625, XJA, 82–84.

15. To guide the process and ensure that the provincial government had direct access to the distant region's mineral wealth, in May 1935 Sheng established a new office, the Altay Mountain Gold Mining Bureau, which officially opened four ore fields in the mountain. Xinjiang jianshe weiyuanhui, ed., *Xinjiang erqi sannian jihua* (Dihua: Ribao Sheyin, 1941), 113–114.

16. See "Zhiling Ashan jinkuangju cheng wang boye kaiban fei yin liu baiwan liang" (March 7, 1935), Republican Collection: 2-7-625, XJA, 59–62; "Chengzhuan Ashan jinkuangju chengbao jiuyuefen xin gong gefei shumu you" (November 1935), Republican Collection: 2-7-625, XJA, 29–31; "Chengzhuan Ashan jinkuangju chengbao bayuefen xin gong gefei shumu you" (November 1935), Republican Collection: file number 2-7-625, XJA, 45–47; "Chengzhuan Ashan jinkuangju chengbao liuyuefen xingong gefei shumu you" (November 1935), Republican Collection: 2-7-625, XJA, 17–19; "Chengzhuan Ashan jinkuangju chengbao qiyuefen xingong gefei shumu you" (November 1935), Republican Collection: 2-7-625, XJA, 9–12; "Chengzhuan Ashan jinkuangju cheng bao wuyuefen xingong gefen shumu you" (November 1935), Republican Collection: 2-7-625, XJA, 1–3.

17. No title (March 4, 1935), Republican Collection: 2-7-625, XJA, 66–69.

18. No title (July 4, 1935), Republican Collection: 2-7-625, XJA, 57–58.

19. See "Chengwei niju huifu Ashan jinkuang banfa yangqi" (March 27, 1935), Republican Collection: 2-7-625, XJA, 68–77.

20. "Sidalin deng yu Sheng Shicai tanhua jiyao: Zhong-Su guanxi" (September 2, 1938) (APRF), in Shen, ed., *Eguo Jiemi Dang'an* 82.

21. Zhang, *Xinjiang fengbao qishinian*, vol. 8, 4423–4424.

22. Ibid., 4675.

23. Ibid.

24. Stephen Kotkin, *Magnetic mountain: Stalinism as a civilization* (Berkeley: University of California Press, 1995), 40.

25. Ibid., 58.

26. "V svyazi s vozbuzhdennym v 1933 godu pravitel'stvom Sin'tszyana voprosom ob organizatsii tekhnicheskoy pomoshchi Sin'tszyanu" (1933), file number 9174-2, RGAE, 59.

27. "Proyekt Dogovor" (no date), file number 7590-726, RGAE, 24–25.

28. Ibid.

29. "Rezyume po predvaritel'nomu otchetu Sin'tszyanskoy geologicheskoy ekspeditsii osobogo naznacheniya po sostoyaniyu rabot na 15 noyabrya 1936" (December 7, 1935), file number 9174-2, RGAE, 1-12.

30. Chairman Miller and Secretary Shchekina, "Stenogramma zasedaniya direktsii IGRY" (February 10, 1933), file number 9174-2, RGAE, 105.

31. Zhao Xinye, "Huiyi Anjihai lianyouchang de chuangjian," in *Xinjiang shiyou gongye shiliao xuanji*, vol. 1, 41–49.

32. "Rezyume po predvaritel'nomu otchetu Sin'tszyanskoy geologicheskoy ekspeditsii osobogo naznacheniya po sostoyaniyu rabot na 15 noyabrya 1936"

33. Ibid.

34. "Programma rabot Sin'tszyanskoy Geologicheskoy Ekspeditsii Osobogo Naznacheniya na 1936 god" (No date), file number 9174-2, RGAE, 53. Piezoelectric quartz had important applications in sonar and telephonic technologies in the 1930s. See also D.E. Perkin, "Predlozheniya po dokladu nachal'nika Sin'tszyanskoy geologicheskoy ekspeditsii osobogo naznacheniya" (no date), file number 9174-2, RGAE, 53.

35. Ibid.

36. Xinjiang weiwuer zizhiqu difangzhi congshu, ed., *Xinjiang tongzhi: dizhi kuangchan* (vol. 9, part 2) (Urumqi: Xinjiang Renmin Chubanshe, 1996), 797–801.

37. D. E. Perkin, "Predlozheniya po dokladu nachal'nika Sin'tszyanskoy geologicheskoy ekspeditsii osobogo naznacheniya" (November 5, 1936), file number 7297-282, RGAE, 406.

38. Pantsev, "Spravka o deyatel'nosti neftekombinata Du-san-dzy na 1 5 1940" (June 25, 1940), file number 8627-4890, RGAE, 15.

39. Huang Jiqing, "Report on geological investigation of some oil-fields in Sinkiang" (English version), in *Dizhi huibao* (English title: Geological memoirs), Series A, no. 21 (February 1947), 40.

40. Ibid. The problem, as far as Soviet officials were concerned, was not the site itself, but rather mistakes made by Soviet geologists and technicians. "Nachal'nik neftekombinata, prikaz po avtokombinatu Tu-Shan-Tszy ot 27/8/1940 goda" (September 3, 1940), file number 8627-4890, RGAE, 38.

41. Litvinov, "Po voprosu ob ekspluatatsii neftyanogo mestorozhdeniya v rayone Shikho provintsii Sin'-Tszyan" (July 23, 1938, file number 8627-4890, RGAE, 19-20.

42. Direktor neftekombinata Du-San-Dzy Pantsev, "Spravka o deyatel'nosti neftekombinata Du-San-Dzy na 1 5 1940" (June 25, 1940), file number 8627-4890, RGAE, 15.

43. Maurice Dobb, *Soviet economic development since 1917* (London: Routledge and K. Paul, 1966).

44. For more on this meeting, see Cai, *Sheng Shicai zai Xinjiang*, 317–322. For Sheng's account, see Whiting and Sheng, *Sinkiang: pawn or pivot?* 244–247.

45. "Excerpt on Xinjiang from minutes No. 21 of the VKP(b) CC Politburo meetings" (October 26, 1940), RGASPI, f.17 op.162 d.23, l. 142, History and Public Policy Program Digital Archive, translated by Gary Goldberg, http://digitalarchive.wilsoncenter.org/document/121880.

46. Cai, *Sheng Shicai zai Xinjiang*, 318–322.

47. Whiting and Sheng, *Sinkiang: pawn or pivot?* 244–247.

48. See Sheng's July 7, 1942 "confession" to Chiang Kaishek, *Waijiaobu dang an congshu jiewulei di sance Xinjiang juan (yi)* (Taipei: Waijiaobu Bianyin, 2001), 29. We might call into question Sheng's supposed patriotism, considering the fact that the archival record shows that he himself would directly offer Xinjiang to Stalin one year later.

49. Cai, *Sheng Shicai zai Xinjiang*, 319.

50. "Concerning the Sin'tszyanolovo concession in Xinjiang" (March 7, 1941), RGASPI, f.17 op.162 d.32, l.115-116, History and Public Policy Program Digital Archive, translated by Gary Goldberg, http://digitalarchive.wilsoncenter.org/document/121882.

51. "Work plan of the Narkomtsvetmet Sin'tszysnolovo concession for 1941" (March 7, 1941), RGASPI, f.17 op.162 d.32, l.150-154, History and Public Policy Program Digital Archive, translated by Gary Goldberg, http://digitalarchive.wilsoncenter.org/document/121883. It should be noted that the Soviet plans also called for exploration in southern Xinjiang with a particular focus on exploration at Kashgar, Khotan, and Yarkand. But the plans for geological exploration in these areas were much less specific.

52. Nachal'nik Planovo-proizvodstvennogo otdeleniya Monin, ekonomist-planovik Banenko, "Plan po trudu Altayskoy gruppy na 1942 god" (no date), file number 9176-19, RGAE, 3; Nachal'nik planovo-proizvodstvennogo otdela upravleniya Monin, ekonomist-planovik Banenko, "Plan po trudu partii Sayram-Nur na 1942 god" (May 13, 1942), file number 9176-19, RGAE, 11; Nachal'nik planovo-proizvodstvennogo otdela upravleniya Monin, ekonomist-planovik Banenko, "Plan po trudu yuzhnoy gruppy na 1942 god" (May 13, 1942), file number 9176-19, RGAE, 17; Nachal'nik planovo-proizvodstvennogo otdela upravleniya Monin, ekonomist-planovik Banenko, "Plan po trudu partii Boro-Khoro na 1942 god" (May 13, 1942), file number 9176-19, RGAE, 25; Nachal'nik planovo-proizvodstvennogo otdela upravleniya Monin, ekonomist-planovik Banenko, "Plan po trudu Borotalinskoy gruppy na 1942 god" (May 13, 1942), file number 9176-19, RGAE, 31.

53. Ibid.

54. For Altay: Nachal'nik planovo-proizvodstvennogo upravleniya Monin, "Kvartal'nyye plany po dobychnym rabotam Altayskoy gruppy na 1942 god" (no date), file number 9176-19, RGAE, 2. For Bortala: Nachal'nik planovo-proizvodstvennogo otdela upravleniya Monin, "Kvartal'nyye plany po dobychnym rabotam Borotalinskoy gruppy na 1942 god" (May 13, 1942), file number 9176-19, RGAE, 13.

55. "Concerning the Sin'tszyanolovo concession in Xinjiang."

56. Mi Taiheng, "*Xinjiang kuangchan jilue*" (Lanzhou: Jingjibu Zhongyang Dizhi Diaocha-suo Xibei Fensuo, 1942), Unpublished report, document 2857, NGAC.

57. "Work plan of the narkomtsvetmet Sin'tszysnolovo concession for 1941" (March 7, 1941), RGASPI, f.17 op.162 d.32, l.150-154, History and Public Policy Program Digital Archive, translated by Gary Goldberg, http://digitalarchive.wilsoncenter.org/document/121883.

58. Mi, *Xinjiang kuangchan jilue.*

59. "Work plan of the narkomtsvetmet Sin'tszysnolovo concession for 1941."

60. Mi, *Xinjiang kuangchan jilue.*

61. Sedinu inzhener-geolog, "Narodnomu komissaru neftyanoy promyshlennosti tov dokladnaya zapiska" (December 11, 1941), file number 8624-4904, RGAE, 108.

62. Weng Wenhao, "Xinjiangsheng Dushanzi youkuang shicha baogao" (July 1942), unpublished report, document 3684, NGAC, 6.

63. Weng, "*Xinjiangsheng Dushanzi youkuang shicha baogao,*" 6.

64. Sheng estimated that he invested four million yuan of precious currency into operations at the site. Subsequent investigations found that that number was too high and that total investment was probably only around US $1 million; see no title (MG 32 [1943], 5/26), Soviet Occupation of China Collection (5): 002-090400-00008-204, AHA.

65. "Concerning signing of an agreement with the government of Xinjiang about the operation of the Dushanzi refinery" (March 20, 1942), RGASPI, f. 17 op. 162 d. 37, l.33-34, History and Public Policy Program Digital Archive, translated by Gary Goldberg, http://digitalarchive.wilsoncenter.org/document/121886.

66. Petroleum products created at Dushanzi were controlled by Sheng Shicai's Office of Military Affairs, which set oil prices for internal sales at 65 fen (there are 100 fen in one yuan) per gallon for military use and two yuan per gallon for commercial use. Also, lamp oil distribution and sale were overseen by the provincial Office of Finance. Weng, "*Xinjiangsheng Dushanzi youkuang shicha baogao,*" 9. See also Wang Lianfang, "Jiu Zhongguo Xinjiang shiyou dashi nianbiao," in *Xinjiang shiyou gongye shiliao xuanji,* vol. 1, 26–27.

67. Weng, *Xinjiangsheng Dushanzi youkuang shicha baogao.*

68. Ibid.

69. Ibid. Weng Wenhao pointed out that oil production at Dushanzi was less than that at oil sites in Yumen or other sites in Gansu province.

70. Ibid., 9.

71. A report from a Chinese official in 1942 suggested that the manager only "assisted in general affairs" and in a separate report that "he had no real power." See Weng Wenhao's telegram to Chiang Kaishek: no title (July 17, 1942), Soviet Occupation of China Collection (5), 002-090400-00008-112, AHA; see also Weng, "Xinjiangsheng Dushanzi youkuang shicha baogao."

72. Ibid.

73. Weng, "*Xinjiangsheng Dushanzi youkuang shicha baogao*"; other reports from Nationalist officials place the number of Soviet workers at only 120 and slightly more than 800 Chinese

workers and managers. See Huang Jiqing, "Xinjiang Wusuxian Dushanzi shiyou ji meiqi kuang-chuang shuomingshu" (1943), unpublished report, document 743, NGAC. It is not clear whether this discrepancy is a product of the fact that Weng's initial report was written nearly five months earlier, or whether he lacked specific access to plant records.

74. Mitchell, *Carbon democracy*, 2.

75. "VKP(b) CC Politburo Decree concerning Xinjiang" (March 22, 1935), RGASPI, f.17, op.162, d. 17, l. 174-179, History and Public Policy Program Digital Archive, translated by Gary Goldberg, http://digitalarchive.wilsoncenter.org/document/121827.

76. "Caizhengbu baogao Xinjiang-Zhong yunhui zuzhi banli Sulian huan Hua wuzi nei-yun qingxing dian" (September 14, 1941), Zhongguo di er lishi dang'an guan, ed., *Zhonghua minguo shi dang'an ziliao huibian*, vol. 5, no. 2 *waijiao* (Nanjing: Jiangsu guji chubanshe, 1991), 255.

77. "Mouluotuofu zhi Sheng Shicai han: Su-Zhong guanxi ehua" (7/3/1942), AVP RF, in Shen, ed., *Eguo Jiemi Dang'an*, 121–123; for a copy in Chinese archives, see Zhongguo Guomindang zhongyang weiyuanhui dangshi weiyuanhui bianyin, ed., *Zhonghua Minguo zhongyao shiliao chubian* (Taipei: Zhongguo Guomindang Zhongyang Weiyuanhui Dangshi Weiyuanhui Bian-yin, 1981), 435. See also Cai, *Sheng Shicai zai Xinjiang*, 326–339.

## Chapter Six

1. "Li ma Wushan yi jiu shi / xiangfeng saiwai bin rusi/ pingsheng yiqi qi wufu / dahao heshan hong huchi." Quoted in Cai Jinsong, *Sheng Shicai zai Xinjiang*, 343. Thanks to Ren Zhi-jun for pointing out the (almost certainly intentional) parallels between Sheng's poem and a twelfth-century poem by the Jurchen leader Wanyan Liang, who "rearing up his horse on Wu Mountain" contemplated the conquest of the Southern Song, and thus the unification of the realm.

2. For more on the potential that the acquisition of Xinjiang had for Chinese officials, see Judd C. Kinzley and Jianfei Jia, "Xinjiang and the promise of salvation in Free China," in Matt Combs and Joseph Esherick, eds., *1943: China at the crossroads* (Ithaca: Cornell University East Asia Series, 2015).

3. To sustain this mission over the long term and eliminate the potential for any future ideo-logical waffling by Sheng or any governor, Chiang sought to recraft the ideological foundation of the province. Provincial schools were given a new curriculum centered around Sun Yatsen's *Three Principles of the People*. He funded cadre and party training institutes equipped to train the three thousand new cadres and twenty thousand new party members who were to serve as the backbone for GMD presence in the province. In addition, party officials regularly held es-say and research competitions over knowledge of the Three Principles; a network of forty-three "Sun Yatsen Rooms" were established around the province to spread the Three Principles gospel and the good news about the Father of the Country (*Guofu*), and a new party printing press was established, which by 1944 was already publishing seven new magazines on topics handpicked by the provincial party apparatus. See Huang Jianhua, *Guomindang zhengfu de Xinjiang zhengce yanjiu* (Beijing: Minzu Chubanshe, 2003), 89. See also Zhang Dajun, *Xinjiang fengbao qishinian*, vol. 10, 5837–5841.

4. V.A. Barmin, *Sin'tszian v Sovetsko-Kitaiskikh otnosheniiakh* (Moscow: Barnaul, 1999), 30.

5. "Panyouxin yu Jiang Jieshi huitan jiyao: Xinjiang diqu wenti" (July 9,1942), AVP RF, in *Eguo jiemi dangan*, 123-124. See also "Jiang weiyuanhui zai Chongqing jiejian Sulian zhu Hua dashi Panyouxin tingqi baogao Sulian zhengfu dui Xinjiang Sheng duban zhi taidu bing biaoshi dan guanyu Xinjiang zhishi ying yu wo zhongyang zhengfu zhijie jiaobu buke yu Sheng duban jingxing tanpan tanhua jilu" (July 9, 1942), in *Zhonghua Minguo zhongyao shiliao chubian*, 435.

6. Huang Jiqing, *Tianshan zhi lu* (Urumqi: Xinjiang Renmin Chubanshe, 2001), 2.

7. See T. K. Huang, C. C. Young, Y. C. Cheng, T. C. Chow, M. N. Bien, and W. P. Weng, "Report on geological investigation of some oil fields in Sinkiang," *Geological memoirs* 21 (February 1947), 104-106. The oldest source consulted was the 1909 Qing gazetteer, *Xinjiang tuzhi*.

8. "Gedi cheng qing kaicai kuangchan" (December 24, 1942), Mining Industry Management Collection, 003-010307-0026, AHA, 25-27. See also "Cha guanyu Xinjiangsheng choushe dizhidiaochasuo yi shi qiangfeng" (October 11, 1943), Economic Affairs Collection, 18-24C, 14-4, IMHA, 3.

9. See Mi Taiheng, "Xinjiang kuangchan jilue" (1942), unpublished report, document 2857, NGAC.

10. "Jiaotongbu guanyu nifa 'xibei shinian jiaotong jianshe jihua' zhi zhongyang shejiju mishugonghan" (October 10, 1942), in Ma Zhendu, Lin Ningmei, and Chen Guang, eds., *Kangzhan shiqi xibei kaifa dang'an shiliao xuanbian* (Beijing : Zhongguo Shehui Kexue Chubanshe, 2009), 220.

11. For more on the role of the northwest in Republican China's nationalist discourse, see Jeremy Tai, "Opening up the northwest: reimagining Xi'an and the modern Chinese frontier" (Ph.D. dissertation, University of California, Santa Cruz, 2015).

12. "Report on geological investigations of some oil fields in Sinkiang," 99.

13. "Jiaotongbu guanyu nifa 'xibei shinian jiaotong jianshe jihua' zhi zhongyang shejiju mishu gonghan," 220.

14. Weng Wenhao, *Xinjiangsheng Dushanzi youkuang shicha baogao* (July 1942), Unpublished report: document 3684, NGAC, 11.

15. As a point of comparison, the old Qing-era refining equipment that had been moved to another site could produce only six tons daily. "Report on geological investigations of some oil fields in Sinkiang," 42-43.

16. For wartime exploration, particularly at the Yumen oilfield in Gansu province, see Taiwei Lim, *China's quest for self reliance in oil: the story of Fushun, Yumen, and Daqing* (Lewiston: Edwin Mellon Press, 2008). William C. Kirby addresses both exploration and synthetic oil production. Kirby, "The Chinese war economy," in James C. Hsiung and Steven I. Levine, eds., *China's bitter victory: the war with Japan, 1937-1945* (Armonk: M. E. Sharpe, 1992), 194-196. For more on synthetic production, see Joseph Needham and Dorothy Needham, eds., *Science outpost: papers of the Sino-British Co-operation Office, 1942-1946* (London: Pilot Press, 1948).

17. Fernando Coronil, *The magical state: nature, money, and modernity in Venezuela* (Chicago: University of Chicago Press, 1997), 237.

18. "Chengbao yu Sheng Shicai duban qiashang jieban Yili wukuang qingxing" (October 5, 1943), Nationalist Government Collection, 001-113100-0004, AHA, 59.

19. Leaders in Chongqing noted in their report for 1944, that regarding "reestablishing engineering operations at all of the mines in Ashan district, Fuyun county in Altay, we fear that

this year it is too late to undertake internal preparations." As a result, they called for focusing on Bortala. "Ziyuan weiyuanhui Xinjiang wukuang gongchengchu sanshisan niandu shigong jihua" (1943), Economic Affairs Collection, 21-14-12-2, IMHA, 1–3.

20. Ibid.

21. In early 1942, China's National Resources Commission produced a report on mining operations at the Yumen oil site in Gansu province, which noted that the establishment of the drilling and refining operation required the import of more than one thousand tons of heavy mining equipment via truck along the bumpy roads that connected the region to Free China. Located 1,300 kilometers west of Yumen, across even rougher terrain and poorer roads, setting up operations at Dushanzi would require an even more herculean effort for the cash-strapped regime. "Jian daidian yi zhun yunshu tongzhiju chadai dian wei tiaozheng tongyi xibei yunshi jigou yian chihe yiju fu dengyin cheng qing jianhe qingan caizhuanyou" (April 11, 1942), Calibrating the Northwestern Transport System Collection, 003-010501-0001, AHA.

22. "Chengbao yu Sheng Shicai duban qiashang jieban Yili wukuang qingxing."

23. Li, Xinjiang dui Su (E) maoyishi, 1600–1900, 520; see also Wang, Under the Soviet shadow, 91.

24. It is hard to assess how much officials in the Chinese Republic supported this campaign in Xinjiang. Chinese archival sources written a few years later blame Sheng alone for the breakdown in relations with the Soviets. While they were certainly suspicious of Soviet intentions in Xinjiang, the Chinese side had little to gain (and indeed, much to lose) from such an aggressive policy. Zhu Shaoliang, no title (November 16, 1946), Sino-Soviet Relations Collection, 001-062000-0005, AHA, 9.

25. No author, no title (January 7, 1943), Manuscript Draft Collection, 002-060100-00172-007, AHA.

26. "Panyouxin yu Jiang Jieshi huitan jilu: Xinjiang wenti" (June 16, 1943), AVP RF, in Eguo jiemi dangan: Xinjiang wenti, 157.

27. "Asitahuofu zhi Jikanuozuofu han: Xinjiang de fan Su huodong" (June 15, 1943), AVP RF, in Eguo jiemi dangan: Xinjiang wenti, 152–154.

28. Quoted in Barmin, SSSR i Sin'tszian, 17.

29. "Panyouxin yu Wu Guozhen huitan jilu: feijichang yu shiyou lianhe gongsi wenti" (May 17, 1943), AVP RF, in Eguo jiemi dangan: Xinjiang wenti, 149.

30. Sheng defended his actions saying he had responded to charges of sabotage coming down from Dushanzi by dispatching three high-level officials to the area who, after questioning the chief engineer and other Soviet officials at the site, found that sabotage had indeed been happening at the site. See Wu Zexiang, no title (January 8, 1943), Soviet Occupation of China Collection (5), 002-090400-008258, AHA.

31. See Liu Yuehua, Minguo Xinjiang shiyou kaifa yanjiu (master's thesis, Xinjiang University, 2002), 28–30. Much of Liu's analysis relies on archival sources from the Xinjiang Uyghur Autonomous Region Archive.

32. See no author, no title (January 7, 1943), Manuscript Drafts Collection, 002-060100-00172-007, AHA.

33. Nationalist officials put the number of Red Army troops arriving in Dushanzi at around two hundred. Wu Zexiang, no title (June 30, 1943), Soviet Occupation of China (5) Collection, 002-090400-00008-220, AHA.

34. See Wu Zexiang, no title (January 8, 1943), Soviet Occupation of China Collection (5), 002-090400-008258 008258, AHA. See also Wang Lianfang, "Jiu Zhongguo Xinjiang shiyou gongye shuyao," in Xinjiang shiyou gongye shiliao xuanji, vol. 1, 15–16.

35. "Panyouxin yu Weng Wenhao tanpan jilu: chengli lianhe shiyou gongsi wenti" (February 18, 1943), AVP RF, in *Eguo jiemi dangan*, 135.

36. "Panyouxin yu Weng Wenhao tanpan jilu: chenli Su-Zhong lianhe shiyou gongsi" (March 8, 1943), AVP RF, in *Eguo jiemi dangan*, 145.

37. Ibid., 146.

38. "Panyouxin yu Wu Guozhen huitan jilu: feijichang he shiyou lianhe gongsi wenti" (May 6, 1943), AVP RF, in *Eguo jiemi dangan*, 148. For the China side, see Zhongguo Guomindang zhongyang weiyuanhui dangshi weiyuanhui bianyin, ed., *Zhonghua minguo zhongyao shiliao chubian*, 449–450.

39. "Panyouxin yu Wu Guozhen huitan jilu: feijichang yu shiyou lianhe gongsi wenti" (May 17, 1943), AVP RF, in *Eguo jiemi dang'an*, 149.

40. "Panyouxin yu Wu Guozhen huitan jilu: Sulian shebei he zhuanjia cheli Xinjiang" (May 24, 1943), AVP RF, in *Eguo jiemi dangan*, 151.

41. Morozov, no title (October 18, 1943), file number 9176-17, RGAE, 3.

42. Vlasov, "Spravka o zaderzhkakh mashin geologicheskogo upravleniya Kitayskimi vlastyami" (May 14, 1943), file number 9176-17, RGAE, 38.

43. Wang, "Jiu Zhongguo Xinjiang shiyou gongye shuyao," in *Xinjiang shiyou gongye shiliao xuanji*, vol. 1, 16.

44. No author, no title (August 26, 1943), Manuscript Drafts Collection, 002-060100-00179-026, AHA.

45. "Wei yifa sheding Wusu Dushanzi shiyouwei guoying kuangyequan yi chi jiansheting dengji you" (November 3, 1944), Economic Affairs Collection, 18-31,109-2, IMHA, 699–700. See also "Jingjibu guoying kuangqu weituozhuang" (September 4, 1944), Economic Affairs Collection, 18-3,109-2, IMHA, 690–691.

46. Wang, "Jiu Zhongguo Xinjiang shiyou gongye shuyao," 18.

47. Li, *Xinjiang dui Su (E) maoyishi*, 511.

48. Lattimore, *Pivot of Asia*, 179.

49. Jack Chen, *The Sinkiang story* (New York: Macmillan, 1997, reprint), 204.

50. Li, *Xinjiang dui Su (E) maoyishi*, 498.

51. Even these items were severely restricted. Ibid., 494.

52. Ibid., 500.

53. Barmin, *SSSR i Sin'tszian*, 27.

54. Cai, *Sheng Shicai zai Xinjiang*, 385.

55. For more on the long-term relationship between Uyghur nationalists and the Soviet Union, see Brophy, *Uyghur nation*.

56. Barmin, *SSSR i Sin'tszian*, 29.

57. The pamphlet was translated into Chinese and reprinted in a Chinese Ministry of Foreign Affairs report. See "Zhu Xinjiang tepaiyuan gongshu baobu Xinjiang Ka, Ta, He, A, ge qu jingchaju zhuohuo Sudie gudong minbian, qing zhuancheng weizuo bing qingshi zunyou" (August 29, 1943), *Waijiaobu dang'an congshu jiewulei di sance Xinjiang juan* (vol. 1) (Taipei: Waijiaobu bianyin, 2001), 202.

58. See Jacobs, *Xinjiang and the modern Chinese state*, 131–153; Wang, *Under the Soviet shadow*; Barmin, *SSSR i Sin'tszian*.

59. In June 1945, Soviet Foreign Minister Molotov approved of the transfer of "rank and file officers who had been demobilized by the Red Army to take part in the insurrectionary movement of Muslims in Xinjiang." The 1946 budget for the Soviet Republic of Uzbekistan, which was

approved in 1945, included five million rubles to fund the "cost of activities in Xinjiang." Barmin, *SSSR i Sin'tszian*, 44–46.

60. Bayiti Wuma'er, "Sanqu geming qijian de Dushanzi," in *Xinjiang shiyou gongye shiliao xuanji*, vol. 1, 83.

61. "Wei liyong tongren yu duan shijian zhengli benwu chu neiwu ji zhangxiang" (February 21, 1945), Economic Affairs Collection, 24-14-12-4, IMHA, 8–11.

62. There is considerable debate over the reasons for the halting of the offensive, though nearly all scholars agree that it was a product of Soviet pressure. While Forbes suggests that it was a product of Soviet fears that the Americans were preparing to involve themselves in the conflict, Wang suggests that the Soviets decided to rein in the Ili National Army in order to consolidate their control over these resource-rich and strategically important areas. Forbes, *Warlords and Muslims in Chinese Central Asia*, 190; Wang, *Under the Soviet shadow*. Drawing on newly uncovered Nationalist government sources, Jacobs argues that the Soviet Union's decision to call a halt to the offensive was prompted by the desire for a new economic cooperation agreement with the Chinese government. When the Nationalist government submitted one, the Soviets immediately stopped the Ili National Army advance. It should be noted, as I will point out below, that the Soviets refused to ratify the proposal. Jacobs, *Xinjiang and the modern Chinese state*, 150–151.

63. "Canxun: Suji yanhu Wai Mengjun rukou Xinjiang, yi shenru liubaili yu jun jiaozhan-zhong" (June 8, 1947), in *Waijiaobu dang'an congshu: Xinjiang juan*, vol. 1, 182.

64. "Hezhong she baodao dui Zhong-Su Xinjiang jingmao jiaoshe Mei dangju jibiao guan-qie" (February 20, 1949), in Xue Xintian, ed., *Zhong-Su guojia guanxishi ziliao huibian* (Beijing: Shehui Kexue Wenxian Chubanshe, 1996), 379; Xue Xintian, *Zhong-Su guanxishi, 1945–1949* (Chengdu: Sichuan Renmin Chubanshe, 2003), 283–284. CIA agents were able to get a sample of the ores being mined in northern Xinjiang in 1947, but according to an analysis, the rocks were nonradioactive beryl and bisthmuthinite (National Archives, Record Group 59, Stack Area 250, Row 50, Compartment 30, Shelf 4, Special Assistant to the Secretary of State for Atomic Energy and Outer Space. "21.17 Country File–China—Nationalist f. Sinkiang, 1947–1949," letter dated August 22, 1947). Thanks to Charles Kraus for the reference.

65. Bayiti Wuma'er, "Sanqu geming qijian de Dushanzi," 95.

66. Ibid., 83.

67. For a list of the scholarly materials sent to Xinjiang in 1946 with the operation, see Kras-nopevtsev, no title (June 13, 1946), file number 7794-606, RGAE, 86.

68. Karpenko, "Svedeniya po trestu No. 5 Ministerstva tsvetnoy metallurgii" (August 22, 1946), file number 7794-606, RGAE, 102.

69. Belokonev, no title (August 1, 1946), file number 7794-606, RGAE, 91.

70. Ge Zhenbei, "Keketuohai kuangmai disanhao kuangmai 1946–1957 nian 1 yue 1 ri dizhi kantan gongzuo ji pi, li tan, ni, yanghuawu deng zonghe chuliang jisuan baogao" (February 2, 1958), unpublished report, document 12984, NGAC, 20.

71. "Guominzhengfu zhuxi xibei xingyuan zhi guofangbu shuoming Sufang daocai Xinjiang kuangzang daidian jielue" (1948), in Xue, *Zhong-Su guojia guanxishi ziliao huibian*, 509.

72. See "Waijiaobu zhu Xinjiang tepaiyuan Liu Zerong cheng waijiaobu baogao Sufang zai Xin caiqu ge kuang qingxing dian" (October 1947); "Guominzhengfu zhuxi xibei xingyuan zhi waijiaobu cheng Wang Yujin 'Sulian shan zizai Keketuohai kaicai kuangshi gaikuang baogao shu' han" (December 16, 1947), in Xue, ed., *Zhong-Su guojia guanxishi ziliao huibian*, 506–507.

Soviet archives largely affirm this report. Soviet sources note that the operations in Xinjiang demanded the import of large numbers of guns to secure the sites and boasted various workshops, labs and electric power stations. For more on the import of guns to the site, see Lyubimskiy, no title (July 9, 1946), file number 7794-606, RGAE, 30. For more on the operation more generally, see Karpenko, "Svedeniya po trestu No. 5 Ministerstva tsvetnoy metallurgii" (August 22, 1946), file number 7794-606, RGAE, 102.

73. In their reports, the former miners asserted that they were mining tungsten and diamonds but their descriptions of the rocks they were tasked with gathering resemble neither tungsten ore nor diamonds. This, combined with the fact that tungsten exists at the site in only trace amounts, suggests that these miners were uninformed. "Waijiaobu zhu Xinjiang tepaiyuan Liu Zerong cheng waijiaobu baogao Sufang zai Xin caiqu ge kuang qingxing dian" (October 1947); "Guominzhengfu zhuxi xibei xingyuan zhi waijiaobu cheng Wang Yujn 'Sulian shan zizai Keketuohai kaicai kuangshi gaikuang baogao shu' han," in Xue, ed., Zhong-Su guojia guanxishi ziliao huibian, 506–507.

74. Ge, "Keketuohai kuangmai disanhao kuangmai," 29. The value of raw beryllium ore in 1949 was US $210,000 per ton. Considering that on the low end beryllium ore contains 3 percent beryllium, the total production at this one ore deposit netted over US $1.575 million in profit.

75. "Waijiaobu zhu Xinjiang tepaiyuan Liu Zerong cheng waijiaobu baogao Sufang zai Xin caiqu ge kuang qingxing dian" (no date), in Xue, ed., Zhong-Su guojia guanxishi ziliao huibian, 506–507.

76. Ibid.

77. See Wang, "Jiu Zhongguo Xinjiang shiyou gongye shuyao," 20–21.

78. "Zhongguo zhengfu guanyu Xinjiang shengnei Zhong-Su maoyi yu jingji hezuo zhi jianyi" (January 1945), in Xue, ed., Zhong-Su guojia guanxishi ziliao huibian, 369.

79. "Xibei xingyuan zhuren Zhang Zhizhong zhi Guomin zhengfu zhuxi Jiang Jieshi dian" (August 3, 1946), in Xue, ed., Zhong-Su guojia guanxishi ziliao huibian, 371–372.

80. No author, no title (August 24, 1946), Russian Occupation of China (6) Collection, 002-090400-00009-288, AHA.

81. Chiang Kaishek, no title (no date), Russian Occupation of China (6) Collection, 002-090400-00009-347, AHA.

82. Zhang, Xinjiang fengbao qishinian, vol. 12, 7223.

83. Xue, Zhong-Su guanxishi, 1945-1949, 271–272.

84. "Migaoyang gei Shidalin de baogao: huifu Su-Xin maoyi he jingji hezuo" (December 7, 1948), AVP RF, in Eguo jiemi dangan: Xinjiang wenti, 281–282.

85. In a joint telegram, the Ministry of Foreign Affairs, the Ministry of Economic Affairs, and the National Resources Commission called for an end to the negotiations. "The surrounding of Xinjiang has already been completed. I fear that a trade agreement will have absolutely no effect," the telegram explained. "Waijiaobu zhaoji jingjibu ji ziyuan weiyuanhui daibiao yijue zhongzhi Zhong-Su Xinjiang maoyi hezuo tanpan chengxing zhengyuan daidian" (August 30, 1949), in Xue, ed., Zhong-Su guojia guanxishi ziliao huibian, 409–410.

86. Scholars have noted that in many respects, the 1949 political divide was a porous one, and that from an institutional and personnel perspective, the early People's Republic closely resembled the Republic of China. This is clearly the case in the context of mineral extraction policies in Xinjiang. For a selection of works addressing this theme of trans-1949 continuities, see Morris L.

Bian, *The making of the state enterprise system in modern China: the dynamics of institutional change* (Cambridge: Harvard University Press, 2005); Mark Frazier, *The making of the Chinese industrial workplace: state, revolution, and industrial management* (Cambridge: Cambridge University Press, 2002); Judd C. Kinzley, "Crisis and the development of China's southwestern periphery: the transformation of Panzhihua, 1936–1969," *Modern China* 38, no. 5 (September 2012), 559–584; William Kirby, "Continuity and change in modern China: economic planning on the mainland and on Taiwan, 1943–1958," *Australian journal of Chinese affairs* 24 (1990), 121–141.

87. Liu Shaoqi, "Guanyu Zhong-Su liangguo zai Xinjiang sheli jinshu he shiyou gufen gongsi wenti gei Mao Zedong de dianbao" (January 2, 1950), in Zhonggong zhongyang wenxian yanjiushi, ed., *Xinjiang gongzuo wenxian xuanbian* (Beijing: Zhongyang Wenxian Chubanshe, 2010), 43–44.

88. See Charles Kraus, "Creating a Soviet 'semi-colony'? Sino-Soviet cooperation and its demise in Xinjiang, 1949–1955," in *Chinese historical review* 17, no. 2 (Fall 2010), 151–152.

89. Hu Houwen, "Xinjiang shi Zhongguo de youku" (June 1950), file number 17515, NHA, 4.

90. Di Chaobai, "Zhong-Su jingji hezuo de yiyi ji qifangshi," *Renmin ribao* (April 21, 1950), 5.

91. The Chinese portion of this capital was in the form of Soviet loans that were to be repaid through the export of natural resources including oil to the Soviet Union.

92. Xinjiang Weiwu'er zizhiqu difang zhi bianzuan weiyuanhui, ed., *Xinjiang tongzhi: youse jinshu gongye* (vol. 42) (Urumqi: Xinjiang Renmin Chubanshe, 2005), 928. For more on the Soviet tungsten industry, see George Rabchevsky, *The tungsten industry of the USSR* (Washington, D.C.: US Department of the Interior, Bureau of Mines, 1988). Rabchevsky notes that Soviet domestic tungsten production doubled from 1940 to 1945, increased by another 10 percent from 1945 to 1946, and then increased by another 20 percent in only the first nine months of 1947. These increases were due in large part to the discovery of productive fields in Soviet Central Asia, and Kazakhstan in particular.

93. *Xinjiang tongzhi: youse jinshu gongye* (vol. 42), 115–116.

94. Ibid.

95. Bai Chengming, "Keketuohai kuangmei di 3 hao kuangchan" (February 2, 1957), file number 12984, NGAC, 27. For more on the uprising and the connections to Chinese policy in Xinjiang, see Justin Jacobs, "The many deaths of a Kazak unaligned: Osman Batur, Chinese decolonization, and the nationalization of a nomad," *American historical review* 115, no. 5 (December 2010), 1291–1314.

96. The central government agreed to foot more than 85 percent of the total price tag of 1.099 million yuan for the project. The project was one of the most expensive infrastructural projects in Xinjiang in the first half of the 1950s. Xinjiang jiaotong shi zhi bianmu weiyuanhui, ed., *Xinjiang gonglu shi*, vol. 2 (Beijing: Renmin Jiaotong Chubanshe, 1998), 18.

97. *Xinjiang tongzhi: youse jinshu gongye* (vol. 42), 639.

98. "Xinjiang diqu de hanyou wenti ji zai Xinjiang wei xunzhao shiyou ying jinxing dizhi diqiu wuli he dixing celiang gongzuo de fangxiang" (1950), file number 10535, NGAC, 21–24.

99. "Zhonggong zhongyang guanyu Zhong-Su shiyou gongsi he Zhong-Su youse ji xiyou jinshu gongsi ruogan wenti de jueding" (May 6, 1953), in *Zhong-Su shiyou gufen gongsi*, 55–56.

100. *Xinjiang tongzhi: shiyou gongye* (vol. 40), 129–155.

101. There were periodic tensions on site and on at least one occasion, Soviet leaders, frustrated by conflicts between Soviet and Chinese at the nonferrous metals operation (described as "serious deficiencies and violations of the principle of equality") completely cleaned house at the site. See "Youjia gei Zuolin de baogao: gaijin Xinjiang gufen gongsi gongzuo wenti" (June 28,

1954), Tsentr khraneniya sovremennoy dokumentatsii, Moscow, in *Eguo jiemi dangan*, 315. Charles Kraus suggests that the company reverted to Chinese control as a concession by Khrushchev to ease mounting Sino-Soviet tensions following the death of Stalin in 1953. Kraus, "Creating a Soviet semi-colony." For their part, Soviet officials complained about the high price they were paying for access to Xinjiang's nonferrous metals in particular.

The prices that Soviet government buyers were paying for the Chinese share of the product was higher than the prices that they could fetch on international metal markets. According to Soviet sources, the market price of beryllium was 2,496 rubles per ton in 1954, but the company was charging 7,000 rubles per ton. Likewise, the global price for lithium was 517 rubles per ton, but the company was charging 1,487 rubles; and the cost of niobium and tantalum was 40,171 rubles per ton, but the company was charging 60,000. "Yiwannianke de diaocha baogao zai Zhongguo de Su-Zhong gufen gongsi qingkuang" (December 11, 1954), in *Eguo jiemi dang'an*, 321–323.

102. *Renmin ribao* (October 12, 1954), quoted in Kraus, "Creating a Soviet semi-colony," 161.

103. Zhou Enlai, "Zhou Enlai guanyu Zhong-Su sida heying gongsi jiejiao wenti zhi guowuyuan youguan bumen dian" (December 24, 1954), in *Zhong-Su shiyou gufen gongsi*, 59.

104. *Xinjiang tongzhi: youse jinshu gongye* (vol. 42), 629.

105. "1955–1958 nian Xinjiang dizhichu baogao chubu sheji" (1960), file number 90131, NGAC, 1.

106. *Xinjiang tongzhi: youse jinshu gongye* (vol. 42), 542.

107. Ibid., 54, 639.

108. "Yizuo xinxing de shiyou cheng," *Renmin ribao* (November 6, 1954), reprinted in *Zhong-Su shiyou gufen gongsi*, 309–312.

## Chapter Seven

1. Wang Enmao, "Zongjie gongye jianshe jingyan, tigao guanli shuiping, wei yingjie da guimo jingji jianshe zuohao zhunbei," in *Wang Enmao wenji*, vol. 1 (Beijing: Zhongyang Wenxian Chubanshe, 1997), 207.

2. Zhou Enlai, *Zhou Enlai xuanji* (Beijing: Renmin chubanshe, 1984), 109. See also Bo Yibo, *Ruogan zhongda juece yu shijian de huigu*, vol. 1 (Beijing: Zhonggong Dangshi Chubanshe, 2008), 200–215.

3. The term "big push" was developed in the Soviet Union in the 1920s by Yevgeni Preobrazhensky. For more on the term in China, see Barry Naughton, *China's economy: transitions and growth* (Cambridge: MIT Press, 2007), 56–59.

4. Bo, *Rouganzhonda juece yu shijian de huigu*, 206.

5. China's first five-year plan (1953–1957) allocated 44.1 percent of its total investment to Manchuria and 25.9 percent of this to the province of Liaoning alone. In contrast, funding for industrialization in the northwest was 16 percent of the government's total allocation, with only 0.2 percent being directed toward projects in Xinjiang. See Dong Zhikai, *Xin Zhongguo gongye de dianjishi: 156 xiang jianshe yanjiu* (Guangzhou: Guangdongsheng Chubanshe, 2004), 413–494.

6. In addition to Xinjiang, they also turned to the Yumen oilfields, which like Dushanzi had been prioritized for production in the Republican period. See Lim, *China's quest for self reliance in oil*.

7. Naughton, *China's economy*, 57.

8. The so-called "oil poor theory" emerged as a discourse in the Republican period but carried over into the early People's Republic. As Grace Shen notes in her work, PRC geologists "labeled the 'oil poor theory' an instrument of imperialism used to retard Chinese development, and the Chinese who accepted the theory as weak or reactionary." Shen, *Unearthing the nation,* 169.

9. "1951–1954 nian dizhi diaochachu gongzuo de jianduan baogao" (July 7, 1955), file number 0717, NGAC, 5. See also Xinjiang Weiwu'er zizhiqu difang zhi bianzuan weiyuanhui, ed., *Xinjiang tongzhi: dizhi kuangchan* (vol. 9, part 2) (Urumqi: Xinjiang Renmin Chubanshe, 1999), 83.

10. A 1953 report from the Sino-Soviet company argued that the underlying geological structure of the region made "it impossible to produce oil deposits," and for much of the life of the company, the site was of a low priority for management. "1952 nian Zhong-Su shiyou gongsi dizhi diaochachu zongjie baogao" (1953), file number 10556, NGAC.

11. Huang Jiqing, "Wo yu shiyou, tianranqi de pucha kantan," in *Huang Jiqing shiyou dizhi zhuzuo xuanji* (Beijing: Kexue Chubanshe, 1993), 172–174.

12. Zhang Wenbin, "Xin Zhongguo shiyou gongye diyi qu zhuangge," in Habudoula, ed., *Xinjiang shiyou gongye shiliao xuanji,* vol. 1, 343–349, 346.

13. Zhang Yi and Wu Qingfu, "Kelamayi youtian de jueqi," in Habudoula, ed., *Xinjiang shiyou gongye shiliao xuanji,* vol. 1, 171–180, 171.

14. Huang Jiqing, "Zhunge'er he Chaidamu pendi de gouzao tezheng ji qi hanyou yuanjing," in *Huang Jiqing shiyou dizhi zhuzuo xuanji,* 107.

15. *Xinjiang tongzhi: shiyou gongye* (vol. 40), 597.

16. Ibid., 49, 234.

17. "Shikou tanjing yipenchu yuanyou Kelamayi zaici bei zhengming shi woguo dangqian zuida youqu," *Renmin ribao* (July 12, 1956).

18. Mitchell, *Carbon democracy,* 2.

19. *Xinjiang tongzhi: shiyou gongye* (vol. 40), 287–288.

20. Chu Anping, "Fang Kelamayi youqu," *Renmin ribao* (May 26, 1956).

21. Xinjiang jiaotongshizhi bianwei weiyuanhui, ed., *Xinjiang gonglu shi,* vol. 2 (Beijing: Renmin Jiaotong Chubanshe, 1998), 63. Officials frequently complained about the fact that they lacked sufficient transport capabilities. Despite a desperate need for equipment, the poor roads and an insufficient number of trucks meant that by late June 1956, large amounts of equipment imported from the Soviet Union were sitting idle at the international border crossing. See "Zai diyijie quanguo renmin daibiao dahui disanci huiyishang de fayan xibei sange youtian de zhuangkuang he cunzai de wenti Zeng Zesheng daibiao de fayan," *Renmin ribao* (June 30, 1956).

22. *Xinjiang tongzhi: shiyou gongye* (vol. 40), 333–334.

23. Keketuohai kuangwuju 701 dizhi kantandui, ed., *Keketuohai kuangchuang 1958 nian dizhi zongjie baogao* (1959), file number 17784, NGAC, 62. Indeed, while the number of laborers working in Koktokay increased steadily in the mid-1950s, the number working at ore fields farther west decreased over the same time frame, as officials in Xinjiang sought to redirect workers and equipment to Koktokay. Additionally, the Altay and Koktokay surveying teams were consolidated into the 701 Group, which was headquartered at Koktokay.

24. *Xinjiang tongzhi: youse jinshu gongye* (vol. 42), 640.

25. Ibid.

26. As Mitchell notes, coal production "flowed along narrow, purpose-built channels. Specialized bodies of workers were concentrated at the end-points and main junctions of these conduits . . . Their position and concentration gave them opportunities, at certain moments, to forge a new kind of political power." Mitchell, *Carbon Democracy* 19.

27. Shu Guang Zhang, *Economic Cold War: America's embargo against China and the Sino-Soviet alliance, 1949–1963* (Stanford: Stanford University Press, 2001), 213–215.

28. For the improvements to the highway network, see *Xinjiang gonglu shi*, vol. 2, 18.

29. *Xinjiang tongzhi: youse jinshu gongye* (vol. 42), 541–543.

30. "Tielu jiang chuanguo Kelamayi youqu dao Aletai," *Renmin ribao* (September 12, 1956).

31. *Xinjiang tongzhi: youse jinshu gongye* (vol. 42), 640.

32. *Xinjiang tongzhi: shiyou gongye* (vol. 42), 234.

33. Total spending from the Xinjiang finance office (*caizhengting*) was 100.3 million yuan in 1956, a number that decreased to 77.97 million in 1957 compared with an increase in spending on oil to 159 million. *Xinjiang tongzhi: caizheng* (vol. 57), 273, and *Xinjiang tongzhi: shiyou gongyezhi* (vol. 40), 516–517.

34. *Xinjiang tongzhi: youse jinshu gongye* (vol. 42), 648.

35. William Cronon, *Nature's metropolis: Chicago and the great west* (New York: W. W. Norton Co., 1991), 52–53.

36. For two examples, see James Millward, *Eurasian crossroads: a history of Xinjiang* (New York: Columbia University Press, 2007), and Donald McMillen, *Chinese Communist power and policy in Xinjiang, 1949–1977* (Boulder: Westview Press, 1979).

37. In 1954, total fixed capital investment in the XPCC was 49 million yuan compared with 31.2 million for Xinjiang's oil industry. In 1957, investment in the oil industry was 180 million versus 122.27 million for the XPCC. While this does not represent investment in Karamay-Dushanzi specifically, considering the centrality of the oil corridor in Xinjiang, it is a fair conclusion that most of this investment would flow to the oil production and refining site. See Xinjiang shengchan jianshe bingtuan tongjiju; Guojia tongjijubingtuan diaocha zongdui, ed., *Xinjiang shengchan jianshe bingtuan tongji nianlan 2013* (Beijing: Zhongguo Tongji Chubanshe, 2013), and *Xinjiang tongzhi: shiyou gongye* (vol. 40), 516–517.

38. Less than a hundred miles north of the town of Kuitun on the Tianshan North Road in 1955 was a small XPCC farm at Xiaoguai town, in territory controlled by the Ninth Agricultural Division (Nongjiu shi) centered in Shihezi. But north of this, for nearly five hundred kilometers along arduous roads there was nothing until you reached the 4,300-man XPCC unit stationed at Balibagai on the banks of the Irtysh River and south of the town of Altay.

39. "Kelamayi shi choubei weiyuanhui chengli," in Kelamayishi dang'anguan bian, ed., *Dang'an zhong de Kelamayi* (Urumqi: Xinjiang Renmin Chubanshe, 2008), 52.

40. *Xinjiang tongzhi: shiyou gongye* (vol. 40), 478.

41. "1957 nian Kelamayi shiyou huatandui chengguo baogao" (1958), file number 14561, NGAC, 2. See also *Xinjiang tongzhi, di sishi juan, shiyou gongye zhi*, 207.

42. *Xinjiang tongzhi: youse jinshu gongye* (vol. 42), 275, 626.

43. Chu Anping, "Zai A'ertai shan zhi dian," *Renmin ribao* (December 16, 1955).

44. Watts, "Resource curse? Governmentality, oil, and power in the Niger Delta," 60.

45. In addition, Wang Qiren, a party cadre since the late 1920s, was brought in to serve as the operation's party secretary in January 1955.

46. Zhang Zikuan was brought in to oversee Koktokay in January 1955 and Wang Congyi, another long-term party member, was brought in as the site's party secretary.

47. "Kelamayi shi choubei weiyuanhui chengli" (January 1957), in *Dang'an zhong de Kelamayi*, 52.

48. "Kelamayi shi shoubei weiyuanhui chengli," in *Dang'an zhong de Kelamayi* 52.

49. "Kelamayi shi chengli," *Dang'an zhong de Kelamayi* 63.

50. Ibid.

51. From 1955 to 1960, the total number of cadres working in the Xinjiang Non-ferrous Metals Company increased approximately five times, from 385 in 1956 to 2,162 in 1960, while the Xinjiang Oil Oversight Office increased from 1,382 to 6,537. *Xinjiang tongzhi: shiyou gongye* (vol. 40), 478. Of these, more than half were party cadres. Ibid., 658.

52. "Sidalin yu Zhou Enlai de huitan jilu" (August 20, 1952), AVP RF, in *Eguo jiemi dangan*, 400–407. Zhou fully agreed with Stalin's assessment and noted that plans for building the line were already well under way.

53. "Tielu jiang chuanguo Kelamayi youqu dao Aletai," *Renmin ribao* (September 12, 1956).

54. "Yumen de shiyou de daxishi," *Renmin ribao* (July 4, 1956).

55. Naughton, *China's economy*, 57.

56. "Kelamayi kuangqu shoujie dangyuan daibiaodahui" (May 5, 1958), in *Dang'an zhong de Kelamayi*, 93.

57. *Xinjiang tongzhi: shiyou gongye* (vol. 40), 598.

58. "Xinjiang shiyou guanliju zhaokai kuangqu yiji dang daibiaodahui de jueding" (April 30, 1958), in *Dang'an zhong de Kelamayi*, 92.

59. Wu Huayuan, "Zai Xinjiang zhaoyou de rizi," in Habudoula, ed., *Xinjiang shiyou gongye shiliao xuanji*, vol. 1, 212–263, 252.

60. *Xinjiang tongzhi: shiyou gongye* (vol. 40), 31.

61. "Dushanzi kuangwuju 1958 niandu dizhi kantan huiyi huibian" (February 1959), file number 17480, NGAC, 1.

62. There is a risk in overdrilling in one oilfield, as the large number of wells could lead to a reduction in pressure that could inhibit the abilities to pump out crude.

63. "Xinjiang Shiyou Guanliju Kezi yanjiu Zhunge'r pendi beibu diqu shiyou kantan yanjiu zongjie baogao" (January 1960), file number 21378, NGAC, 82–86.

64. *Xinjiang tongzhi: shiyou gongye* (vol. 40), 122.

65. Keketuohai kuangwuju 701 dizhi kantandui, ed., *Keketuohai kuangchuang 1958 nian dizhi zongjie baogao* (1959), file number 17784, NGAC, 3.

66. Figures from the Xinjiang Non-ferrous Metals Company seem to bear out this assertion. In terms of lithium and beryllium, the largest shipments to the Soviet Union in aggregate occurred in the years in 1958–1960. *Xinjiang tongzhi: youse jinshu gongye* (vol. 42), 640; "Wei jianli duli de wanzheng de xiandaihua de guomin jingji tixi er jixu fendou" (December 4, 1963), *Renmin Ribao*.

67. Zhang, *Economic Cold War*, 214.

68. *Xinjiang tongzhi: youse jinshu gongye* (vol. 42), 273–280.

69. Ibid., 288.

70. "Gaoju hongqi yue Tianshan danao Talimu," *Xinjiang shiyou gongren* (July 23, 1958), 1.

71. "Zizhiqu difang shiyou gongye huiyi zai Dushanzi zhaokai," *Xinjiang shiyou gongren* (May 19, 1958).

72. "Lianyouchang shilian yong 'tubanfa' lianyou chenggong," *Xinjiang shiyou gongren* (May 13, 1958), 1.

73. Ibid. In order to further spread the technology and the message, at least one meeting was organized by officials in Xinjiang for local officials living in oil-rich counties in the Tarim basin. See "Quanmin banshiyou de gaochao ji jiang chuxian," *Xinjiang shiyou gongren* (August 26, 1958), 1.

74. At Kucha, local officials recruited a team of more than 140 locals to dig; similar teams were sent out in the area around Baicheng and Kashgar. Additional teams were recruited to participate in refining operations. See "Nanjiang ge de fenfen ban shiyou gongye," *Xinjiang shiyou gongren* (September 19, 1958), 2.

75. See *Xinjiang tongzhi: youse jinshu gongye* (vol. 42), 145–151.

76. *Xinjiang tongzhi: shiyou gongye* (vol. 40), 209.

77. "Danao Talimu daxiang diyipao," *Xinjiang shiyou gongren* (October 12, 1958), 1.

78. *Xinjiang tongzhi: shiyou gongye* (vol. 40), 626.

79. Ibid., 224.

80. While the ratio of earth processed to ore produced was slightly less than 1 ton of ore to 1 square meter of earth in 1957, that ratio dropped drastically, to the range from 1:4.7 to 1:5.1. *Xinjiang tongzhi: youse jinshu gongye* (vol. 42), 288.

81. Ibid., 517, 489–490.

82. "Guanyu Xinjiang youse xiyou jinshukuang jinhou shengchan jianshezhong de ji ge wenti," quoted in *Xinjiang tongzhi: youse jinshu gongye* (vol. 42), 23. For the shift in focus toward tantalum-niobium, see Zhongguo kexueyuan Xinjiang xiyou yuansu dizhidui, ed., *Xinjiang Keketuohai kuangqu disanhao weichang yanmai 1964 nian yewai diaocha baogao* (October 1964), file number 52354(1), NGAC, 6. Tantalum-niobium is a steel alloy frequently used in jet engine components, rocketry, and capacitors, while lithium ore, in addition to being a critical element in the production of rocket fuel, is also a central component in the production of thermonuclear weapons.

83. *Xinjiang tongzhi: youse jinshu gongye* (vol. 42), 275–279.

## Chapter Eight

1. As Deng argued, "Developed areas will continue to develop, and help underdeveloped areas vigorously by various means, e.g., paying more profits and taxes and transferring technology." See Heike Holbig, "The emergence of the campaign to open up the west: ideological formation, central decision-making, and the role of the provinces," *China quarterly* 178 (June 2004), 335–357, 336–337.

2. By 1994, coastal provinces received 59 percent of state investment, compared to 41 percent for the interior. See Debasish Chaudhuri, "A survey of the economic situation in Xinjiang and its role in the twenty-first century," *China report* 41, no. 1 (2005), 10.

3. In 2004, the western region accounted for only 17 percent of China's GDP. Henryk Szadziewski, "Commanding the economy: the recurring patterns of Chinese central government development planning among Uyghurs in Xinjiang," *Inner Asia* 13 (2011), 101.

4. See Chaudhuri, "A survey of the economic situation in Xinjiang," 9–10.

5. Hu Angang and Wang Shaoguang in particular advocated for a reexamination of policy. See Holbig, "The emergence of the campaign to open up the west," 338–341. See also David S. G. Goodman, "The campaign to 'open the west': national, provincial-level, and local perspectives," *China quarterly* 178 (June 2004), 326.

6. David Bachman argues that demand for oil, the emergence of Tibetan opposition, and the collapse of the Soviet Union all served as driving factors behind the new emphasis on Xinjiang. See Bachman, "Making Xinjiang safe for the Han?" As far as Nicolas Becquelin is concerned, the integrationist effort is in fact primary and the desire to balance out patterns of development is complete whitewash. See Becquelin, "Staged development in Xinjiang," *China quarterly* 178 (June 2004), 358–378.

7. Cited in Henryk Szadziewski, "The open up the west campaign among Uyghurs in Xinjiang: exploring a rights-based approach," in Trine Brox and Ildiko Beller-Hann, eds., *On the fringes of the harmonious society: Tibetans and Uyghurs in socialist China* (Copenhagen: NIAS Press, 2014), 74.

8. The relatively low domestic demand for oil in the 1970s and 1980s meant that China enjoyed vast oil surpluses and exported twenty-seven million tons of crude oil as late as 1985. Naughton, *The Chinese economy*, 340.

9. Heike Holbig refers to the campaign as "soft," "an amorphous set of diverse policy agendas and instruments not designed to form a complete and coherent programme, but rather to appeal to as many interests as possible simultaneously." See Holbig, "The emergence of the campaign to open up the west," 336.

10. The term was coined by Cao Huhua. See Cao, "Urban-rural income disparity and urbanization: what is the role of spatial distribution of ethnic groups? a case study of Xinjiang Uyghur Autonomous Region in western China," *Regional studies* 44, no. 8 (October 2010), 975.

11. As of August 2016, the Number 3 ore vein was not being actively worked, though the infrastructure remained in place to reopen quickly. Decisions about the operation were based on shifting market prices for lithium and other minerals.

12. The Chinese government began seeking access to Kazakhstan's oil wealth in 1997, when the China National Petroleum Corporation purchased a 60 percent stake in the country's fourth-largest oil and gas company. In the early 2000s, Chinese state-owned and private enterprises purchased stakes in various Kazakh oil companies and offered loans to the Kazakhstan government. Experts speculate that these loans were paid down using raw petroleum shipped directly to Dushanzi. See Michal Meidan, *China's loans for oil: asset or liability*, in Oxford Institute for Energy Series, no. 70 (December 2016), 6.

13. Jones, *Routes of power*, 233.

14. Cao, "Urban-rural income disparity and urbanization," 971. The category is calculated based on county incomes when measured against the highest county-level incomes in the province.

15. If you eliminate the highest and lowest prefectural per capita GDP from each of the north and south categories as outliers, the number is even more stark, as the GDP for the north is nearly three times that of the south (9,294 v. 3,526). See Chaudhuri, "A survey of the economic situation in Xinjiang and its role in the twenty-first century," 6.

16. See ibid.; see also Cao, "Urban-rural income disparity and urbanization"; Stanley W. Toops, "The demography of Xinjiang," in S. Frederick Starr, ed., *Xinjiang: China's Muslim borderland* (Armonk: M. E. Sharpe, 2004), 260–262.

17. See Ernst Gellner, *Thought and change* (Chicago: Weidenfeld and Nicholson, 1964). Thanks to Angel Ryono for the reference.

18. For more on inequalities experienced by Uyghurs in the 1950s, see Jacobs, *Xinjiang and the modern Chinese state*, chapter 5.

19. For more on this, see James Millward, *Violent separatism in Xinjiang* (Washington, D.C.: East West Center, 2004); see also Bovingdon, *The Uyghurs*.

20. In his work on the ways in which economic "normalization" in Xinjiang has fueled Uyghur unrest, Thomas Cliff notes that there are "multiple vectors of differentiation" that have promoted greater Han-Uyghur tensions since the 1990s. Thomas Cliff, "Lucrative chaos: interethnic conflict as a function of the economic normalization of southern Xinjiang," in Ben Hillman and Gray Tuttle, eds., *Ethnic conflict and protest in Tibet and Xinjiang: unrest in China's west* (New York: Columbia University Press, 2016), 131.

21. For more on the formation of ethnic identities more generally, see Michael Omi and Howard Winant, *Racial formation in the United States*, 3rd ed. (New York: Routledge, 2014); Frederik Barth, *Ethnic groups and boundaries: the social organization of difference* (Long Grove: Waveland Press, 1998). For more on the formation of ethnic identities in China and the role that the state plays in shaping that formation culturally, see Dru Gladney, "Representing nationality in China: refiguring majority/minority identities," *Journal of Asian studies* 53, no. 1 (Feb. 1994), 92–113; see also Dru Gladney, *Dislocating China: Muslims, minorities, and other subaltern subjects* (Chicago: University of Chicago Press, 2004).

22. It should be noted that not all do. Becquelin cites the Xinjiang party secretary Wang Lequan, who rejected a strategy of relying on economic development alone to resolve the ethnic problem in Xinjiang. As Wang argued, supporters of an economic development strategy for Xinjiang "believe that after Xinjiang's economy develops, people's living standards will improve so the issue of stability will be resolved naturally. This belief is wrong and dangerous." Quoted in Becquelin, "Staged development in Xinjiang," 374.

23. Recognizing this reality, the new plans unveiled in 2010 sought to target funds to the local areas with the highest concentrations of poverty and minorities. Indeed, more than half of the "pairings" that connect wealthy administrative entities in east and central China with subdistricts in Xinjiang are located in southern Xinjiang, and nearly 98 percent of the 39.5 billion yuan had already been earmarked for the south by the middle of the twenty-teens. See Stanley Toops, "Testimony before Congressional Executive Commission on China roundtable on China's far west: conditions in Xinjiang one year after demonstrations and riots" (July 19, 2010), http://www.cecc.gov/sites/chinacommission.house.gov/files/documents/roundtables/2010/CECC%20Roundtable%20Testimony%20-%20Stanley%20Toops%20-%207.19.10.pdf.

24. For a detailed accounting of this process, see Cliff, "Lucrative chaos," 129. See also Bhajan S. Grewel and Abdullahi D. Ahmed, "Is China's western region development strategy on track? an assessment," *Journal of contemporary China* 20, no. 69 (2011), 180.

25. Andrew Martin Fischer, "Labour transitions and social inequalities in Tibet and Xinjiang: a comparative analysis of the structural foundations of discrimination and protest," in Trine Brox and Ildiko Beller-Hann, eds., *On the fringes of the harmonious society: Tibetans and Uyghurs in socialist China* (Copenhagen: NIAS Press, 2014), 29–68.

26. For more on the nineteenth-century pursuit of coal and an exposition on the connection between coal and empire, see Wu, *Empires of coal.*

27. For more on foreign influence in Manchuria, see David Holm, "Russia, the Soviet Union, and the China eastern railroad," in Clarence Baldwin Davis, Kenneth E. Wilson, and Ronald Edward Robins, eds., *Railway imperialism* (Westport: Greenwood Press, 1991); for an overview of Japan's role and the creation of a Japanese "enclave" in Manchuria, see Peter Duus, "Japan's informal empire in China, 1895–1937: an overview," in Duus, Meyers, and Peattie, eds., *The Japanese informal empire in China, 1895–1937;* Ramon H. Meyers, "Japanese imperialism in Manchuria: the South Manchuria Railway Company, 1906–1933" in Duus, Meyers, and Peattie, eds., *The Japanese informal empire in China*, 101–132.

28. Tibet's major commodity exports in the nineteenth and twentieth centuries were wool and livestock, which, as the major products produced for export (to China-proper, and into global markets), did not require large-scale capital investment; they largely promoted patterns of development and state investment that clung to extant market towns.

29. See Paul Baran, *The political economy of growth* (New York: Monthly Review, 1968 [1957]). See also Andre Gunder Frank, *Capitalism and underdevelopment in Latin America: historical studies of Chile and Brazil* (New York: Monthly Review, 1967).

30. There are a wide assortment of works addressing the "resource curse." For a selection, see Jeffrey D. Sachs and Andrew M. Warner, "Natural resource abundance and economic growth," Working Paper No. 5398 (Cambridge: National Bureau of Economic Research, 1995); Michael L. Ross, *The oil curse: how petroleum wealth shapes the development of nations* (Princeton: Princeton University Press, 2012). For a different perspective on the curse, see Ellis Goldberg, Erik Wibbels, and Eric Mvukiyehe, "Lessons from strange cases: democracy, development, and the resource curse in the United States," *Comparative political studies* 41 (2008), 477–514.

31. Xinjiang was able to avoid this affliction, with its high political, economic, and social costs, due to the fact that the resources were not generating precious revenue but rather paying down Soviet loans. After the Sino-Soviet split, the resources were shielded from global markets because of China's political and economic isolation.

32. For more on the U.S. and Mexico, see William J. Fleming, "In the path of progress: railroads and moral reform in Porfirian Mexico," in Davis, Wilson, and Robins, eds., *Railway imperialism*; for more on Soviet investments in Persia, see Sara Brinegar, *Baku at all costs: the politics of oil in the new Soviet state* (Ph.D. dissertation, University of Wisconsin-Madison, 2014); for Venezuela, see Coronil, *The magical state*.

# Index

Academia Sinica, 125, 140
agricultural reclamation, 18, 23–42, 196nn2–3, 197n4, 197nn8–9, 197n13, 198n29. *See also* grain
Altay Mountain mining: gold, 64–68, 103–5; nonferrous metals, 109, 115–16, 137–40, 156–58, 163, 166–73
anti-Han sentiment. *See* ethnic tensions
Anti-Rightist Movement, 166
anti-Soviet sentiments, 78–79, 123–24, 129–33, 216n24
arms trade, 83–90, 156

Baku, 59, 108–9, 118
Ban Chao, 123
beryllium production, 18, 101–16, 122–24, 133–45, 155–57, 173, 219n74, 220n101, 224n66. *See also* nonferrous metals production
big push development strategy, 150, 221n3. *See also* Preobrazhensky, Yevgeni
black gold. *See* oil
Bogdanovich, Karl Ivanovich, 46, 50, 67
border policy in Xinjiang: agricultural reclamation and, 18, 23–42, 196nn2–3, 197nn8–9, 197nn13–14, 198n29; assimilationist, 4, 24; competition for natural resources and, 1–19, 196n31, 197n19; endurance of layers and, 178–89; foreign capital and, 43–69, 205nn89–90; informal empire and, 99–121; integrationist, 3–4, 82, 226n6; Soviet resonances and, 122–49; state power and, 150–77
Bortala, 107, 115–19, 123–28, 133–38, 145, 148, 215–16n19
Bountiful Xinjiang Local Product Company (Yu-Xin Tuchan Gongsi), 90–93, 210n92
Boxer: Protocol, 33; War, 38

British Empire, 10–15, 46, 61–70, 79, 83, 86, 128, 185–87, 204n67, 205n89, 205n3; India and, 68–70, 122, 128, 205n3
Burhan Shahidi, 83, 90
Burqin, 139, 145, 158. *See also* Irtysh River; riverine shipping
Burultokay (Fuhai) reclamation site, 34–36. *See also* agricultural reclamation

Chen Deli, 87
Chiang Kaishek, 6, 81, 87–89, 118–28, 135–37, 141, 214n3. *See also* Guomindang Party (GMD); Republic of China
"China miracle," 178
China National Petroleum Corporation, 226n12
Chinese civil war, 142–43
Chinese Communist Party (CCP), 2, 5–6, 18–19, 68, 89, 134, 142–52, 162–66, 176–84, 188, 196n31. *See also* Mao Zedong; People's Republic of China
Chinese Green Standard troops, 30
Chinese Ministry of Geology, 148, 153
Chinese Republic. *See* Republic of China
Christian humanism, 200n63
coal production. *See* mining
Coal Tar Mountain, 153–54. *See also* Karamay
colonialism, 7, 10–11, 62, 159–60, 195n23, 197n4. *See also* imperialism
commerce war, 71, 206n8
Cooper, Frederick, 10, 195n23
Cultural Revolution, 175

Daqing oil field, 174
decentralized mining, 38, 50–54, 66–67, 105, 171
Dekanozov, Vladimir, 120